MORE ADVANCE PRAISE FOR *SMART SALES MANAGER*

"This remarkable book demonstrates what it really takes to build and manage a high-performance inside sales team today—when the competition is tough and the customers are tougher. This is the ultimate playbook. No hype, no B.S.—not a page without some real value for the reader. It's insightful, relevant, well-researched, and, with just the right blend of anecdotes, examples, stories, and tools, it gives you everything you need to get the job done."
—DAVE STEIN, CEO & Founder, ES Research Group, Inc.

"*Smart Sales Manager* is a top-notch guidebook to help those who are serious in their desire to improve sales team performance. I recommend it to all my sales leads."
—BILL GRIFFIN, VP of Worldwide Manufacturing and Channel Sales, Autodesk, Inc.

"Interested in sales tools that will ignite your revenue? Don't limit yourself to smart selling tools . . . look for smart selling books, too! Josiane Feigon's new book, *Smart Sales Manager*, fits the bill, and couldn't come at a more perfect time."
—NANCY NARDIN, President, Smart Selling Tools

"*Smart Sales Manager* reconnects managers with their teams and offers managers the latest trends and the practical, tactical strategies, skills, and guidance they need to run a high-performance inside sales team, and to carry their organizations to the next level of excellence."
—CHRIS CABRERA, CEO, Xactly Corp.

"Josiane Feigon has created a comprehensive guide for today's inside sales managers. She's condensed years of valuable knowledge and insight into an interesting, easy-to-read, how-to manual. Simply outstanding!"
— LARRY REEVES, Chief Operating Officer, AA-ISP

"The sales world is in a constant state of change, and managers must come equipped to manage their teams from a new perspective to meet the inevitable challenges. *Smart Sales Manager* is their guide to excellence in today's 2.0 world."
—CARRIE MARTINEZ, CFO Sales Gravy

"Every inside sales manager should read *Smart Sales Manager*. Josiane provides specific, actionable advice grounded in real-world experience. This is a terrific guide that has helped Carahsoft make the right investments in our sales leaders and their abilities to develop highly effective inside sales teams."
— CRAIG ABOD, President, Carahsoft Technology Corp.

"Josiane Feigon has set a new standard and raised the bar in *Smart Sales Manager* as she encourages managers to press 'refresh' when it comes to managing their teams to navigate today's social, virtual, and mobile sales environment."
—FRANCES EVENSEN, Director of Sales, SAP

"For years, an inside sales position has been considered as the bottom rung on the sales ladder. Not anymore. Today's breed of inside sales professional is bright, qualified, and well-rewarded. Their commercial bandwidth is much, much wider, and their skill sets are, at the very least, the equivalent of their 'outdoor' colleagues. The migration is gaining momentum, and this, in turn, is creating the need for new, more sophisticated management skills. Josiane Feigon's excellent new book, *Smart Sales Manager*, will seem like a gift from above: the definitive guide for both new and seasoned inside sales managers."
—JONATHAN FARRINGTON, Managing Partner at Jonathan Farrington & Associates; and CEO at Top Sales World

"*Smart Sales Manager* focuses on the human side of managing: watching, observing, learning from, and motivating teams. It also covers the core elements that lead to sales success: the right mindset, the right skills set, and the right tool set."
—GERHARD GSCHWANDTNER, CEO, Selling Power

"The pressure for managers to produce is crushing, but guidance is minimal to none. Until now. *Smart Sales Manager* is a practical playbook that helps managers get up to speed fast on leading inside sales teams to success in the 'New Normal' totally wired Sales 2.0 world."
—ELAINE CHAN, Sales Development Director, Jive Software

"Managing an inside sales team today demands a new understanding of sales, sellers, and customers—and especially the sales management function. Whether you're currently in charge of a sales team or are looking to move into sales management, *Smart Sales Manager* should be the next book you pick up. Josiane Feigon fully examines the new reality of managing inside sales, and presents a solid path to becoming the smart sales manager today's inside sales teams need."
—PAUL McCORD, President, McCord Training and Development

"Josiane Feigon has done it again! *Smart Sales Manager* is the new trusted friend for managers. It will live on as the AP Style Manual for managers just like her first book, *Smart Selling on the Phone and Online*, the must-have manual for teams. These books are written by one of the smartest inside sales minds today."
—ANDY CREACH, Director of Mid Market Sales, ServiceMax

"I purchased a copy of Josiane Feigon's *Smart Selling on the Phone and Online* for every one of my reps because I believe it is truly THE essential guide for anyone selling on the phone. I am thrilled to have her new book, *Smart Sales Manager*, because it is the perfect next step to further reinforce the concepts, and provide the managers with critical, relevant, and practical guidance for coaching and developing high-performance teams. Josiane gets it, and we are very fortunate that she is willing to share her amazing expertise!"
—STACY ERB, Director Inside Sales, Apple Inc.

"It's a 2.0 world, and *Smart Sales Manager* is the most comprehensive sales and management book out there today. It provides managers with the secret sauce when it comes to managing their teams that are selling in a social, mobile, and virtual sales environment."
—TODD MCCORMICK, SVP of Sales, Silverpop

"Sales isn't the same game that it used to be. What's a sales manager to do? Read Josiane Feigon's newest book. It offers useful suggestions, framed with contexts that explain why her ideas make so much sense."
—JOHN COUSINEAU, President, Innovative Information Inc.

"The Internet has dramatically changed the way people buy, and thus how great salespeople sell. *Smart Sales Manager* is THE instruction manual on how to find and lead today's sales professionals toward greatness. You'll discover practical strategies you can immediately implement to motivate, guide, and hold accountable your sales team toward record performance. Feigon brings fresh insight into today's selling world, with creative ideas that will generate results."
—SAM RICHTER, bestselling author of *Get the Cold Out of Cold Calling*; and #1 ranked speaker

"I've been following the Sales 2.0 movement for several years, and Josiane Feigon's description of the Sales 2.0 ecosystem is spot on. She's got the inside scoop on the customer, the talent, the tools, and the 'potent prospecting' it takes to succeed."
—LORI RICHARDSON, President, Score More Sales

"*Smart Sales Manager* is a book that will empower sales managers to transform their salespeople into effective social selling teams. Feigon's playbook on the Sales 2.0 environment and the coaching process required to win is exactly what so many salespeople and sales managers are missing."
—JON FERRARA, CEO, Nimble LLC

"It's vital for managers to embody the spirit they want from their teams. *Smart Sales Manager* walks the talk about motivating and building an innovating team of disruptive, inside sales superheroes who will take our business to the next level of excellence."
—TOM SCONTRAS, VP of Sales & Marketing, Glance Networks

"One of the first things I do when building a sales organization is buy a copy of *Smart Selling on the Phone and Online* for every one of the SDR's account executives. Josiane's unique take on hybrid sales in the social era quickly becomes a go-to guide for the sales team. *Smart Sales Manager* creates the same level of value for the Sales Manager, Director, and VP, detailing best practices and unlocking the secrets of how to recruit, train, coach, and develop members of the millennial generation in today's demanding and fast-paced environment."
—BEN NACHBAUR, VP of Sales, PeopleMatter

"My brain lights up when I come across a book that is so engaging and comprehensive. *Smart Sales Manager* answers all the questions sales managers have about how to lead their teams in today's 'New Normal' landscape. Prepare to be challenged, to be inspired, and, ultimately, to be a better professional."
—PATRICK SWEENEY, President of Caliper; and *New York Times* bestselling author of *How to Hire & Develop Your Next Top Performer*

"With roughly 60-70 percent of the buying process happening before sales is involved, and buyers continuing to ignore phone calls and emails from people they don't know, Josiane Feigon's book helps sales leaders understand what they need to do to ensure that their salespeople adapt to this new reality. This is a must-read for any sales leader who realizes that what worked yesterday is no longer working today."
—BARBARA GIAMANCO, President and Social Sales Strategist; and coauthor of *The New Handshake: Sales Meets Social Media*

"The sales leaders of the future must read *Smart Sales Manager* today. As Josiane Feigon reminds us, the virtual, social, mobile world is changing everything you thought you knew about sales. Read this book, and get with the program!"
—MARTY FUNK, **Director of Sales for the Americas, Informatica**

"The search for top inside sales talent is increasing, but the talent pool is shrinking. *Smart Sales Manager* provides an innovative 'always-be-recruiting' ecosystem that transforms old and tired hiring and recruiting habits. Everyone wants a sales superhero on their team, and Josiane Feigon's book is a roadmap to the superheroes."
—JEN COLOSI, **President, Colosi Associates Executive Search**

"Executives leading their company's journey from Sales 1.0 to Sales 2.0 recognize that an inside sales team can fast-track a transformation to more effective and efficient selling, but only if the team's management is innovative and up-to-date for today's customers and sales teams. Josiane Feigon, who challenged old-school thinking in her first book for inside sales reps, now brings managers welcome new ideas and practical strategies with *Smart Sales Manager*."
—**Anneke Seley, coauthor, *Sales 2.0: Improve Business Results Using Innovative Sales Practices and Technology***

"*Smart Sales Manager* is thought provoking, well written, and extremely insightful. Managers must read the strategies, ideas, and insights into Sales 2.0 this book has to offer. Their professional success depends on it."
—GARY READ, **President and CEO, Boundary**

"Feigon casts a spotlight on the Sales 2.0 ecosystem that will permanently transform sales as we know it. *Smart Sales Manager* is one of the few must-reads of the year!"
—GARY AMBROSINI, **President, Timetrade**

"Customers have changed; younger inside sales reps are different and demanding; sales tools and intelligence have never been more plentiful—or more confusing to navigate. In *Smart Sales Manager*, Josiane Feigon reveals how to align 2.0 buying-and-selling environments to develop a team that turns the human connection into a pipeline accelerator. If you want to amplify inside sales performance, this book is your guide."
—ARDATH ALBEE, **B2B Marketing Strategist; and author of *eMarketing Strategies for the Complex Sale***

"The most compelling business books aren't the ones that just convey knowledge or advocate doing certain things. As important as those are, the most compelling business books encourage readers to do something. *Smart Sales Manager* is destined to change the way managers think about their teams—and, more important, to change the way professionals view themselves."
—DEBRA KEITH, **Director, Global License Compliance and Inside Sales, Autodesk**

"Having spent the last 25 years building and managing inside sales organizations, I have seen the need for sales managers to adapt to new ways of thinking in the world of Sales 2.0. Today's effective leaders must think differently, and Josiane Feigon has written an effective blueprint for both experienced and brand new inside sales leadership to motivate their inside teams to new levels of effectiveness. While there are hundreds of choices for sales management books out there, this is the one that is the most current, and really helps both the new and the experienced inside Sales 2.0 sales manager."
—MITCH STEWART, **Inside Sales Director, Meraki**

"*Smart Sales Manager* is a powerful, practical roadmap for building world-class sales teams and the leadership practices that empower results. From her insights on the new realities facing customers to innovative techniques for motivating excellence and managing perform-ance, Josiane Feigon delivers insightful and actionable strategies for success. This book is a must-have for new inside sales managers or those simply looking to sharpen their skills."
—JOHN HOAGLAND, **Director, Client Delivery, ServiceSource**

"Top performing professional sports team don't run the same plays over and over—they innovate. *Smart Sales Manager* provokes you to think the same way in business—from understanding your customer to creating your own playbook for hiring, training, and coaching sales reps who challenge the old way of selling."
—BILL BINCH, **Senior VP of Sales, Marketo**

"In this Sales 2.0 world, we often see 1.0 sales managers. In her first book, *Smart Selling on Phone and Online*, Josiane Feigon provided inside sales reps with a clear roadmap to success in today's selling environment. In *Smart Sales Manager*, she does the same thing for their managers. This is a comprehensive guide with tips and checklists covering all the essentials to manage and coach your reps to attain their full potential."
—BARRY TRAILER, **Managing Partner, CSO Insights**

"Josiane Feigon has done a brilliant job of aggregating the collective experience and wisdom of hundreds of inside sales leaders and managers. This is not a book that you read and put on your shelf. This is a book that is meant to be used; a book that lives on your desk, and gets tattered pages."
—STEVE RICHARD, Co-Founder, Vorsight

"Josiane once again demonstrates that she is a master of the new sales game. *Smart Sales Manager* delivers wisdom that is relevant to today's reality, and practically applicable immediately. Her insights into buying behavior, technology enablement, and most important, the new game of work, are tack sharp and delightful to consume. Every sales manager, no matter their tenure or whether they manage an inside or field team, needs to read this book. I expect this work to change the lives of sales managers across the globe."
—STU SCHMIDT, Chief Revenue Officer, ConnectAndSell

"Just as inside sales itself is different from selling face-to-face, managing a professional inside sales team requires a sophisticated set of skills and specialized knowledge different from typical sales management. Luckily for anyone tasked with building and managing inside sales, Josiane Feigon has assembled THE guide to help you do it the right way in today's ever-changing environment. This is not a book to be just read; USE it as your playbook for successful inside sales management."
—ART SOBCZAK, author of *Smart Calling*

"The world of inside sales is changing! Josiane Feigon knows exactly what is needed to harness its power and to take our great profession to yet new heights. Her passion and energy around transforming inside sales for the future is uplifting and contagious."
—BOB PERKINS, Vice President, DataSite

"No one knows inside sales like Josiane Feigon does, and her penetrating insights, meticulous observations, and wonderful storytelling ability make a manager's daily challenges come alive. For each of us, this book marks the beginning of the journey in becoming a truly better sales manager"
—DAVID STERENFELD, Principal and Founder of CORPORATE DYNAMIX

"Too many sales leaders are operating with the old rules, and wondering why they no longer work. *Smart Sales Manager* helps them understand and learn the fundamentals of inside sales that drive sales today. Josiane Feigon provides the strategies and tactics to help field sales professionals transform their careers to the next level of professionalism and performance."
—CHAD BURMEISTER, Director, Corporate Sales, ON24

"If your task is to lead a young inside sales team, you will find Josiane Feigon's *Smart Sales Manager* an essential guide. Covering all the bases of the 'New Normal,' it delivers for both experienced front-line managers and young professionals transitioning to sales management."
—TIBOR SHANTO, President, Renbor Sales Solutions Inc.

"Josiane Feigon has written the definitive book on how to manage the modern inside sales team. Her innovative strategies leave other sales management books in the dust. Awesome!"
—KEVIN GAITHER, VP of Inside Sales, uSamp

"Josiane Feigon really knows her stuff, and has a knack for delivering it in a format that's easy to follow, easy to implement, and highly likely to drive greater results across your sales organization. Put this book at the top of your reading list!"
—MATT HEINZ, President, Heinz Marketing Inc.

"If you are an inside sales manager who wants to make your team more effective, I highly recommend *Smart Sales Manager*."
—CRAIG ROSENBERG, Founder, Funnelholic Media

"*Smart Sales Manager* is written in the same humorous, knowledgeable, and cutting-edge style as Josiane Feigon's first book, *Smart Selling on the Phone and Online*. It tackles the entire Sales 2.0 ecosystem from the sales manager's point of view: everything from the new rules for selling to hiring, motivating, training, coaching, everyday management basics, and the skills it takes to create an effective inside sales team and lead it to success."
—CAROLYN BETTS, CEO of Betts Recruiting

"As a result of reading *Smart Sales Manager*, my sales team is utilizing social media tools to connect with and engage prospects—building long-term relationships versus transactional sales."
—BRUCE TUCKER, President and Founder, Patriot Technologies, Inc.

SMART SALES MANAGER

The Ultimate Playbook for Building and Running
a High-Performance Inside Sales Team

JOSIANE CHRIQUI FEIGON

AMACOM

American Management Association

New York • Atlanta • Brussels • Chicago • Mexico City • San Francisco
Shanghai • Tokyo • Toronto • Washington, D.C.

Bulk discounts available. For details visit:
www.amacombooks.org/go/specialsales
Or contact special sales:
Phone: 800-250-5308
Email: specialsls@amanet.org
View all the AMACOM titles at: www.amacombooks.org
American Management Association: www.amanet.org

This publication is designed to provide accurate and authoritative information in regard to the subject matter covered. It is sold with the understanding that the publisher is not engaged in rendering legal, accounting, or other professional service. If legal advice or other expert assistance is required, the services of a competent professional person should be sought.

Library of Congress Cataloging-in-Publication Data
Feigon, Josiane Chriqui.
    Smart sales manager : the ultimate playbook for building and running a high-performance inside sales team / Josiane Chriqui Feigon.
        pages cm
    Includes bibliographical references and index.
    ISBN-13: 978-0-8144-3283-9
    ISBN-10: 0-8144-3283-2
    1. Selling. 2. Success in business. 3. Teams in the workplace. I. Title.
    HF5438.25.F44 2013
    658.8'102–dc23   2013010823

About AMA
American Management Association (www.amanet.org) is a world leader in talent development, advancing the skills of individuals to drive business success. Our mission is to support the goals of individuals and organizations through a complete range of products and services, including classroom and virtual seminars, webcasts, webinars, podcasts, conferences, corporate and government solutions, business books, and research. AMA's approach to improving performance combines experiential learning—learning through doing—with opportunities for ongoing professional growth at every step of one's career journey.

Printing number
10 9 8 7 6 5 4 3 2 1

To my daughter, Briana

CONTENTS

ACKNOWLEDGMENTS

It has taken me 20 years to gather up all the courage to write a book like this one, and it wouldn't exist if it wasn't for my editor, Bob Nirkind at AMACOM, whose unabashed enthusiasm and support for this book made it happen. My master collaborator, friend, and editor, Naomi Lucks, demanded extreme excellence with a no-tolerance zone for mediocrity and always helped me stay the course.

As the inside sales world continues to explode, I'm so grateful to hold onto my front row seat in this extremely exciting space. I want to thank Larry Reeves and Bob Perkins, the founders of AA-ISP (American Association for Inside Sales Professionals), for creating a growing community that is *the* place to be if you live and breathe inside sales. There are tons of new chapters all over the world where the brightest bunches come together to share and network. I also thank the true thought leaders who have dedicated their careers to making significant contributions in this field, such as Trish Bertuzzi, President of the Bridge Group Inc. and manager of the extremely vibrant Inside Sales Experts LinkedIn group; Steve Ricard from Vorsight; Anneke Seley from RealityWorks; Dave Elkington and Ken Krogue from Insidesales.com; and Art Sobczak from Business by Phone.

Support is everything, and I assembled a top-notch advice council—a group of managers/directors/VPs/CEOs who really *got* this complex space. My *peeps* were always there for me with generous advice, great insights, and wisdom that helped me fill those empty pages. Thanks for the graphic wizardry and training help of Martha Acosta, whose capacity for brilliance and understanding never ceases to amaze me. My thanks go to Deb Keith, Elaine Chan, Mitch Stewart, Shelly McNary, Carolyn Betts, Ben Nachbauer, Melanie Fitzgerald, Chad Burmeister, Jim O'Halloran, Kevin Gaither, Brett Wallace, Andy

Creach, Stacy Erb, Dan Aldridge, Dave Sterenfeld, Jen Colosi, Nancy Nardin, Gwen Wagner, Brody Paul, David Stein, and Ted Weinstein.

I took a chance writing this book. The sales profession is a very crowded space, and this book requires a major overhaul in old thinking. So I want to thank the Sales 2.0 pioneers who are leading this charter of change, especially Gerhard Gschwandter, Founder of Selling Power and Sales 2.0 Conference, who continues to spread the sales love, sprinkled with tools, social media, and marketing, and reminds us that sales as we know it will never be the same, and Jill Konrath, author of *SNAP Selling* and *Selling to Big Companies*.

My deepest gratitude goes to my clients, the ones who never lose trust in my work and who continue to choose TeleSmart as their primary inside sales training solutions provider. I am always inspired when I'm in the trenches training the new hires, existing teams, and managers, because they are the ones who live it—I'm there to help make their work easier, faster, and much more productive.

Finally, I thank my loving family and cherished friends who never lose faith when I drop off the grid for months and months of writing, and welcome me back with open arms when I return.

MANAGING INSIDE SALES IN A 2.0 WORLD

You have a $75 million sales quota for the quarter, and you are responsible for managing and driving revenues for your team of 14 direct reports. You've got a full team of lead development, inside sales, and renewals reps. You manage a unique, complex system of CRM, tools, processes, talent, and technology that powers the organization. Your job is to make sure that your people are running on all cylinders and at maximum capacity—charging forward, making tons of calls every day, and closing all the deals in their pipeline. It should be a snap, right? But . . . that's not exactly the case, and you're not exactly sure where to start to fix that.

If you're like most managers today, you were promoted because of your skills as an individual contributor and thrown into your job with little or no management training. It would be so *easy* if you could just grab your reps' customer calls and show them how it's done. But your young team is impatient—the members just want answers. *Now*. Meanwhile, 25 percent of your deals don't close because of "no decision," only 40 percent of your team is actually making quota, and win rates are under 50 percent due to significant discounting. New prospects won't pick up the phone, your loyal customers are canceling appointments left and right, and that phone buzz you love to hear has been replaced with the punctuated silence of clicking keyboards.

So far, your survival strategy is to just keep moving ahead while looking in your rear-view mirror on the theory that what was done in the past has to work sometimes. But managing a high-performing inside sales team in the dynamic Sales 2.0 ecosystem—a digital, diverse, connected world where customers do their own research and talent expects work to be F-U-N—requires you to have all the answers, in a Siri sort of way.

MANAGING IN THE SALES 2.0 ECOSYSTEM

Inside sales has burst through the cubicle walls with seemingly unstoppable momentum. In fact, it's on course to overtake and, even, replace field sales by 2015. The need for more inside sales managers usually means that top sales reps are being promoted—but as with so many promotions, many managers are in way over their heads. They know sales, but they don't know *managing* sales. The pressure from above for these managers to produce numbers can be crushing—and the training provided is minimal to none.

As social selling, digital communications, and innovative visual content take the place of simple cold calling, the new inside sales organization has become a large, complex, and delicate operation that needs skilled management to make it run effectively, efficiently, and profitably. Everything is different in this new world: New customers who want to self-educate and who buy on their own sales cycle, not yours. New tech-savvy talent who hate the phone and want it all now. New tools that seem to proliferate faster than you can keep track of them, let alone learn them. And, new prospecting rules and even metrics that turn everything you know upside down.

Managing these organizations and these young diverse teams is increasingly more complicated. The old rules absolutely do not apply. A whopping 90 percent of managers used to be individual contributors, but the skills that got them there aren't the ones they will use in their leadership roles. So they are scrambling to figure out the best way to effectively manage and drive revenues with their teams.

A BOOK WRITTEN JUST FOR YOU

For the past 20 years, I've been a thought leader and solutions provider for global inside sales organizations with my own company, TeleSmart Communications. My best-selling book, *Smart Selling on the Phone and Online*, has become the go-to sourcebook for inside sales teams that need to quickly pick up speed on their sales skills. It's their trusted friend in the cubicle and *Smart Sales Manager* is the big brother version for you!

If you are an inside sales manager who is stepping out of a career as a successful rep or just inherited a new team from a recent acquisition and must hit the ground running, *Smart Sales Manager* is designed to get you up to speed quickly on what you need to know to manage effectively, coach like a leader, and create and drive engaged high-performance teams that know what it takes to win in today's Sales 2.0 Ecosystem.

Smart Sales Manager is your playbook for leading your young, eager inside sales teams in the Sales 2.0 Ecosystem: the new rules for everything from everyday management basics to selling to hiring (and firing), motivating, training, coaching, the new metrics . . . all the skills it takes to create an effective inside sales team and lead it to success. You'll find references to the latest trends and the practical, tactical strategies, skills, and guidance you need to run a high-performance inside sales team and to carry your organizations to the next level of excellence.

The chapters in Part I, "The New Normal," bring you up to speed on the players in the Sales 2.0 Ecosystem:

- The care and feeding of the new independent and elusive Customer 2.0

- The multitasking and technically wired Millennial Talent 2.0

- The social-mobile-video Sales 2.0 tools

- The new Sales Superheroes in all of their Prospecting 2.0 nurturing and blitzing action

The chapters in Part II, "The Compassionate Manager 2.0," constitute your playbook for building an integrated, sustainable, and effective hiring, training, and coaching system. This section is about human capital—your talent:

- Finding, hiring, and retaining good talent

- Building a sustainable training structure and establishing a comprehensive sales skill system

- Building an integrated coaching program

- Trust-based coaching that gets the most out of your teams

- Metrics 2.0—metrics that work in the wired world and make sense to Talent 2.0

The chapters in Part III, "Motivate Fast!" turn the spotlight on you, Manager 2.0—leader, motivator, Fun Meister, and the one who has to make the tough decisions. These four chapters are filled with how-to strategies and loaded with tips, ideas, and checklists that managers need quickly. They focus on:

- Reinventing sales meetings: recapturing the team spirit, enhancing sales team communication, and delivering your message loud and clear. You'll get dozens of new ideas for agendas, topics, organization, and flow to keep the teams engaged and ensure that you make a strong positive impact.

- Course correcting the 1:1 forecast review as it happens: new ways to assess team members' skill sets and to dissect and reframe the objections they are struggling with, as well as new questions to ask that elicit real information.

- Creating incentives that work: dozens of new, innovative, and highly motivational contests, spiffs, and incentives you can roll out each month, plus motivating with mobile text messages.

- Learning to let go: how to stop procrastinating on those tough talks with problem members of your team, and how to know when it's time to let them go.

Smart Sales Manager is your new trusted adviser and friend who will lead you if you want to follow. Now take this playbook and run with it!

PART ONE

THE NEW NORMAL

Managing the Sales 2.0 Ecosystem

It seemed so simple in the beginning. . . .

Moving into an inside sales management role meant hiring a team, giving the members territories, designing their comp plans, and setting them up in their cubicles with landlines, PCs, headsets, and whiteboards. You would hold weekly team meetings, 1:1 forecast reviews, walk the sales aisles to listen for the daily dialing buzz, and update your dashboard regularly. Your teams would make quotas, set record-breaking numbers of appointments, expand their product line, and not have to rely on their field partners. Your trusty dashboard would be your lifeline, keeping you accurate and in control.

But your plans, which were based on everything you've learned about sales over the years, have somehow gone awry. And the well-honed skills that got you this job in the first place don't seem to be working their old magic—not with customers, with new sales teams, with new tools, and even with prospecting:

- Gone are the days when customers answered their phones and receptionists put your calls through.

- Gone are the days when customers patiently sat through demos, accepted appointments, and even insisted that you walk them through the entire sales process.

- Gone are the days when you hired a professional team of solution-selling salespeople and geo-aligned them with the field.

- Gone are the days when sales reps valued hard work, put in time and paid their dues, engaged in meaningful conversations with their prospects, and were so excited when you gave out Starbucks gift cards as a little bonus.

- Gone are the days when investing in tools meant purchasing the latest noise-canceling headsets, getting multiple lines on your phone, buying new PCs for your teams, and switching from old legacy systems to the latest sales CRM with sales-centric features that no one had access to—not even the marketing department.

- Gone are the days when cold calling and prospecting meant "butts in seats" for 75 outbound daily dials and averaging four hours of talk time per day—and mailing out 25 VITO letters each week was your biggest outreach effort.

Welcome to the New Normal world of the Sales 2.0 Ecosystem.

In this section, we'll introduce you to the elements of this dynamic environment—the new independent customers, multitasking millennial sales talent, social-mobile-video tool choices, and prospecting approaches that nurture with curated content. We'll explore how they work together to create the sales synergy that has permanently transformed inside sales and give you the play-by-play vision on what it takes to manage your team for success.

CHAPTER 1

CUSTOMER 2.0 IS MAD AS HELL!

Understanding the New Independent Buyer

It's the usual Wednesday 4 pm meeting, time to catch up with the sales team. John watches nervously as the members of his team straggle into the conference room and drop into chairs, distracted, discouraged, detached, and restless. The forecast numbers have continued to slide and the end of the quarter is only weeks away. He hired this team last year, but the members haven't produced the way he had hoped. It's getting demoralizing, and his boss has made it clear that their lack of productivity is reflecting badly on him.

John takes a deep breath. He knows what he's going to hear but feels helpless to do anything but listen to the bad news. He starts with Ashley, who is sitting next to him.

"Ashley, how did your demos go last week? I think you had three strong ones scheduled, right?"

Ashley twirls a strand of hair. "Well," she says, "two of them got canceled and the other one lasted only ten minutes because his boss never showed up. This happens all the time!" She rolls her eyes.

John moves on to Brad, who looks more confident than Ashley.

"Brad, did you work things out with that customer who blasted you about phone stalking him?"

"Yeah, bro, no problem. I sent him some swag from our marketing department, and it's all good." He grins, two thumbs up, satisfied that he's got it covered.

John can feel his stomach acid heating up. "Tara," he says, pressing on, "you've got some very large accounts coming up for renewal within the next few weeks. We're counting on this revenue for the quarter. How are things moving along?"

Tara gets to the point fast. "The purchasing department isn't returning my calls, and all my old contacts there are gone. I keep trying to find someone who owns this contract but no luck so far. All the names I have are no longer there, and no one can point me in the right direction"

John nods and turns to his slacker rep. "Mario, your talk time is very low—about 45 minutes per day. Why aren't you making any outbound calls?"

"Dude," Mario shrugs, "I can't get anyone on the phone! They're all on email or texting. I use the robo, but every call seems to get DENIED."

Just a few reps left. "Alex! How's it going with that customer you told me about? Did the PO come in on Tuesday like they promised?" Alex is smiling. "I spoke with him this morning and things are A-W-E-S-O-M-E, John. He told me I should get the PO by later today or tomorrow."

Lucy walks into the meeting late and frazzled, rushed but excited. "Lucy, what's up? This meeting started fifteen minutes ago. Why are you coming in now?"

"Good news! I just closed a deal that I didn't even have forecasted. I talked with this guy about seven months ago and he just called me and said they were ready to buy now. It's CRAZY."

John looks around the room wondering what's wrong with his sales team. Why has the sales cycle become so unpredictable? Do they need more training? Does he need a new team? Why can't they get through to the customer?

* * *

Most sales managers are used to customers who want and need them. So the attitude of the New Normal Customer 2.0 is jarring: They're just not that into you. At least, not yet. In this chapter, we'll discover what drives these customers, what drives them away, and what brings them back.

MEET THE NEW CUSTOMER 2.0

Today's customers are super busy, super mobile, super connected, and independent. They don't return calls, they see the phone as an interruption, they are too smart for promotional incentives, and they cancel appointments. Digitally astute, these DIY'ers are quickly weaning themselves *off* salespeople altogether in favor of doing their own research and making purchases unassisted. They often claim that they don't need salespeople anymore, and they don't— at least, not the traditional ones.

The biggest message salespeople get from customers today is *stay away*. We're just trying to get a pulse, but the closer we get the more annoying we seem to become. Senior team members are baffled. Why don't their tried-and-true sales approaches work anymore? Junior new hires are offended. Why is this customer so rude? Managers order their teams to charge forward despite the uncertainty, hoping for a sudden turnaround. But the old sales approach not only doesn't work on them; it makes them *mad as hell*.

Today's busy prospects are independent, self-sufficient, and self-educated. These hard-working multitaskers don't want to be crowded and held in a sales headlock. They don't want to be "sold" to. They have radically different buying habits and expectations. They actually *control* the buying process, creating their own unique—and hidden— sales cycle: They buy when they're ready to buy.

Is this frustrating? Yes. Is it hopeless? Not at all. You just have to understand what they're trying to tell you. But love them or hate them, they are here to stay. As one astute report sums it up, "This educated consumer is not just your best customer, it's your only customer."[1] In this chapter, you'll step into the mind of Customer 2.0 to learn why they seem so annoyed with salespeople, and how you can help your team make them happy again.

FIGURE 1-1 | The New Independent Customer 2.0

DECODING CUSTOMER 2.0

Today's top sales effectiveness initiative is capturing new customers. That means keeping up with Customer 2.0's rapidly changing expectations, and this puts a huge amount of pressure on sales organizations. Managers who climbed the sales ladder over the course of the last five years or more can remember customers who actually sat through sales presentations, answered their phones, called you back, and kept you informed throughout the sales process. Getting a handle on what Customer 2.0 wants—and needs—can be challenging. They just seem so angry.

The better you get at decoding Customer 2.0's messages, the faster you can understand their new habits and requirements and recognize what annoys them. Once you have the ah-ha! moment, you can effectively coach your team on how to listen, respond, and course-correct.

It's a safe bet that you and your team have heard Customer 2.0 say most of the following statements—or variations on them—over and over again. We'll decode each one to find out what they're really saying, and then we'll follow up with coaching essentials you can use with your team so you never have to hear these mad-as-hell messages again.

Get real. Start decoding!

"Sales intelligence means doing some homework about me before you call!"

Decoding the message: *"Only an intelligent, well-informed, and relevant call will earn time with me."*

Customers are no longer forgiving when it comes to unprepared sales calls. Research indicates that more than 90 percent of prospects will not accept a meeting if it's from a cold call or email by a sales rep. Information today is transparent and public, so customers have a right to be upset. There's really no excuse for not knowing everything you can before you call.

Coaching your team: Salespeople must take time to research the prospect before the first call and then integrate that information into their call. With the deluge of information out there, there are no more excuses for not knowing who a prospect reports to, what their email address is, and their direct dial. The salespeople who will earn time on the call are the ones who come in prepared and knowledgeable. Insist that pre-call research is essential, and make sure they know how to use the tools they have to the best effect. Watch that they don't spend too much time on research. Some may spend up to twenty minutes to an hour per contact, a task that can generally be accomplished in two minutes.

"Oh, another one? It must be a call blitz day. Stop stalking me!"

Decoding the message: *"I'm very busy, and you're interrupting me. I'm tired of feeling manipulated and pressured by desperate reps on call blitz days."*

Incredibly, there is something even worse than getting an angry hang-up like this one. So often, when reps actually get that rare live voice on the line, they are startled into silence or unintelligible mumbling; they zoned out long ago, convinced no one would ever pick up. Customers especially don't want to hear from robots. Do you? So when reps hide behind robo-dialers during their calling rampage, the customer who picks up feels like they're just #348 on some rep's call radar. Then things get *really* ugly.

Coaching your team: You may want to put your team on a blitzing call campaign to get call numbers up. That's fine, but it won't work if it's just desperate calling to anyone and everyone. And the rare live call will quickly become a failed attempt if your salespeople are not well prepared to focus on quality and not quantity. The days of meaningless cold calling are dead—blitzing, done correctly, is a double-espresso prospecting shot. It's proven to increase numbers, productivity, and revenues.

> *"Stop harassing me with Outlook meeting*
> *requests! Don't you know that I cancel*
> *four out of five appointments each week?"*

Decoding the message: *"Don't think I'm going to make your meeting if you can't do your job right."*

Customer 2.0 often seems to cancel appointments for no apparent reason. But there's always a reason: reps schedule appointments too far in advance, ask for too much time, invite too many people to attend, forget to "sell" the value of the appointment, or fail to confirm the appointment through social media as the date gets closer.

Coaching your team: Help them understand that having an effective appointment strategy will help avoid cancellations. Appointment setting is more than just sending an invite; it includes nurturing with contagious content, socially securing the appointment, and doing some preliminary outreach before the appointment.

*"I don't let any outsiders in. Dip into
my social circle and maybe I'll listen."*

Decoding the message: *"I don't know you, and neither does anyone
else I know. How can I trust you?"*

Socially savvy Customer 2.0 is easily influenced by peers. They
begin their buying journey by tuning to their social networks, and
they base their purchase decisions on what others say about your service or solutions. They will listen and trust their social network of
peers, friends, and colleagues before they listen to your sales team.
The DemandGen report "Breaking out of the Funnel"[2] found these
telling statistics on this customer:

- 59 percent engaged with a peer who had addressed the challenge.

- 48 percent followed industry conversations on the topic.

- 37 percent posted questions on social networking sites looking
  for suggestions and feedback.

- 20 percent connected directly with potential solution providers
  via social networking channels.

- 44 percent conducted the anonymous research of a select group
  of vendors.

- 41 percent researched papers and postings from thought leaders.

Coaching your team: Many sales leaders do not fully realize the potential of social selling as an effective prospecting strategy for sales,
but they should. They discourage their team members from using social media because they believe that it is a major waste of time. They
would rather have their teams cold calling because they can see tangible results. But they are failing to respond to the new ways that customers are buying. What they don't realize is that today's customers
are ready to buy; the rep just has to be there at the right time during
the sales cycle to be part of it. And that means interacting regularly
in the social world these customers live in.

Encourage your team to develop a strong and relevant digital footprint. Make sure that they clean up their Facebook presence (no party pictures, please), join the customer's favorite LinkedIn discussion groups and blogs, and write some appropriate tweets. Once they identify the customer's tight circle of peers, they can leverage or "name-drop" these connections, but remind them to do this naturally and professionally.

> *"You really expect me to read a whitepaper?*
> *Can you send me a YouTube video instead?*

Decoding the message: *"I don't have the time or inclination to read."*
This customer would rather watch a two-minute video on their iPhone or iPad than read a 20-page whitepaper.

Coaching your team: Provide the tools for your team to include more videos that they can share with their customers. Make sure the videos are fun; these customers like to be entertained. And remind your reps that web conferencing and Skype meetings mean that customers can see (and judge) them. They need to start looking good from the waist up.

> *"Give me the sound bite, not that marketing garbage."*

Decoding the message: *"I need you to make the message easy to understand."*
Customer 2.0 lives in a 135-character world and needs everything broken down into bite-sized pieces. These customers are busy, impatient, and too savvy for marketing fluff. They need you to make all information about your product or solution easy for them to understand, download, and implement. Documents filled with lots of data and big attachments do not get their attention, and may even aggravate them. Long emails get deleted without being read because they have a short attention span. Reading, sorting through, and analyzing lots of data and information is just not going to happen.

Coaching your team: Remind your team that it is essential to condense information into minibites. Tell your sales team to send out one-page documents and one-paragraph emails only and to make sure to spell out the essential information right at the top. The easier and faster it is for customers to understand your product or solution, the more quickly they can make a decision about it being a potential match.

"You've got to be kidding. No way am I sitting through one more 'death by PowerPoint' presentation!"

Decoding the message: *"Don't waste my time."*

Customer 2.0 does not want to be sold to. They do not want to be bored by long presentations, and they do not want their time wasted. Nothing makes them run faster than a long-winded sales pitch or an endless, deadly PowerPoint presentation. They are very sophisticated at diagnosing their own problems through online demos or proofs, opinions, and case studies.

Coaching your team: Discourage your team from presenting anything that sounds like a sales pitch. And make sure they toss that 170-slide PowerPoint demo for one that has fewer slides, less text, and more engaging visuals. Promote a collaborative culture with your team and encourage live collaboration opportunities with their prospects. Reinforce the point that they may never have a second chance.

"An eight-person committee signs off on this, not just ONE person."

Decoding the message: *"I don't think I can make this decision by myself."*

Today's decision-makers are not easy to find—even though there are a lot more of them floating around. Today's customers are defensive and protective of their turf, and they are uncertain of how much power and influence they really have, regardless of their job title. According to Marketing Sherpa,[3] as many as 21 people might work together to make a purchase decision over $25K.

Coaching your team: Most opportunities are lost because salespeople do not talk with enough people. Encourage your teams to call deeper and wider. Have them build out the org chart in the 2 × 2 mode, which requires them to reach out to a minimum of eight contacts per company.

> *"Don't push me! I can scope out the market on my own. Clearly, I know more about your product, service, company, and process than you do."*

Decoding the message: *"Give me some credit! I can find out everything I need to know by shopping online."*

Customer 2.0 likes to self-educate—and why not, when all the information is out there waiting to be found? These independent and self-sufficient customers are more informed than ever before; their claim to know more about your product than you do might actually be true. A study by Hubspot[4] showed that 93 percent of buying starts with an online search. They do all their own research—by participating in discussion forums, asking peers, reading reviews, and watching product video demos.

Coaching your team: Your team must stay one step ahead of these customers by anticipating their needs throughout the sales cycle. Remind them about each customer's hidden sales cycle—a customer may seem extremely interested one day, and go radio silent the next. But the customers haven't vanished; they are still paying attention. They're just in their own cycle, not yours, and they engage on their own terms.

Work with your teams to develop content-nurturing strategies that build interest in your solution slowly by dripping information to prospects in small, entertaining, and digestible bites. Hook their curiosity and then engage them with contagious content that is strategically planted and anticipates their needs throughout the sales cycle. Remind your team that enterprise deals require eight to twelve and that each touch has a unique value proposition that educates, sells, and drives their value as a trusted adviser.

"I'm not taking any risks!"

Decoding the message: *"I don't want to lose my job because I made the wrong decision."*

Customer 2.0 doesn't take risks, and for good reason: They have survived tough economic times; if they make a bad purchase, they can lose their jobs and maybe even their homes in today's economy. No surprise—they're cautious and smart enough to know how to shop for value and not just wait for the bargains. But it's important to remember that even though they are low risk, they are sitting on a stash of cash—money ready to spend. Because they are so risk averse, they want to know exactly what they will get from their investment; they want to see the most value for their money and see returns years later.

Coaching your team: Remind your team that very few customers will go out on a limb for a new solution. They want to know that they are guaranteed a return on their investment. Have team members show these customers some ROI, let them read some case studies, hear customer testimonials, and download a free evaluation first. To keep the customer feeling safe and cared for, reps must engage in these ROI discussions on each call, and even long after the services have been delivered.

"Yeah, yeah, I know I said I wanted your solution now, and I did. But that was last week. See ya!"

Decoding the message: *"The ball's in my court, not yours. I don't have to call you back."*

This customer is a game changer *and* a mind changer. Customer 2.0 can stop and start the buying process whenever they want, and they will abuse that advantage. It's not unusual to engage with the customer and have them completely vanish on you the same day. The "call back" is a thing of the past.

Coaching your team: Remind your team members to treat each call as if it's their only call. Independent customers lose track of time. They may have engaged with customers through demos and presentations or conversations five months ago, but they've lost track of that time and the lead life has lost some power. Reviving old leads is one of the most efficient sales efforts reps can make.

Encourage your team to use a multiple-attempt email strategy that maintains momentum for up to nine months or long after the lead is closed. Make sure they don't close the lead too soon: These customers will come back; they just have their own rhythm.

> *"Wait! Don't close that opportunity.*
> *I may be interested after all!"*

Decoding the message: *"Your deadline woke me up."*

Crazy-busy Customer 2.0 fears loss and wants to be included, and this makes them respond positively to decision deadlines. Research suggests that as many as 77 percent of buyers who might buy, do— eventually. The best way to capture cooperation and get response is to create a deadline.

Social customers want to belong. When salespeople tell them that they are going to be "removed" or "eliminated" from something, they panic. They still want to belong and be part of the club! When they are threatened with a lead being closed, they suddenly want it. The "going, going, gone" or "last attempt" message will suddenly wake them up to say, "Wait, wait! Don't close that opportunity. I may be interested after all!"

Coaching your team: Encourage your team to stay with it. Don't give up too soon! Most customers are bombarded early in the sales cycle with introductory voice mail scripts and email templates. These early first, second, and third attempts focus on the beginning of the sales cycle. Most salespeople give up after the fourth attempt, but it's often the seventh attempt that gets the job done. Just when your team members are ready to close the lead, coach them to leak the "going, going, gone" message. More times than not, the prospect will suddenly wake up and buy.

> ### *"I know it's been nine months since we last spoke, but I'm ready to buy NOW."*

Decoding the message: *"I create my own sales cycle, and it's not when you think it is."*

Customer 2.0 prefers to engage much later in the sales cycle, creating their own "hidden" sales cycle. Sales Executive Board shows that 57 percent of B2B buying steps are completed before buyers connect with a salesperson. Before they come to you, they have searched through competitors' products, talked in discussion forums, and downloaded their own demos. When they come to you, they know what they want and when they want it. When they decide they are ready to buy NOW, it happens NOW. They are ready to spend these dollars immediately and want it shipped yesterday. That means that they are not sitting around waiting for your "desperate discounting" to make their purchase.

Coaching your team: When customers are ready to buy, sell! Stress the importance of reacting to these messages immediately and wrapping up the deal quickly to prevent a change of heart. They will rarely get a second chance.

> ### *"You are the eighteenth vendor who has described herself as a 'value-added solutions provider with a strong product portfolio.' Very original!"*

Decoding the message: *"I have no idea what you're really saying, and it just sounds like recycled marketing fluff."*

When reps fail to distinguish themselves from all the other salespeople out there, customers get confused, and they bail. When salespeople take the extra misstep of describing themselves in generic jargon, they are saying "I am boring and unimaginative." The most important part of your team's role is branding and evangelizing your solution and sounding persuasive and intelligent enough to make it stick.

Coaching your team: If you hear your reps speaking in Vendor Gobbledygook, stop them. If you hear them using endless, prewritten marketing intros, stop them. If your product offerings are too broad, condense the focus. Remind them how important it is to be clear, to get to the point quickly, and to make sure it's understandable. Role-play and practice with your team members to sound unique and authentic with their intros and to make them short and to the point. The more fancy or wordy intros are, the more generic and confusing they will sound.

Have them practice, practice, practice the intros they are using, and recraft them if necessary. Make sure each member of your team can easily verbalize what makes your product/service unique in the marketplace and articulates it in a way that the customer can understand and engage with.

> *"I almost never respond to cold calls*
> *and emails, but yours caught my eye."*

Decoding the message: *"You are doing something right."*

According to research conducted by Insidesales.com,[5] 4 percent of voice mails result in a call back. Customers are so angry and demoralized that when something good comes their way they appreciate it. When a salesperson times it right and gets the message right, these grateful customers will go out of their way to let you know how much they appreciate it.

Coaching your team: Talk to your team about looking for positive ways to stand out. Remind them that well-crafted voice mail messages and well-written—short!—emails are no-fail. Customer 2.0 is extremely receptive to intelligent, well-prepared, and well-packaged messages.

Mixed Messages: Understanding the
Needs of Today's Complex Customer 2.0

Okay, here's the rub: Customer 2.0 seems to be pushing us away and sending out clear signals to give them space. Right? Not exactly. They are very complex. They send out "Don't bug me and stay out of my way" messages, while simultaneously asking you to keep your sales lifeline open.

This phenomenon is counterintuitive to everything we know about them—but it's just as true! It pays to understand their mixed messages, and coach your team not to give up. Some of the following mixed signals may sound familiar:

- They travel light—but they still want company. The customers who ask for very little are actually the ones who need the most.

- They are reluctant and cautious about spending—but they have tons of cash stashed away.

- They are busy and have short attention spans—but they take the time to self-educate and devour content when it's fresh, relevant, and easy to digest.

- They don't trust vendors—but will trust their social networks. Peer approval is vital to them.

- They see phone calls as an annoying interruption—but they will accept demos.

- They cancel appointments—but they request conference calls at a moment's notice.

- They have short fuses and short memories—but over time, they forget what they were "mad as hell" about!

- They are not loyal or monogamous—but they are starved for a relationship. They crave long-term relationships with business partners they can trust, especially if it's virtual.

- They lose interest in the beginning of the sales cycle—but they pay attention at the end.

- They are independent buyers who do their own research and don't need salespeople—but when an intelligent one appears, they are unrestrained with appreciation and eager to share and collaborate.

THE TEAM MEETING: TAKE TWO

John felt beaten down and discouraged from his team meeting and his reps' passive and clueless responses to his questions. They didn't seem to really care if they made the sale or not. Unfortunately, his job was on the line too. He was tempted to press "refresh" and hire a new team, but this is the brand-new team he hired last year.

The more John thought about it, the more he realized that all of their issues were customer related. But these customers were different from the ones he'd cut his sales teeth on— they just didn't respond to tried-and-true sales techniques. No wonder his team members felt everything they were doing with this customer was WRONG; they weren't even speaking the same language!

John decided to call a meeting to educate his team members on what this new customer wants and how to decode what the customer is really saying. He also talked to them about why the old sales tactics they'd all been using—and he was as guilty as the rest of them—were actually driving the customers away. Then he gave each of them some customized Customer 2.0 advice for next steps.

Ashley's canceled appointments: *"Ashley, you can expect at least a 50 percent cancellation rate with today's customer, so don't take it personally. Instead, go back to all the appointments you booked this month, draw out an org chart for each target company, identify at least six people you would like to invite for a demo, and ask for no more than six minutes. Ask for less. You might get more. And be sure to explain what they will learn from the demo. Once you have scheduled each appointment, go through LinkedIn and socially surf through to confirm. Reconfirm again 24 hours before the demo and send them a great two-minute video to prepare them."*

Brad's phone-stalking issues: *"Brad, lay off the phones with this prospect. Customer 2.0 doesn't want to feel harassed and stalked. Instead of calling, I want you to put together some personalized, rele-*

vant content, send it to your prospect over the course of three weeks, and 'drip' it to them slowly. Vary the content. Make it all fun, relevant, short, and memorable."

Tara's purchase department problem: *"Tara, stop trying to contact the purchase department. It's pointless. This customer makes decisions by committee, and those committee members may be all over the state or even the country and difficult to find. Start by reaching out to the end-users. Get some intelligence on how they are using the product, check with technical support to see if they've had issues, and put together a cost analysis of how much they have saved in support costs with their renewals. Then contact the CFO's admin. Get the admin live, don't leave a message. Ask if she can help you confirm the org chart of names.*

Mario's low talk time: *"Mario, look. Whatever you've heard, the phone isn't going away in inside sales right now. But robotic call campaigns turn today's customer off. I want you to stick to your non-negotiable power calls and make intelligent and well-researched introductory calls. Back them up with emails and leverage LinkedIn. This will make your outbound call strategy more robust. I also want you to have all your sales productivity tools set up and ready to go. This momentum will help you hit your call time, create new leads, and eventually generate new appointments and quotes."*

Alex's never-arriving PO: *"Alex, have you ever heard of the No-Po Zone? That's when a rep is stuck talking to people with no power and no potential. They have no influence. That's where you are now. You've been talking to someone who keeps giving you false promises—someone who probably doesn't even have the power to issue a PO. They may just not want to hurt your feelings, or they may be purposely keeping you out with this tactic. Whatever, it's time to cut the cord! Call above them, below them, around them, and engage more influencers."*

Lucy's surprise $BlueBird$: "*Lucy, pay attention and react quickly to this new order. Do whatever it takes to help bring in a smooth close. Thank your customer with a LinkedIn connection and stay in touch with them even after the sale closes.*"

MANAGEMENT TIPS

- When you understand what Customer 2.0 wants and needs, you can reframe your approach to meet those needs.

- Customer 2.0 creates their own hidden sales cycle, so be creative. Don't be attached to old habits in the sales cycle.

- Listen and diagnose what your team members are saying about how their customers are responding, and help them adjust their approach based on what you know about Customer 2.0.

- These busy, independent customers want the attention of salespeople. All of it. Urge team members to be unique and authentic about their intentions when they reach out to Customer 2.0. Watch out—they will be mad as hell if salespeople drone on with a generic and meaningless message.

CHAPTER 2

TALENT 2.0

Why Millennials Make a Winning Team
of Disruptive Inside Sales Superheroes

It was the first worldwide sales kickoff for Ellen's inside sales team and they were going to Vegas! Her team of 72 young reps was beyond excited to be flown out for this huge company event in an exciting city. They were a supportive team who loved to be together, and this would be the first time her remote workers would have an opportunity to meet the rest of the group.

Ellen was proud that her awesome young team was getting the recognition it deserved. There would even be awards in store for some of them on this trip. She heard a few members of her team joking that "What happens in Vegas stays in Vegas, right?," and she laughed along with them. At breakfast on the first day of meetings, Diego and Jared showed up in flip-flops; they had remembered there was a pool but had forgotten to pack their dress shoes. She sent them shoe shopping immediately. Then she heard a tiny bark and saw that Molly was holding a bright pink dog carrier, with her miniature Yorkshire terrier peeking out. How did she manage to get that on the plane? Ellen made Molly promise to keep her dog in her hotel room.

On day two, during one of the product demos, Sadia and Caitlin abruptly ran out of the room to console Lauren, who was sobbing uncontrollably because her boyfriend had just broken up with her by text during the meeting. As Ellen surveyed the room, she could tell that almost all of her team had their heads down and fingers tapping, gchatting away. Later on, Manny asked the product managers if they've ever watched Hunger Games, *because they felt the new products had a postapocalyptic feel to them. By the third day, Colby, her rising star, was so hung over that he got up to puke loudly in the back of the meeting room. And Ellen wasn't feeling that well either; inhaling Stella's perfume all day was making her sick. Going over the roster of disasters in her head, she noted Nick, who drank his five-hour energy drinks every afternoon and wouldn't stop talking, and Betsy's special diet, which seemed to consist exclusively of edamame that she'd brought from home and ate at the banquets.*

The last straw was the final awards ceremony—and not because they lost out. When the sales contest winners were announced, her winning team members bounced up to the podium, beaming with pride and high-fiving each other. They loved recognition. But when they were presented with their prizes—new iPads—their faces dropped. "I already have an iPad," said Ryan, limply shaking the CEO's hand. Lyla asked, in all seriousness, "Um, can I trade this for a MacBook Air?"

Ellen had a headache. She knew she'd be hearing from her own boss. Bad news moved fast. But it was almost over. Not much more they could do to damage their reputations, thought Ellen. Then, at the closing cocktail party, she saw Adam introduce himself to the company's startled CEO with a fist bump and a happy "Sup, brahh? Great party!" She looked away and caught a glimpse of Maggie, her quietest rep, dressed to kill in a leopard-print miniskirt, five-inch stilettos, and a sheer blouse that showed off her black bra.

The evening dragged on. Ellen could not wait to get home and pull the covers over her head until Monday.

* * *

Make way for Talent 2.0. The Millennial Generation—Generation Y, the Wired Generation—is flooding inside sales organizations. They bring a renewed sense of economic optimism, a tone of extreme self-confidence, and an acute desire to challenge the traditional ways of doing business.

They can embody the very best sense of "disruptive selling": un-expected, bold, innovative, and tenacious salespeople who are not afraid to try new approaches that take customers by surprise and wake them up to your solution's possibilities. But these savvy, successful sellers can also be disruptive in the traditional meaning of the term: distracting, unruly, unsettling, and counterproductive. Older managers in particular can be confused and annoyed when their fresh new team members bring in sales like pros one minute and act entitled, snarky, blasé, and self-involved the next. They seem like they're still living with one foot in the frat house, or expecting you to rescue them like mom and dad would.

In this chapter, we'll see how managers can rewire their teams' innate talents and begin to transform them from Sales Slackers into Sales Superheroes, using the best disruptive sales tools to make it happen.

FIGURE 2-1 | Socially Savvy Millennial Talent 2.0

MEET TALENT 2.0

Ready to chill? Meet your new friends. These young men and women, born roughly from 1980 to 1993, make up about 25 percent of today's workforce. This number is estimated to grow to 75 percent by 2025. With roughly 10,000 people turning 21 each day—that's 42.5 million Millennials[1]—you'll soon be seeing 100 percent Millennial sales teams. These digitally savvy natives are socially connected, have extremely high expectations of themselves and of you, and they want it all NOW. They embody a can-do attitude, are extremely motivated for success, and are on track to be your top performers. They just need a smart manager to transform them into a truly disruptive team of inside sales innovators.

Do you sometimes catch yourself thinking thoughts like these, or even saying them? "When I was a rep, I kept my mouth shut and never asked for . . ." or, "When I first started in my sales career, I always took the time to show respect and develop relationships. . . ." Suddenly, you feel prehistoric—and you are too young for that! But it can be frustrating trying to figure out the best way to relate to this new wave of young workers who bring new values and challenges to the sales enterprise, especially those who view life like one big video game where they are always winning.

Millennials will always question, challenge, and want to do it better. Hey, isn't that what managers want from these spunky sales warriors? But it comes at a cost. They tend to be high maintenance, have little fear of authority, demand constant feedback, and want instant gratification. And—brace yourself—some DON'T LIKE THE PHONE!

But here's the good part: Millennials like clear, firm leadership, and they look up to experience. They already believe that you have something to teach them. It's up to you to take hold of the reins, guide them in the right direction, and put their disruptive energy to good use.

DECODING TALENT 2.0

As an inside sales manager, your success depends on your ability to retain and promote excellent talent. So harnessing this talent and driving revenue with your team is essential. With a basic understanding of how Talent 2.0 thinks and what they need to succeed, you can learn how to effectively manage, coach, and motivate them to align with Customer 2.0.

"That's not part of my job responsibility, is it?"

Decoding the message: *"Tell me exactly what I need to do, and I'll do it."*

A whopping 61 percent of Millennials say they need *specific directions* from their boss to do their best work.[2] Although it seems as if they want to defy authority, they can be Generation WHY when it comes to their employers. As children, their time was generally structured for them—they knew what they were doing every hour of the day—and that makes them risk adverse. They don't want to make a mistake on the job that could cost them future success.

Coaching your team: Never expect your millennial team to read your mind or to do a task you haven't asked for; that's a recipe for disappointment and frustration. Give them clear instructions about everything you need them to do. Be as transparent as possible and double-check to make sure you understand each other's expectations.

"I've been here three months, and
I think I deserve a promotion."

Decoding the message: *"I'm goal oriented, impatient, and want to get ahead."*

It's easy to mistake statements like these for pure entitlement. The truth is, Millennials are self confident and ambitious. When asked, "What are the top two things your company can do to make you more successful?," Millennials chose the answer. "better defined career path."[3]

Millennials are ready to take on the world. Their parents told them they can do it, and they are confident that they can. They walk in with high expectations of themselves, their employer, and their manager. They want to see growth potential in their job, and they want to be able to explore different career paths. Eventually, or sooner, they want to have your job.

According to one study, 76 percent of Millennials think they could do a better job than their boss.[4] It's irrelevant to them that their supervisor may have had to spend many years in a position to advance in their career. They're ready to take over as CEO anytime. They don't want to be judged by their experience or qualifications, but by their ability to do the job. Because of this, they rarely get caught up in traditional hierarchal organization and command-and-control management methods. Despite all their talk about promotion and increased responsibility, however, many do nothing with it and still focus only on quota attainment.

Although you may be tempted to doubt their loyalty, Millennials like to race to advancement—often within the same organization. A study conducted by Vorsight and The Bridge Group asked Millennials, "How does Gen Y's perception of paying their dues match previous generations?" Many responses indicated a desire to move into sales, engineering, marketing, and product management within their existing companies.[5]

Coaching your team: Mentor your Millennials to help them to understand what it takes to get ahead. Help them understand the skill requirements for advancement and the value of longevity.

Then develop a structure that defines a career path. Create roles within the sales organization, such as Team Lead, Mentor, Coach, Senior Coach. You can use these to help them feel they are moving forward and to let them know that their ambition and success is duly recognized. Design detailed job descriptions for each role, so that teams understand the expectations for each role. This will provide a solid framework for expectations and advancement that they can follow.

"Huh? What did you say?"

Decoding the message: *"I'm multitasking right now."*

Millennials are born multitaskers. They may be talking with prospects (with a phone headset in one ear while listening to music through an earbud in the other ear), sending out emails, setting up a demo, scheduling an appointment, IM'ing their SE with questions, and answering questions from their manager—all at the same time. Without all these tasks going at one time, they get bored.

Coaching your team: Even if a salesperson is really good at sending a text while talking on the phone, that doesn't mean they should do it. Reports have shown that no matter how good the multitasker may be, mistakes inevitably get made and information gets lost. In her whitepaper "The Rewired Resolution," Camille Preston, PhD, writes about being "overwired"—overtaxing our brains and bodies by multitasking and multithinking and never being present. For every $100K employee, she says, companies are finding that $46K of productivity and quality of work is being compromised.[6]

More devices and more tools are great when used correctly, but they also increase the distraction level. And when you consider that 60 percent of workplace distractions come from email and social networking and 14 percent of workers say they will tune out a meeting to tweet or update their status on a social network, this is serious. Help them focus on unitasking—focusing on one thing at a time. For example, encourage them to shut off their phones during nonnegotiable call times. Whether they are writing, reading, speaking, or listening, they need to make sure that everything gets completed.

"Hey, boss, how am I doing? How did that go?"

Decoding the message: "I need daily affirmation and attention."

Millennials may seem needy, but this group expects to be told how they are doing on a regular basis. They need daily affirmation. They especially crave attention in the form of constant feedback on their performance levels.

According to one study,[7] 80 percent of Millennials want regular feedback from their managers. Yes, 8 out of 10 of your team want regular feedback from you at least once a week. They especially want managerial attention as a way to make sure they are on the right path to move ahead.

Coaching your team: This group will demand far more of your time than any other generation. In general, they crave guidance, love, support, structure, and attention. Specifically, they need constant coaching and mentoring. That's your job.

They can be surprisingly literal in their understanding. They respond very well to structured processes and instructions, so don't be vague:

- On their first day of work, give them a welcome card and letter, an office tour and introductions, an outline of their first day, and an on-boarding guide.

- Have their cubicle already set up (desk, phone, double monitors, business cards).

- Send an email that introduces them to everyone.

- Take them out to lunch (or encourage team members to do so) every day for the first week to help them settle in.

- Provide performance feedback instantaneously, not in an annual review.

- Make your appreciation personal and meaningful. Some managers, for example, take the time to walk the rep into their office, close the door, and tell them how important their contribution is to the team and company. Other managers send handwritten notes praising them for their hard work.

Email Appreciation for Talent 2.0

Appreciation, personally expressed, goes a long, long way to motivating Millennials and creating loyalty to the organization. Below is a real email sent by the Director of Corporate Culture at Beachbody to an employee who had completed four years of working for the company. Note that it's written in the language of the specific corporate culture and pulls out specifics the employee will recognize.

Subject Line: Sandi We Want to Say 400 Thanks for Your Hard Work!

Dude!

There was a day, nearly FOUR YEARS ago, which was recorded in the Beachbody history books—a day that signified a new beginning, presented a life-changing challenge, and culminated in a powerful personal decision. The date?

Monday, May 14, 2007

Do you recognize it?

On that day, you—Sandi—DECIDED to become a Dude—an ambassador of personal growth and the member of an outstanding organization dedicated to helping people change their lives for the better. . . .

On that day, you COMMITTED yourself to a great challenge—the challenge of making a great organization even greater not only by joining our award-winning team, but by pledging to bring on a daily basis what only YOU could bring—your unique combination of skills, vision, passion, and personal determination . . .

And beginning on that day, and for the last FOUR YEARS, you have more than SUCCEEDED in meeting this challenge. Having demonstrated time and time again the initiative and passion to consistently deliver on your promises, you have SUCCEEDED not only in helping to make Beachbody one of our nation's leading providers of personal growth solutions, but you have, by bringing the unique and outstanding qualities that only YOU can bring, SUCCEEDED in making Beachbody a more extraordinary place to work . . . and THAT is something that we (and the rest of us Dudes) are very grateful for indeed.

Thanks, Sandi, for all your hard work and dedication. And as a humble token of our thanks, please accept the forthcoming ANNIVERSARY AWARD of $400 (a hundred bucks per year of service), which will be included in your 5/5/2011 paycheck.

All the Best.

"Hey, look over here! Watch this"

Decoding the message: *"I need **public** recognition."*

One of the many names for Millennials is the "trophy" generation. They grew up getting awards for everything. There are no losers in kindergarten, and everybody graduates from the fifth grade, complete with diplomas. Millennials—also known as the Echo-Boomers—have the most child-centric parents ever. Largely Boomers, these loving parents scheduled their entire lives around watching their kids' activities, supporting their sports and performances, and cheering them on.

So, no surprise, Millennials like to be congratulated, and they always want to be winning. They thrive on public recognition, glowing with pride even about a group email announcing their attainment. On the other hand, when they are not recognized—even if they got wild praise just the week before—they are not good sports about it. Very often, as one manager told me, "They will take their marbles and go home." They don't like to fail. If they do, or even perceive that you think they have failed, they tend to get defensive, blame others or things beyond their control, and spiral downward.

Coaching your team: Give Millennials public and visual displays of recognition. Keep them engaged with perpetual small wins and milestones; give them more ways to earn status and respect among peers. For example, they like to point to the scoreboard and brag about their name at the top. Decorate the sales boards, TVs, and sales monitors with trophies, gold medals, small prizes, and so on. Schedule small, winnable contests. And create team spirit. They love swag, and they'll wear team shirts proudly. Anything with the company logo, name, or other inside info gives them a sense of family and group unity. Start ordering extra large t-shirts!

"I can't work on Saturdays. I actually have a life."

Decoding the message: *"I want a healthy work-life balance."*

After years of watching their parents put in 60-hour workweeks for faceless corporations, Millennials are not interested in "paying their corporate dues." They want more than a paycheck; they value work-life balance: 93 percent of Millennials say that they want a job that works with their lifestyle.[8]

They also value flexibility; autonomy is key. Eight-hour days no longer exist in today's global economy. It is becoming harder to justify the old 9 to 5 workday when technology allows us to work from any place at any time. Remote inside salespeople, or those who split their time between the office and home, are gaining more traction in an already exploding area. Accordingly, sales organizations are revamping their corporate workspaces to include open cubicles, pods for collaboration, open kitchens, and recreation sites like foosball and ping-pong.

According to a Cisco study, 70 percent of college students and professionals don't feel that it's necessary to work at an office anymore.[9] They want to spend their time in meaningful and useful ways. They will come in early, stay late, and work during lunch when necessary but they want the option to work at home some days and hit the gym during lunch.

Coaching your team: Be adaptable to work scenarios outside the norm. Reward your teams with flexible hours, performance-related bonuses, and even vacation days off for their birthdays or special occasions.

"I saw our CEO's wife on Facebook. She's hot!"

Decoding the message: *"I don't know the difference between personal and professional. Aren't we all online and available?"*

Even the most socially awkward Millennials are extremely social in the virtual world. They don't see a difference between LinkedIn and Facebook and, according to a study by Millennial Branding,[10] 4 million Gen-Y and Facebook profiles from Identified.com's database of 50 million are inadvertently using these profiles as an extension of their professional personality. Unfortunately, they are very open about their private lives and sometimes fail to see the distinction between business and personal. Many will tell you EVERYTHING—way more than you want to hear, and often things that are professionally damaging.

Coaching your team: Inside salespeople have become their company's chief customer officers. If their digital footprint has beer spills all over it, that beer is also spilling all over your company's reputation. Before hiring a Millennial, be sure to check out their digital footprint and social graph. Facebook will provide insights into their personal life, hobbies, friends, and so on. LinkedIn will provide insight into their professional life.

Capitalize on their affinity for networking, but guide them on the best ways to use professional sites, such as LinkedIn, and the mistakes they need NOT make on their personal sites. Millennials can often act as great social megaphones for your company. But keep in mind they can also post positives and negatives about their employers, and this too carries lots of social clout.

> *"I'm bored here. I was learning so much more when I was in college."*

Decoding the message: *"I want a colorful career trajectory that includes tons of life and professional experiences."*

When asked about the top two things that motivate them professionally, Millennials say that their second biggest motivator is "building my skill set/resume."[11] A full 22 percent saw training and development as the most valued benefit from an employer, and 65 percent said the opportunity for personal development was the most influential factor in their current job. Their commitment to their continued education is impressive. In today's economy, they are one of the most educated and underemployed groups out there.

Millennials like challenges when it comes to building their skill sets and resumes. They are willing to put in the hours if it means onboarding and development to acquire new skills.

Coaching your team: Because this group likes a challenge, they rarely push back when you set high goals or quotas, and they are motivated by success in reaching them. Create opportunities for them to learn, and offer continued education that supports their development: provide spot training, lunch 'n' learns, call recording reviews, product training, etc.

"My friends are making more than me.
How much paid vacation time do you offer?"

Decoding the message: *"I am motivated by money, and I want more of it."*

Research from Sibson Consulting[12] has shown that Generation Y performs as well or better than other generations when incentivized correctly. Fortunately, they are motivated by more than money; meaningful work, high pay, and a sense of accomplishment also get them going.

But money still continues to be the prime motivator. When they get incentives and bonuses, they take advantage of all the accelerators instead of banking them for the next measurement period. The vast majority of sales reps are focused on the short-term income potential of their job. This attitude makes them cautious when committing on deals when forecasting. They are reluctant to commit until customers say they are sending in the contract.

Coaching your team: Have some incentive strategies in place, such as giving Millennials incremental raises, sales accelerators, contests, incentives, and different types of perks. But remember they also must do their jobs well and not just rely on incentives to get them going.

"I never leave voice mail messages.
The phone isn't happening right now."

Decoding the message: *"I live and breathe online. Why use the phone?"*

This group will never know what it was like to wait in line for the nearest pay phone, wait at home for a boyfriend or girlfriend to call, or wait to get phone messages at the office on a landline's answering machine. They assume that face-to-face meetings can be inconvenient and are replaceable with teleconferences, Skype calls, webinars, texting, instant messaging, and email formatted for delivery to a mobile device. Most Millennials view meeting and interacting online as comparable to face-to-face meetings.

Coaching your team: Millennials are not big phone fans. They are so technically proficient that just calling someone on the phone is out. They prefer lots of bling—automated dialers, Gmail chatting, Skype, video. . . . But as long as they are in inside sales, the phone will never disappear altogether: it is a primary communications tool, essential in the sales and engagement cycle. Coach them to develop new strategies:

- *They are impatient.* They quickly tire of getting voice mails instead of live voices. Help them diversify their outreach efforts to get better response: VM + EM + Social + Text + Video.

- *They are socially wired.* They'd rather reach out to people and learn about their lives than leave impersonal messages. Encourage them to do some research on prospects and leave customized voicemail.

- *They don't understand rejection.* They're tough enough to weather rejections, but not wise enough to learn the meaning behind customers' objections. Encourage them to reflect on what they might have done or said to bring on the objection.

"Is it happy hour yet?"

Decoding the message: *"My coworkers are my friends, and we want to be in the fun zone!"*

This a social bunch: 88 percent of Millennials want their coworkers to be their friends, and 89 percent want their workplace to be social and fun.[13] They place high value on friendships, and they want friendships to happen in the workplace. They will choose a job just to be with their friends. They want to laugh, go out with workplace friends for lunch, and help plan the next company event or committee. They are peer oriented and driven by a desire for social connection. They are eager to learn from peers and best practices and are very supportive of each other.

And for better or worse, they love to drink together. They go to company-sponsored happy hours and then stay together doing pub crawls until late into the evening.

Coaching your team: "Gamification"—the use of game techniques in nongame contexts—motivates behavior with rewards, recognition, and a dose of fun. Perfect for video-game-raised Millennials, who learn best when information is presented in a game-like format. Here are the Seven Rules of Sales Gamification[14]:

1. *Entertain.* Must be fun and interesting.

2. *Simplify.* Pick a few behaviors to motivate and measure.

3. *Keep it top of mind.* Share status updates regularly.

4. *Provide real-time results.* Allow salespeople to always know where they stand.

5. *Don't depend on it.* Always encourage the right behavior and layer on rewards to amplify it.

6. *Make it social.* Encourage team members to share how they're doing.

7. *Offer real rewards.* Give them real prizes, not just tokens.

Provide a fun, employee-centered workplace. Design games that include things like team videos, tournaments, contests, spiffs, spot bonuses, and monthly team outings. Then cheer them on and let them play. You'll be pleased with the results.

"Can I get this NOW?"

Decoding the message: *"I am used to instant gratification."*

This is a group that is accustomed to getting answers NOW. They can Google or ask Siri for information that would have taken hours of research only a few years ago. But their need for instant gratification may also mean that they get impatient with time-consuming projects, and they rarely need to do any independent thinking.

Coaching your team: Many managers feel the iPhone's "Siri effect" when it comes to responding to Millennials. They feel compelled to provide ready-made answers to their questions. While team members may expect answers delivered immediately to their email inbox, they need to learn that managers cannot rescue them. Teach your teams how to think, analyze, create, engage, and close opps on their own. Basically, you are helping them learn to think for themselves. Provide them with feedback, but be prompt and make it specific.

"I partner with an integrated sales team."

Decoding the message: *"I work well with others."*

Millennials have been collaborating with each other since they were in elementary school. They are used to working in groups and teams, and they believe that a team can accomplish more and do it better than an individual. The downside is that individual thinking can be stunted. The upside is that they treat coworkers as partners rather than rivals. They get involved in team meetings, especially if it is to work on something innovative where they can be collaborative. Collaboration comes easily to reps on a team where cooperation is reinforced.

Coaching your team: Millennials love teamwork, so do everything you can to encourage it. Mentor, engage, and train them as a team. Group meetings are great. And whether they are working with their friends in the office or remotely, they can connect to their projects and each other from any location—which means constant collaboration.

They are active and like to participate in sports as a group, so encourage softball, soccer, basketball, or hockey teams, and more personal activities like cycling together And don't stop there. They also like more offbeat activities, such as beer brewing, rock climbing, and camping. For example, PeopleMatter held a company-wide Olympics-style meet in which its employees competed in office events, such as Table Tennis (over the conference table), Stressball Throw, Office Chair Lunge, and Paperclip Football.

Being connected is more than a desire; it's an important part of their nature, and it can only benefit their work.

"What's happening next?"

Decoding the message: *"I am in danger of getting bored."*

"What's happening next?" is the Millennials' mantra. They are used to filling their lives with multiple activities, and they seek ever-changing tasks within their world. They may play on sports teams, walk for multiple causes, spend time as fans at company sports leagues, and enjoy lots of time with family and friends. They are used to a high level of activity, and when they don't have it they get bored. Boring is bad.

Coaching your team: Provide your team with an ever-changing environment to keep them engaged. Structure their day to include a variety of activities—calls, list building, marketing campaigns, and more. Have them travel to other offices to meet other team members; schedule them to go on appointments with their field partners; give them the opportunity to work the booth at tradeshows.

"What's wrong? Why does he want to see me in his office?"

Decoding the message: *"I must have done something wrong. I don't want to lose my job."*

Millennials can be tough on themselves. They function on assumptions and tend to obsess about things beyond their control. Fear is a constant companion. They will panic at any sign, real or imagined, that their jobs may be in danger; they get defensive in an instant; and they are quick to assign blame. They see their world as black and white, without much introspection or self-reflection.

Coaching your team: Always keep their sensitivities in mind, especially when you are trying to help them course correct. If you give Millennials a performance plan—no matter how positively you frame it—they may immediately decide they are going to look for another job. If you actually fire them, they will be very vocal with their peers about how it's not fair; they will blame the company and try to get other reps fired up about how the company is trying to screw them. Stay one step ahead of them; don't let yourself get blindsided by their reaction. Keep them focused on what they can control versus what is beyond their control.

Mixed Messages: Understanding the Contradictory Nature of Talent 2.0

As PeopleMatter's whitepaper "Getting the Best out of Gen Y" confirms,[15] the seemingly contradictory behavior of Millennials can be quite perplexing: "They can be positive, multi-tasking team players or a bunch of unmotivated egoists who spend all day texting one another." Don't let their mixed messages take you by surprise:

- They are extremely impatient about career advancement but they have a sense of entitlement when work is required of them.

- Sometimes they say "gimme, gimme, gimme," but when you give it to them, they don't run with it. They want to advance in their career but are short term on their attainment strategy.

- They are big multitaskers but they lose focus quickly, relying on mentoring and feedback to help them prioritize and know what to do next.

- They are fearless when it comes to authority but they depend heavily on structure and guidance, leadership from mentors, and regular feedback.

- They don't like talking on the phone and are not fluid when it comes to the art of conversation. They are, however, masters at networking. They would rather reach out to people and learn about their lives than leave impersonal messages.

- They don't like land lines but they love automated dialers, gmail chatting, Skype, video . . . and the more color, the better.

- They are very opinionated and want constant and immediate feedback, but they don't always take it gracefully.

- They want work-life balance and never want to come into work on a Saturday but they will easily go for a round of drinks with office peers after work.

- They are extremely social on Facebook, but are slowly adapting to LinkedIn and haven't discovered the power of blogs yet.

- They hate rejection but they're not reflective and insightful enough to learn the reasons behind customers' objections and what they can do about it.

- They say they are not motivated by money but they respond to financial perks, overachieve quota, and always want to come out winning.

Customer 2.0 and Talent 2.0 are a perfect match. They both work virtually, socially, and globally, and they both want your attention. The reason is demographics: Just as Millennials are naturally moving into sales positions, they are also moving into positions of influence and decision making in business. Figure 2-2 shows how they match up.

FIGURE 2-2 | Customer 2.0 + Talent 2.0 = We Have a Match!

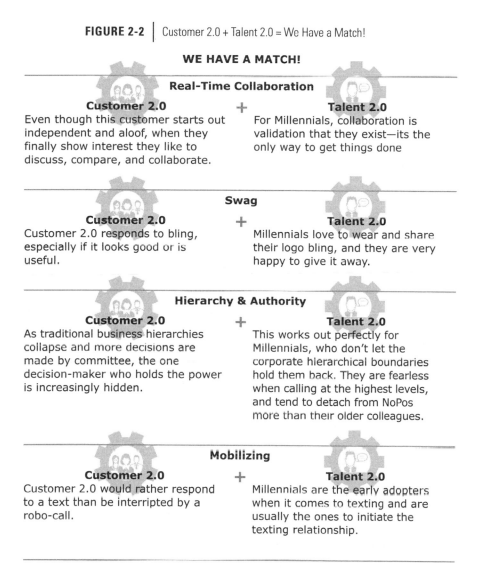

WE HAVE A MATCH!

Real-Time Collaboration

Customer 2.0   +   **Talent 2.0**

Even though this customer starts out independent and aloof, when they finally show interest they like to discuss, compare, and collaborate.

For Millennials, collaboration is validation that they exist—its the only way to get things done

Swag

Customer 2.0   +   **Talent 2.0**

Customer 2.0 responds to bling, especially if it looks good or is useful.

Millennials love to wear and share their logo bling, and they are very happy to give it away.

Hierarchy & Authority

Customer 2.0   +   **Talent 2.0**

As traditional business hierarchies collapse and more decisions are made by committee, the one decision-maker who holds the power is increasingly hidden.

This works out perfectly for Millennials, who don't let the corporate hierarchical boundaries hold them back. They are fearless when calling at the highest levels, and tend to detach from NoPos more than their older colleagues.

Mobilizing

Customer 2.0   +   **Talent 2.0**

Customer 2.0 would rather respond to a text than be interrupted by a robo-call.

Millennials are the early adopters when it comes to texting and are usually the ones to initiate the texting relationship.

(continues)

FIGURE 2-2 | Customer 2.0 + Talent 2.0 = We Have a Match! *(continued)*

WE HAVE A MATCH!

Technology & Tools

Customer 2.0   +   **Talent 2.0**

The most effective way to reach out to today's elusive Customer 2.0 is through the right tools used correctly.

Millennials were born with game controllers in their hands. They understand technology, they're comfortable using it, and they always look for the cutting edge.

It's Gotta Happen NOW

Customer 2.0   +   **Talent 2.0**

Customer 2.0 calls the shots—they want to close the deal on the spot, the minute they are ready.

Talent 2.0 is impatient for things to happen. It's important for them to see that they need to align their idea of NOW with the prospect's idea of NOW and be ready to either wait or pounce.

Relationships

Customer 2.0   +   **Talent 2.0**

Customer 2.0 seems standoffish but is really starved for personal relationships.

Talent 2.0 loves to be with their friends but has a tendency to speed-date prospects. A little guidance can help them see that customers are people too.

Social Media Engagement

Customer 2.0   +   **Talent 2.0**

Customer 2.0 is socially wired, and they value working with someone who has a strong social graph.

Millennials are networkers. They are very eager to engage socially, but may need guidance in making their digital footprint more professional.

The Fun Factor

Customer 2.0   +   **Talent 2.0**

This busy customer loves to be entertained—they much prefer a short, fun informational video to death by PowerPoint.

Millennials are the Little Emperors of Fun. Encourage them to engage customers with entertaining product videos and other fun informational visuals, but remind them to keep it professional

THE KICKOFF MEETING: TAKE TWO

Ellen came back from Las Vegas somewhat angry and demoralized. She wasn't their mother! Then she calmed down. She realized that while they had an awesome online presence, many of her team were not so skilled at actual, face-to-face encounters. Some had gone straight from home to college to work and knew little of how the business world operates outside their earbuds. She'd done a good job of motivating them—the sales awards and quota levels were proof of that—but she'd just assumed that they knew the difference between their personal lives and their professional lives.

She knew that they responded well to instructions and expectations. She just needed to be clear about her expectations of professionalism and how best to achieve it. She just needed to be clear about her expectations of professionalism and how best to achieve it. So, she sent everyone a wrap-up email, staying friendly and positive but firm:

Re: Sales Kick-off Guidelines—Please Review

Hi Team—

Thanks for your participation at last week's kick-off. Our ISR team has made a memorable impact! And, after all the recognition and kudos we received, we are an influential force in driving sales revenues this year and beyond. All your excellent sales efforts have helped us get to the next level. The future growth of our group looks extremely promising. All eyes are on us, and that's awesome.

Now is the time to crank up the volume when it comes to professional conduct so that we shine even brighter the next time we go to Vegas—and believe me, we will. The office is home, and we're all comfortable with each other here. But out in the world, you represent the company. I had a few comments concerning professional behavior, so I just want to go over some areas we can tighten up before our next company kick-off. Please watch the video and review the following guidelines. You will be tested!

• *Dress code.* Please dress in business casual during meetings. That means no flip-flops, miniskirts, shorts, or weekend beachwear. Business casual means Dockers, slacks, or nice jeans with shirts, blazers, jackets. Think of what you'd wear to your grandmother's house for Thanksgiving.

- *Hygiene.* We are in close quarters, so be sensitive. Some people are allergic to strong perfumes and aftershave and extra deodorant is never a mistake!

- *Food and alcohol consumption.* We are surrounded by food during these events, and we will never run out. Enjoy your meals, but don't pig out, and limit your drinking to what you know you can handle.

- *Communication.* When you meet people face to face it's super important to make eye contact and shake hands (use your right hand even if you are left-handed). Please don't bury your head in your iPhone. Speakers see that as rude, even if you really are listening at the same time. Repeat: NO texting or IM'ing during meetings.

- *Timeliness.* Show up early and remember to bring a pen, laptop, and materials. Be alert and ready to learn.

- *Chill.* You will learn something new. Ask questions and listen to the answers. Don't interrupt, and don't share your opinion. That just puts the speaker on the defensive. Be politically correct. That will get noticed.

Read, review, and think about all this, and we'll all talk about what it means together in our team meeting on Wednesday.

Thanks for an awesome job! I know this year you will shine even brighter.

Ellen

MANAGEMENT TIPS

- Millennials like structure, so give it to them. Make sure they know what's expected every day.

- Clarity is crucial with these literal thinkers. Say exactly what you mean, and don't leave out the details.

- Millennials love collaborating, and they like fun and games. Encourage them to work in teams and play in teams after hours.

ition and personal encour-
ith increased motivation.

ut make sure they un-
nd professional net-
ofessional network

CHAPTER 3

TOOL POWER 2.0

Sales 2.0 at Work

Frank walks out of a long, grueling meeting with his new Global Sales VP, who has decided to clean house. He has asked Frank for sales forecasts, territory summaries, and stack rankings of his inside team of 29 reps. His VP is not convinced that Frank's team can take the company to the next level. He believes that they're stuck in the Sales 1.0 world, AKA Sales BC (before computers), and thinks they will never survive. "I gave you a stack of our best leads and asked your team to close them," he reminds Frank. "They didn't. I think it's time for you to clean house and get some people in there who can do the job. That's your job, not mine."

Frank is frazzled, scared, and anxious about what the future holds. His loyal inside sales team has been with the company for more than 15 years and has never experienced a tougher time in sales. They haven't hit their numbers for the past few quarters and continue to struggle to close deals. Their market share has eroded in the last few years, and many of their companies have taken a hit from several years of dwindling sales. In addition, the company's product suite has become extensive. They've made several acquisitions, forcing the inside teams to sell the entire product suite without relying on their field counterparts.

Frank's team hasn't had to actively prospect for new accounts in years. They've prided themselves on high-touch versus high-tech sales, and their strong relationships with high-profile "named accounts" has carried them through year after year with predictable revenue. This team has always put its customers first: going the extra mile to get orders through the system, extending deadlines on discounts, and providing extra consulting services. Over the years, they developed friendships—sending customers birthday cards, including them on their fantasy football betting pools, and even sending out large popcorn buckets for Christmas. But their customers have grown up. They've become independent and self-sufficient, preferring to shop online by downloading their own trial evaluations. They're socially active now too. His team feels irrelevant, outdated, and forgotten.

*   *   *

Sales 1.0—and its outdated and ineffective sales tactics—has left the building. Today's Sales 2.0 is fueled by tools. Make sure your team understands how to use them throughout the sales cycle; it is vital to their success. As Gerhard Gschwandtner, CEO of *Selling Power* and sponsor of the Sales and Marketing 2.0 Conference, says, "Sales 2.0 brings together customer-focused methodologies and productivity-enhancing technologies that transform selling from an art to a science."[1] In this chapter, you'll learn about the rich vein of sales productivity tools, sales intelligence tools, and social tools you can mine to maximize your teams' efficiency and create a seamless and positive virtual customer experience.

THE POWER OF TOOLS

The tools we use throughout the sales cycle have created a serious shift in how inside salespeople communicate, aggregate, monitor, collaborate, engage, present, quote, nurture, and sell. In the last five years, literally hundreds of new sales tools have entered the market, all promising greater productivity and revenue growth. CSO Insights reports that "revising sales tools" ranks among the top sales effectiveness initiatives for 2012–2013. Yet 46 percent of salespeople use fewer than five tools in their sales efforts.[2]

Five just scratches the surface.

Stepping into this world—often referred to as a "technology flea market"—can seem daunting and overwhelming. The rapid proliferation of tools means that some will survive and some will lose their power quickly. With so many options, and more each day, it can be difficult for sales managers to identify the tools that will help their teams most.

Inside sales now generates up to 50 percent of company revenues and is being tasked with more responsibilities and expectations—to grow their territories, form partnerships, and generate new business. In 2009, there were 800,000 inside sales departments. By 2013 there will be 2.3 million.[3] They no longer can rely on outdated sales tactics, other departments, and stale habits. Their survival depends on who has the most tool fuel to make it through today's rugged Sales 2.0 terrain. Making sure that teams have the right tools is the first step in supporting their sales success. Even improving the top 20 percent of your sales team by providing them with better tools will create a more competitive group.

Understanding and using tools correctly is vital, for you and your team. These days, it's safe to say that it's more important for inside sales talent to have a high Tool IQ than a nice phone tone:

- Sales 2.0 has put inside sales in the driver's seat. Once the "data hounds" of information, now they are the new content curators, finding and capturing customers through sales intelligence and lead nurturing.

- Customer 2.0 wants us to know everything about them before we call, and why not? These DIY customers know everything about us. The right tools help your team know what they want and meet them when they are ready to engage, collaborate, and buy.

- Today's Talent 2.0 Superheroes are technologically and digitally wired. They already love to use tools and expect to access them whenever and wherever they want.

- As connect rates continue to drop, the few seconds we have on a live call are simply not enough. Tools power up our engagements and buy us more time to connect virtually.

- Tools create new standards of knowledge and expertise. We must approach tools with a marketing mindset while monitoring and analyzing responses.

Tools drive the inside salesperson's selling life, helping them to stay close to the customer, watching, listening, and tracking their every move. With this kind of intelligence, salespeople are not caught off guard by customers who want to engage later in the sales cycle. No problem! The tools not only replace the lost time we have with our customers; they enhance the virtual relationships customers prefer. But managing these tools isn't all about selling. Remind your team that sales also requires a marketing mind, a social mind, an analyst mind, a detective mind, a listening mind. And tools help with all of these.

Tools Increase Marketing and Sales Alignment

Marketing 2.0 no longer provides one-dimensional whitepapers and glossy data sheets. Today it is chartered to deliver success pieces, such as industry trends, buying guides, product success roadmaps, and business analysis tools; captivating infographics, slide shares, social communities, and interactive ebooks; and expert webinars, podcasts, and how-to guides. Sales must complement and enhance these marketing efforts and add their own sales outreach flavor.

A strong alignment between sales and marketing sets a strong foundation for consistently branding and evangelizing the solution. The best way for sales and marketing to coexist is by sharing tools. Sales managers must be in regular communications with marketing, and in agreement about which department is responsible for what tasks. Together, sales and marketing must create a strategic vision that translates into tactical, well-executed marketing campaigns and processes.

It's time to share the road. Both sales and marketing must have access to the primary tools, especially CRM and marketing automation tools. Make sure you and your team work closely with marketing to rank prospects, nurture leads, monitor customer activities, and so on.

Social media is a huge customer relations tool, and marketing has already jumped into it. Here are some quick facts about the role social media is currently playing in the business world, courtesy of the 2012 Social Media Marketing Industry Report[4]:

- 94 percent of all businesses with a marketing department used social media as part of their marketing platform.

- Almost 60 percent of marketers are devoting the equivalent of a full work day to social media marketing development and maintenance.

- 43 percent of people aged 29 to 29 spend more than 10 hours a week on social media sites.

- 85 percent of all businesses with a dedicated social media platform as part of their marketing strategy reported an increase in their market exposure.

- 58 percent of businesses that have used social media marketing for more than three years reported an increase in sales over that period.

Today's customer has a loud social voice. If a prospect has a poor customer experience, the first place they turn is to social media. Partner with marketing to make sure that both sales and marketing are delivering the same positive message about your solution.

TOOL FUEL POWERS THE *ENTIRE* SALES CYCLE

Aberdeen research confirms that most "Best in Class" inside sales organizations—traditionally, the early adopters of technologies—plan to deploy sales effectiveness tools now and in the foreseeable future.[5] That means it's more important than ever to learn how you can integrate tools throughout the sales cycle: from beginning, to middle, and straight through to closing. The tools in Figure 3.1 are mapped to the TeleSmart 10 skills featured in my book *Smart Selling on the Phone and Online.*

HOW TOOLS HELP MAKE SALES

The variety of tools available covers the entire sales cycle, from organizing your time and planning your approach right through to

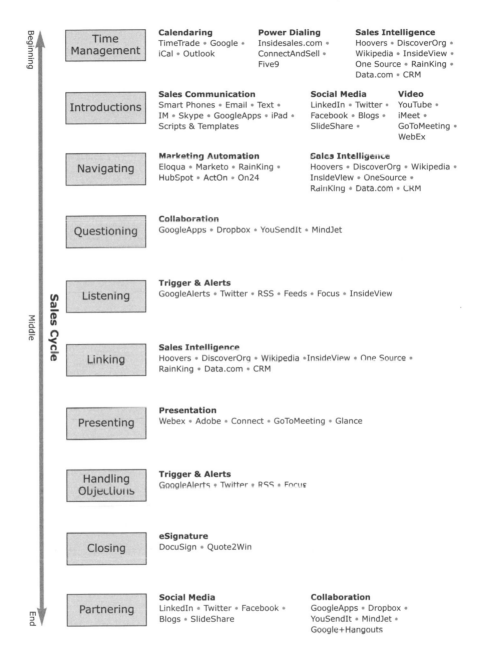

FIGURE 3-1 | Using Tools Throughout the Inside Sales Cycle

closing the deal. You'll find tools for everything from trigger alerts to collaboration, sales productivity, and much much more. That's why depending on just five tools won't cut it. Your team needs the most effective tools for every part of the sales cycle. Take tools seriously and encourage your teams to use them regularly as their sales right arm.

Take time to understand how tools can be used effectively throughout the day, then do your research. Make it a priority to learn about the tools that are out there—read reviews, ask your colleagues what they use, and go to the Sales 2.0 Sales and Marketing Conference.

And remember: You do not have to spend your entire budget on tools. Some very effective tools we use everyday—LinkedIn, Google, YouTube, for example—are absolutely free.

Trigger Alerts

Today's salespeople are Chief Listening Officers, keeping ahead of breaking news, trends, and discussions and gathering information about companies, solutions, and customers. Listening means being informed, and information capture is critical. Listening is about absorbing, organizing, and sorting through tons of data that is specific to your prospect. It's having the intuition and timing to capture and extract the salient points of this data. But knowing what type of information you need is just as critical: Who was just promoted? Who won a business award? And in today's new economy, who was just hired back or jumped to another company?

Tool Types: GoogleAlerts, Twitter, RSS feeds, Focus, InsideView

Tool IQ: Customers demand that we reach out to them based on trigger events. Alert tools are all about instant, minute-by-minute notification of the latest breaking news. This gives salespeople the opportunity to stay ahead of them. When they suddenly decide they want to buy NOW, the rep is way ahead of them. This increases the chances that your teams will engage with pinpoint timing, which will lead to more meaningful interactions—and more sales.

Calendaring

Too many salespeople spend too much time calendaring—coordinating, confirming, and scheduling appointments, demos, presentations, web conferences, and proposal reviews—just to have the customer cancel. According to research conducted by Insidesales.com, reps who schedule appointments can expect a 20 to 45 percent no-show rate. But that number *decreases* by 20 percent when they use Google or Outlook invitations. A good calendaring tool lets individuals and business teams publish their time availability for online access and keep their personal lives private and controlled at the same time.

Tool Types: iCal, Outlook, TimeTrade, or Google

Tool IQ: Customer 2.0 cancels appointments for many reasons mentioned in Chapter 1, and one of the big ones is the tedium and annoyance of back and forth scheduling and confirmation. Having a calendaring tool ready automatically increases the chance that appointment will stick.

Collaboration

What happened to those attachments you had your team send out? Most customers probably didn't even open them. And forget about getting them to sit through some long demo. Too-busy-to-read customers have made collaboration solutions one of the fastest growing application categories today. An online repository (such as corporate intranet or SharePoint) for all processes and procedures, documents, templates, and so on, can be kept up to date by content owners and made easily accessible to everyone who needs the information.

Tool Types: GoogleApps, Box.net, Dropbox, YouSendIt, MindJet

Tool IQ: Today's busy and distracted customers are on email overload. You've probably already noticed them reducing their paper intake and reading time. They do not want to sit through long

PowerPoint presentations, and they are reluctant to open up large attachments. And, since they are also very elusive, we never know when we will get them back. Real-time collaboration, such as file and document sharing, instantly ensures that everyone is "on the same page," increasing efficiency and productivity.

CRM

A reliable customer relationship management (CRM) system is the basic tool in every inside sales organization, the one through which sales teams must manage every customer interaction. A companywide CRM system must be accessible and used by everyone who touches the prospect-to-customer process. CRM maps sales processes and workflow in order to:

- Support a volume, transaction-oriented environment

- Provide visibility on pipeline values and velocity

- Enable forecasting consistency and accuracy

- Capture key data for market knowledge and marketing support

- Provide reports and dashboards with up-to-the-minute performance

According to Gartner Research, CRM will total 7.6 billion in 2012,[6] so get to know it and use it wisely!

Tool Types: Salesforce.com, Microsoft, NetSuite, BPMonline, Oracle, SAP, Pivotal, Sugar CRM

Tool IQ: In a culture where customers are able to gain access to information anytime and anywhere, sales force automation provides an advantage over competitors. First, it allows salespeople to organize marketing strategies based on demographics and preferences. Whether this is by phone, email, Internet, or letter, targeting your desired audience helps generate more quality sales leads. And, when you incorporate a structured follow-up, sales happen.

Dialers

With connect rates dropping below 6 percent,[7] salespeople are desperate for live conversations. According to The Bridge Group 2012 Inside Sales Metrics and Compensation Report for B2B technology companies, 24 percent of the companies surveyed are utilizing dialing technologies, and they recommend these as a "massive technology boom." This power dialing software accelerates calls and successfully connects live prospects with salespeople.

Tool Types: Insidesales.com, ConnectandSell, Five[9], M5

Tool IQ: Today's customers are difficult to reach by phone, and the chance of getting them live continues to decrease. Salespeople are getting discouraged, and dialers are their special outbound enhancers. They work, but they can also backfire when reps begin to sound too robotic and hide behind these dialers.

Get Creative and Disruptive with Messaging

Do some of your team members think that just because a few email templates are loaded into their CRM they can call it a day? Remind them that marketing does not own email, and the email template designed six months ago is stale. Worse, too much time is spent crafting or adjusting messaging that, in the end, has little consistency. This kind of messy approach will only work by accident.

Truly disruptive marketing and sales approaches have a big, tangible goal and a bold way of reaching it. Work with marketing and your inside sales team to create a variety of unique and targeted messaging templates—both email templates and voice mail scripts—to help with strong introductions and multiple-attempt follow-ups. Guide them in crafting sharp, succinct, well-written, *short* email templates. Design each email as part of a progression, each one building on the previous email. This informational approach makes sense with today's customers, who like to self-educate and are paying attention.

Today's leads seem to be converting after six to eight attempts, so it makes sense for email templates to match this cycle. That means using a different email for each attempt. Here's an example of what to include on four multiple-touch email templates over a ten-day period:

- *First-attempt email.* This is the "lite" version. Make it short: one paragraph fishing for potential interest and doing some preliminary qualification.

- *Second-attempt email.* This is a bit more robust. Say more about the company. Brand them in their space and include some award-winning facts and wins.

- *Third-attempt email.* This gets down to specifics. Include some ROI information, with results the company has achieved in their space.

- *Fourth-attempt email.* This is the "last call" or "going, going, gone" email. Make it direct and to the point, gauging their interest and level of cooperation. You might use a subject line like "Is [name of company] still on your radar?" or "Final attempt for [name of company]."

    Don't stop here. Consider adding these to your team's email template library:

- Navigating to find the right contact

- Request for appointment

- Lead response; follow-up on webinar, case study, whitepaper download

- News and announcement

- Title-specific

- Vertical-specific

Marketing Automation

A sales-friendly lead nurturing-and-marketing automation tool gives you a sixth sense about when sales leads are ready by automating frequent distribution of varying content—such as trend reports, webinars, articles. Marketing automation extends insight and action to the front lines by letting sales reps send personalized email campaigns, get instant updates when prospects open email or visit the website, and see detailed profiles on online behaviors.

This includes lead scoring. According to IDC Research, 25 percent of sales time is spent on unproductive prospects.[8] Vorsight and The Bridge Group found that 84 percent of reps follow up on the marketing-generated leads when they already know that 70 percent of them don't fit their "sweet spot,"[9] so it's no surprise that lead scoring has become a hot topic. The right tool helps efficiently prioritize lead effectiveness and determine a follow-up strategy by determining which call to make next and sending automated marketing response emails that look more human and personalized.

Tool Types: Eloqua, Marketo, RainKing, HubSpot, ActOn, ON24

Tool IQ: Customer 2.0 likes to self-educate. It's important for salespeople to continually drop content that evangelizes, educates, and informs them on your solutions. These customers also prefer bite-sized pieces of information, and "dripping" informative bits of content works like magic.

Mobile

Forrester projects that by 2015, smartphone adoption will grow 150 percent and 82 million consumers will own a tablet.[10] That's a lot! It also means that mobile will become a primary way to speak to customers and prospects. The growth of mobile technology is huge and, by 2014, it's expected that mobile will overtake the PC.[11] IDC has estimated that the mobile workforce will be 1.19 billion people in 2013.[12]

Tool Types: Smartphones, Androids, iPads.

Tool IQ: You can expect that at least 50 percent or more of all opportunity and lead management will be conducted from a smartphone or tablet. Today's mobile and portable salespeople regularly make things happen from their iPads, smartphones, and other devices, so make sure they use them wisely.

Sales Intelligence

Umberto Milletti, President of InsideView, is enthusiastic about how sales intelligence has changed the face of prospecting. His formula:

sales intelligence + the right people + the right message + the right time = relevance. But some salespeople get stuck right at the beginning of that equation and never make it to the solution.

Pre-call research and sales intelligence tools are staples in most sales organizations, but reps have to use them correctly and integrate them into the call with finesse. Dropping connect rates mean that salespeople literally have only seconds on a live call. If they are not prepared, they will never have another chance. The chance of getting that customer back on the line is slim to none.

Sales can also use the intelligence gained from social media and traditional editorial sources to speed up sales productivity. These tools provide real-time access to relevant news alerts, relationship analysis, and company information on prospects. They continually aggregate and analyze relevant executive and corporate data from content sources, including emerging social media content and traditional data providers. And some tools even notify sales reps in real time about compelling business events and provide key company insights about their prospects.

Tool Types: Hoovers, Google, InsideView, OneSource, Discover.org, Peoplemaps, Data.com, Zoominfo, Netprospex, LinkedIn, RainKing

Tool IQ: Customers today expect salespeople to do their homework before contacting them. According to Forrester Research, only 13 percent of customers believe that a typical salesperson can demonstrate an understanding of their business issues and solve them.[13] Help your team understand how important it is to have this information beforehand, and how easy it is to gather it.

eSignature

Business today is more dynamic and global than ever before and most of it happens remotely. Electronic signature tools gain commitment fast.

Tool Types: DocuSign, EchoSign

Tool IQ: In the real world, with real paper and pens, it takes forever to get something signed off and initialed. Why wait until the customer has changed his or her mind?

Social Media

Forrester research found that 86 percent of business technology decision makers use social media for professional reasons.[14] With longer sales cycles, social media can actually reduce the number of touch points needed to close a sale. According to an article in *Forbes*, "The perception of social media marketing has shifted quickly—no longer viewed as a trendy or passing fad, having a flexible and well-managed presence in each of the 'big three' (Facebook, Twitter, and Google+) has become a must for any business seeking to secure a place in both the traditional and digital marketplace."[15]

Forrester research[16] shows that 81 percent of online adults use social media. Regardless of whether your business is B2B or B2C, it is people who ultimately make the purchasing decisions, and 81 percent are using social media.

- In 2010, consumers consumed 5.3 pieces of content before making a purchasing decision. In 2011, that number jumped to 10.4.

- 33 percent of B2B marketers have fully embraced social media marketing.

- B2B customers contact a sales rep after 60 percent of the purchasing decisions have been made.

According to the Reality Works (previously PhoneWorks) 2011 Inside Sales Metrics Snapshot, 34 percent of companies have social media as part of their inside sales process— this adoption rate is slow.[17]

Tool Types: LinkedIn, Twitter, Facebook, Slideshare, blogs, YouTube

Tool IQ: Social media serves a purpose in the B2B space as it increases sales and brand awareness, drives leads to the pipeline and traffic to websites, reduces customer service costs, and improves customer satisfaction, retention, and loyalty.

LinkedIn is the primary corporate social media tool. With 135 million users as of this writing and two more added every second, plus a targeted audience, it is the single largest corporate tool for prospecting. Put it at the top of your list as a social and sales intelligence prospecting tool.

LinkedIn

How LinkedIn Works Overtime for Inside Sales

LinkedIn is not "Facebook at work." According to The Bridge Group's 2012 Inside Sales Metrics and Compensation Report for B2B technology companies, LinkedIn is the preferred social media choice for inside sales organizations. They have found it to be an essential prospecting, messaging, presenting, and relationship sales tool. LinkedIn must be at the top of your list as a social and sales intelligence tool.

How to Get Up to Speed on LinkedIn

- *Complete your profile 100 percent.* This provides you with a 40 percent greater chance for networking success.

- *Upload a professional picture of yourself.* Choose an image that shows you from the waist up, dressed professionally—no beach or party photos, please! Then gather about six new photos and rotate them every two months.

- *Create a compelling headline.* Example: If you are an inside sales rep working for a virtualization company, you can put "expert in virtualization and cloud computing" as your headline.

- *Gather some recommendations.* Give recommendations in order to get some. This should be easy! All you have to do is ask a few people who have worked with you to recommend you.

- *Join professional groups.* You can join up to 50 groups. Make sure to include those your prospects belong to so you can start gaining visibility.

- *Beef up your current role in your job.* Your current role should stand out more than all the rest on your resume. Make it sound as good as possible without compromising the truth.

- *Complete the specialties section in your profile.* This helps with search terms of key words.

- *Add some apps, such as Twitter, Blog, or Book Recommendations.*

- *Change up your status regularly.* This must be professional! No "in a relationship" or "looking for love" posts.

- Change up the standard invitation to connect. Personalize it to show you are a real person who wants to connect.

How LinkedIn Really Pays Off:

- Always confirm appointments through LinkedIn.

- Vet your customer's career trajectory through LinkedIn.

- Check out the "people who viewed your profile also viewed" connections.

Video

Video rules, and it's not going away. By 2020, 85 percent of buyer-seller interactions will happen online, through social media and video.[18] Everyone goes to YouTube to learn, develop, educate, and watch some good (or bad!) presentations. While you are thinking about that, take a look at these stats from a Nielson report that explains why video matters:

- Over 60 hours of video per minute is downloaded and watched on YouTube every day (every minute of every day). This equals about 9.1 million minutes a day of video watched on YouTube.

- Over 1 billion subscriptions exist in YouTube. That means they subscribe to your channel to be emailed updates and new video!

Tool Types: iMeet, Skype, YouTube

Tool IQ: Everyone likes to be entertained, and we are used to taking in visually presented information. Would you rather read a 20-page attachment or watch a video that gives you the gist of all that information—and a demo to boot—in just a few minutes? Busy customers will opt for the video every time.

Web Conferencing

Presentations can happen anywhere in the sales cycle:

* Early (when you are educating),

* Middle (when you want to deeply qualify), and

* End (when you want to review proposals and timelines).

Web conferencing tools allow salespeople to instantly conduct demos and launch one-click product demos. They make it easy for your team to create, manage, and deliver on-demand multimedia presentations.

Tool Types: Webex, GotoMeeting, Adobe Connect, Glance

Tool IQ: Prospects want to view presentations on their own, at a time of their choosing and without the presence of a salesperson. (Don't worry, they still want a virtual relationship as their travel budgets continue to get cut!)

Deciding on Tools: Your Selection Criteria

Which tool is the one to select? Use these criteria to evaluate tools before you buy them.

* It must be inside sales-centric.

* It must be easy to download.

* It must offer risk-free trials or low monthly fees.

* It must be Web based or cloud based.

* It must be compatible with your CRM.

- It must be user-friendly and easy to implement.

- It must align with the field sales organization and the marketing departments.

- It must have a proven track record.

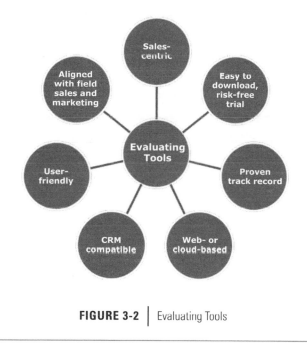

FIGURE 3-2 | Evaluating Tools

TOOLS: TAKE TWO

Frank isn't ready to let go of his loyal inside team just yet, but he doesn't have much time left—for his team, and possibly his own job. His VP suggested that Frank might benefit from attending the Sales 2.0 Sales and Marketing Conference. This is the number one industry event devoted to excellence in leveraging tools and technology from a sales perspective. It's packed with speaker presentations, vendor demonstrations, and networking opportunities. At the conference, Frank realizes that he's not alone. Many sales managers are grappling with the same issues that he is, trying to figure out how to move their teams to the next level. He's definitely in the right place.

Afterward, Frank feels like he's entered a new world of possibilities and, for once, he actually has some hope that he can save his team. The conference helped him see his world from a different angle, and the thing that seemed to be missing was tools. It was a shock to learn how much more there was than just CRM. He knows that he needs to introduce a new work culture that's powered by tools—the right tools. So instead of shopping for a new team, he goes shopping for new tools: sales productivity, sales intelligence, social tools, and all the rest. He invites Sales 2.0 vendors to meet with him and asks marketing to be part of these meetings. His VP gives him the thumbs-up.

After explaining the new lay of the land to his team members and getting them on board, he introduces the essential tools they are going to be working with. Frank works with his team to quickly on-board them on their new tools. He gets Millennial interns to come in to help train on "Tools Tuesdays" and helps them learn the tools.

Frank was worried that some members of his team might quit in frustration or be annoyed that they needed to learn from interns, but they're all for it. They get up to speed quickly and the next quarter's sales look much stronger—just like the old days.

MANAGEMENT TIPS

- The key to your team's survival is a high tool IQ. Having the right tools and knowing how to use them is essential to your team's success.

- Include a good mix of sales productivity/communication tools, sales intelligence tools, and social tools.

- Tools create intelligence, productivity, and customer insight. They are the virtual hand-shake that creates relationships.

- Make sure your team's tool adoption rate is strong.

CHAPTER 4

PROSPECTING 2.0

Inside Sales Superheroes in Action

It's Monday, the first day of Gina's March Madness call blitz. Her teams are ready, they have calling lists and scripts, and she's announced cash prizes. The rules: five hours of outbound calling = 175 calls during this nonnegotiable time. Ready, set, dial!

Gina walks around, observing. Everyone is in their cubicles but the loud buzz that usually defines her energetic and fun team has disappeared. She checks in, popping her head into everyone's cubicle and asking what's going on.

"Hey, Raj, why aren't you on the phones?"

"My field rep called and needs me to adjust a couple quotes for him immediately."

"Taylor, you're usually the star, how are you doing?"

"I'm already done. Do you have more leads I could call on?"

"Carter, I haven't heard you make any calls this morning."

"It's brutal out there. No one's answering their phones. I have better luck with email."

Finally, she hears Katy calling—and she gets a live one! "Hi, is this Majid Hadeem? Oh, I'm sorry, I meant Daljeets Hadim . . . I'm calling to invite you to our webinar on data warehousing. Are you the person who manages this for your company? Sure, sure, I can call you back. When would be a good time? Do you have a current project or initiative around data warehousing?"

Gina keeps walking, a little more slowly now. *"Whitney, is there anything I can help you with today?"*

"Its taking me forever to input my notes into five different systems, and my computer decided to freeze up on me."

"Ethan, have you called down on your list of names?"

"Yeah, right. They're clueless. These are lousy leads. There's nothing in my territory."

"Jacqueline, I heard you on the phones earlier. Did you get some leads?"

"I got a few, but many of them don't have any projects happening in the next six months."

Will is always talking—and here he goes. *"Hey, this is Will. Did I catch ya at a bad time? Do you have a minute? Gotcha, I can definitely call you back, fo' sure. When's a good time? Um, how's next Thursday? We're Goodrich Corp. No, no, we're not the tire company, we're a data company, the leaders in our space. Listen, do you guys have a data project goin' on?"*

Elad shouts out, *"Hey, do you know where I can find the web page on our products? I don't know where to point customers on our website, it doesn't make any sense."*

Why isn't anyone picking up the phone? Gina walks into the break room and sees three of her reps standing near the refrigerator, talking about going for happy hour with the few hundred dollars they are about to win just for picking up the phone during their blitz.

* * *

According to Vorsight's 2012 whitepaper, "The True Cost of Poor Prospecting,"[1] VPs of Sales continually cite their three top priorities as:

1. Revised lead generation programs

2. Building sales pipeline

3. New customer acquisition

For the sales organization, that means pressure to bring in new business. But approaching prospecting with stale habits and outdated techniques will guarantee failure.

Prospecting should be the beginning of a great adventure. But often, salespeople complain that it's boring and robotic. Who wants to call customers who refuse to answer their phones or, if on the rare occasion they do answer, they answer them by accident? Day after day inside salespeople make outbound dials waiting for a LIVE voice, only to get rejected within thirty seconds of that rare connection. Teams become frustrated and impatient, starved for real guidance. They are desperate to reach the C-level buyer but are lost on the best way to get into their inner circle. They spend hours crafting long emails and choose empty subject lines that guarantee an instant trip to the trash, unopened. And when they finally do get someone on the phone, they hold them in a headlock with off-topic questions and annoying "self-selling utopia" pitches.

If this is your experience, you may be tempted to go out and hire a new team. Yet in many cases, it is the manager who needs to embrace a new model of prospecting. Prospecting isn't dead; it's just different. Without prospecting, nothing happens: no new opportunities, no new leads, and no new business. This chapter is designed to reprogram managers' sales and marketing brains, laying out the essential requirements for building an intelligent Prospecting 2.0 playbook.

BUILDING AN INTELLIGENT PROSPECTING 2.0 STRATEGY

Prospecting 2.0 does not exist in a vacuum. It brings together everything we know about the rest of the Sales 2.0 ecosystem—the customer, the talent needs, and the tool power. It includes a working alignment with marketing and focus as well as a familiarity with best 2.0 prospecting practices and processes. Powering it all is a sense of positive team energy that keeps the momentum going; a real sense of curiosity about the customer, loyalty to the solution, and a comprehension of what's expected and how to go about it. And all of that is driven by you: manager, coach, and cheerleader. This tight strategy sets the tone for potent prospecting.

Embed Prospecting in the Sales 2.0 Ecosystem

Prospecting begins with understanding Customer 2.0. They have money to buy, but they don't want to be stalked by mindless sales androids. They want a relationship and lots of attention, but they still want to come to you on their own terms. For them, prospecting means engagement, collaboration, education, mobilization, and application. A special bonus is if this happens through a shared connection or respected peer. They hate being sold to. So:

- Make sure that your salespeople are equipped with well-researched, timely, and intelligent introductions to earn their time.

- Encourage them to stick to their prospects with a strategic multiple-attempt strategy that nurtures with content over time.

Talent 2.0 has energy and social enthusiasm, and they are on an aggressive career path that has no boundaries. They are ready to robo-call with an earbud in one ear and a telephone headset in the other while researching prospects online and managing their CRM. They just need effective guidance and direction from you:

- Encourage your young teams to see prospecting as a game of skill, patience, precision, and focus, not a robo-chore.

- Frame prospecting as a hunt that they must approach with respect and insight and the right tools, not as a competition for volume calls.

Tools 2.0 do not replace the phone, but they do increase engagement throughout the sales cycle—especially on the front end, where prospecting happens. Educate yourself and your teams about all of the best tools out there, and determine which you will adopt into your sales process. Encourage your teams to get to know what their tools can do for them and to use them productively throughout the sales cycle. Start by implementing a core CRM system.

- Make it clear to your team that CRM is their primary tool. Customer intelligence and relationships are based on a substantial CRM.

- Make CRM the foundation for many other tools, including email templates, calendaring, data integration, sales intelligence, dialers, lead management, collaboration, sales analytics, and forecasting.

Align with Marketing on Your Prospecting Strategy

Marketing is usually active on both the front end and the back end of the sales cycle. It always has consistent and ongoing activities through the company's website, including tradeshows, whitepapers, webinars, podcasts, research studies, ebooks, and managing the website. Why let all this go to waste? The inside sales world easily straddles both functions. Your team's prospecting must continue to brand and evangelize your solution in alignment with the marketing efforts. Many inside sales organizations are already staffed with team members (lead development) who report into the marketing organization and inside sales teams who report into marketing. Make sure sales and marketing speak the same universal language.

- Deliver a cohesive marketing and prospecting message. Make sure that your prospecting efforts are not repetitive or conflicting; have your salespeople sell as an integrated sales team.

- Communicate regularly with marketing and collaborate on a strategic vision that translates into tactical, well-executed marketing and prospecting campaigns.

The Sales and Marketing Love/Hate Relationship

There's a thin line between love and hate when it comes to the relationship between sales and marketing. There's always some fingerpointing from sales when it comes to marketing support—sales needs them and when they step in, it's never good enough. Here are some common love/hate issues:

FIGURE 4-1 | The Sales/Marketing Love/Hate Relationship

Sales Loves About Marketing	➤	Sales Hates About Marketing
Lots of leads	➤	Too many leads to keep up with
Vertical-specific case studies	➤	Case studies with accounts that are not relevant to specific territories
Competitive comparisons	➤	Comparing the wrong competitors
Voice mail and email templates	➤	Templates that have too much marketing gobbledygook
Help design PowerPoint slides	➤	Slide deck is too big to present
Great company videos	➤	Videos are too long and technical
Lead scoring	➤	Not in agreement on lead qualification
Landing pages and calls to action	➤	Confusing website
Mass mailings	➤	Spams customers
Offer road shows in region	➤	When sales has to help invite people to road shows

Embrace the Future with Potent Prospecting

Building an intelligent Prospecting 2.0 strategy means leaving behind strategies that are past their sell-by date. Make sure your strategy hits these marks:

- *Leads:* Fill your team's buckets with good leads. Bad leads equal volume calls, but they also create instant discouragement and apathy for team members.

- *Messaging:* Make sure the message your team sells is clear and simple; it must engage and persuade. Don't throw tons of data at them or confuse them with complex messaging that isn't supported by any Web presence.

- *Qualification:* Make sure your teams know how to qualify quickly and effectively, using the Trust Thermometer (page 179). Communicate these criteria at all levels within the sales and marketing organizations. Giving teams minimal qualification criteria will result in low-quality leads.

- *Email and voicemail:* Provide your teams with prewritten email templates that have strong subject lines, and refresh this library of templates every few months. Work with your team on an integrated multiple-attempt strategy that includes variety: four-to-six attempts with emails, voicemail, social media, and video over the course of the prospecting cycle.

- *Social media:* It's time to jump in. Social media is not a fad. In fact, banning social media in a Sales 2.0 world is an epic fail. The trick is to control how your team swims in the professional B2B social river and uses it for their outreach efforts.

- *Quality versus quantity:* It's still a numbers game, but Prospecting 2.0 is more about skill, intelligence, and relevance. Your team wants prospects to stick, not avoid them. Setting unrealistic expectations for them to blitz three times per week for three hours per day looking for high-volume calls or expecting team members to set three appointments per day with anyone who has a pulse will get you exactly nowhere.

- *Perks that work:* Despite your best efforts, prospecting can sometimes be mindless, and it can lose its luster after a while. The remedy? Make sure your Millennial team is living in the fun zone! Create excitement, and be their cheerleader as well as their wise guide. Remember that senseless perks drive the wrong behavior. Provide perks that work.

Use the Best Prospecting 2.0 Practices and Processes

An effective Sales 2.0 prospecting strategy makes sense to both your sales team and your customer. It is built on a sound foundation of alignment with your solution's marketing message, and it allows your inside sales Superheroes to use their superpowers wisely in these three major prospecting practices and processes.

1. Outbound call campaigns and blitzing

2. Lead generation and content nurturing

3. Sales skills alignment

Remember that, as the team's manager, you set the pace. Your primary tasks are to develop a coherent approach, communicate it to your team, guide them through the process you want them to use, and confirm they have the tools and information they need to do a good job. Make sure that everything you do in your prospecting efforts embodies the fun and games factor that drives Millennials to do better, and embody this spirit yourself as their leader.

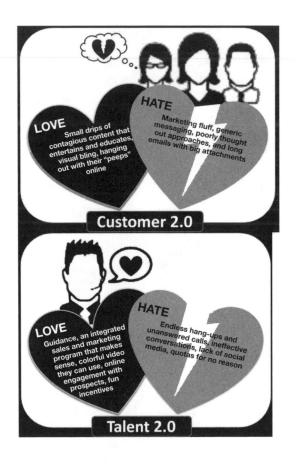

FIGURE 4-2 | Prospecting 2.0's Love/Hate Relationships

OUTBOUND CALL CAMPAIGNS AND BLITZING

Call campaigns and call blitzing are the face of Prospecting 2.0. The intention is to get the call volume up, but if that's your only criteria for success, your campaigns will probably not succeed. To have a potent impact, you must approach call campaigns and blitzing with intelligence: plan your campaign, communicate its goals, and determine your marketing alignment.

Planning

Take the time to plan your campaign in advance. It boils down to two things: the lists and leads your team will be calling on. Make sure team members know the target audience, whom they're calling, what the titles are, the industries, and the size of the companies. Help them understand the difference between calling on lists versus leads: Leads have raised their hand since they have engaged in some level of pre-qualification, and lists have never heard of your company. Have them plan their approach based on this knowledge.

Goals

Communicate the goals of the campaign, and work with team members on succinct call objectives. What type of campaign will it be: an awareness campaign, a product-specific campaign, a leads campaign? These are all different animals. Is the goal to up-sell, cross-sell, invite people to a webinar, or schedule an appointment? Knowing all of this up-front gives team members something to build around and aim at.

Marketing Alignment

Work with marketing to provide teams with details on the campaign, dates, locations, and so on. Sales and marketing must agree on and define the various sales stages. This is vital, because the team has to understand how to move something along and through the sales funnels. Marketing must also create support for the campaign through the company's website. They will need to build landing pages, calls to action, and marketing calendars, and provide these reporting analytics that measure lead conversions. Campaigns need to be prioritized and summarized so that team members can grasp the most important elements and effectively support them.

Marketing must support these efforts by aligning the campaign with the sales team's sales stages. Vorsight and The Bridge Group's Sales Speaks: 2012 whitepaper, "Perceptions and Ponderings on Marketing Leads,"[2] provides a simple outline.

Day 1

- Marketing rolls out the campaign details and tells the story.

- Inside Sales asks questions to make calling most effective.

Day 3

- Inside Sales reports initial results.

- Marketing commits to deliver additional resources as requested by Inside Sales.

Days 6 to 10

- Teams update "where are we," identify obstacles, and commit to assistance.

Day 14

- Teams debrief by retelling actual conversations, sharing results, and making future commitments.

LEAD GENERATION AND CONTENT NURTURING

It's an old story that sits at the crux of the sales and marketing standoff: Reps complain to managers they don't have enough leads; managers complain to marketing they don't give them enough leads; and marketing complains to sales that they are not following up and converting the leads they do receive. And then it really starts to go downhill. Once salespeople start working the leads, many tend to let go too fast or spend too much time holding on to weak leads that never convert. They complain that their leads are bad because they are not qualified and stop following up on the leads that marketing has generated. But salespeople often don't bother communicating this to marketing, which continues its lead generation efforts and blames the salespeople for poor closing efforts.

According to Insidesales.com,[3] most sales professionals give up trying to reach a lead after an average of 1.29 attempts, but 61 percent of leads go into the pipeline after the second call. This is a lot of wasted effort because it takes from 6 to 24 interactions with you or your company before a customer makes a purchase decision.[4]

The solution, as discussed in Chapter 3, is lead nurturing: dripping bite-sized morsels of information to entice and engage prospects over time. Leads can be nurtured to align with the sales stages in this way:

- Not contacted

- Qualified

- Unqualified

- In process

Managers must establish a lead management strategy that includes response rates, follow-up efforts, and qualification criteria and communicate this throughout their organization.

- According to Vorsight and The Bridge Group,[5] sales reps believe that roughly 70 percent of the leads they receive have a low probability to purchase: "Smart organizations realize that the job of a sales rep is not to just 'follow up on leads,' but rather to 'create opportunity.'"

- According to Insidesales.com,[6] 78 percent of sales go to the companies that respond first. Contact rates decrease 100 times if you wait 30 minutes as opposed to 5 minutes to call back.

- According to the lead response management research conducted in 2007,[7] a sales rep is 100 times more likely to make contact with a new lead and 21 times more likely to progress that lead into the sales pipeline if live contact is attempted within the first five minutes of a lead being submitted.

Don't let your teams sit on fresh leads without giving them any attention. This should be a primary focus of their job, especially when statistics prove that slow follow-up is detrimental to potential lead conversion. Remember to prioritize recycled leads over time, as today's Customer 2.0 likes to engage later in the nurture cycle.

Customer 2.0 likes to self-educate and be engaged. Good content stimulates curiosity. Managers must become the conversation leader and content leader. Help your team members nurture their curiosity and engage them with contagious content strategically planted throughout the sales cycle to control how informed you want them to be. Work with marketing to diversify these outreach efforts by aligning the right mix of content with delivery. Effective content nurturing strategies build interest in your solution slowly by dripping information to the prospect in small, entertaining, and digestible bites. Content that initially nurtures can include webinars and general introductions. Later, whitepapers, case studies, and more direct content, such as an ROI calculator, can help them to close the deal.

Ten-Week Nurturing Plan

This two-and-a-half-month nurturing strategy is specifically designed to capture the attention and commitment of Customer 2.0. Spend time carefully selecting the most interesting, most popular, most newsworthy, and most intriguing bits of information you can. Look for variety, color, clarity, and fun, but be sure that you also include substantial industry information and peer testimonials that support your solution as the best one to buy.

- *Week 1: Send a video.* Look for some relevant company or YouTube videos you can send them. Make sure they are short and entertaining, so they'll keep watching.

- *Week 2: Send a solution infographic.* Send a cool, colorful infographic that visually explains what your solution will do for them. *Much* better than a data sheet.

- *Week 3: Send industry research/surveys.* What does third-party research have to say about your industry, field, solution? Is growth predicted? Does it substantiate a need for your solution? Let them know that research supports your solution.

- *Week 4: Send customer testimonials.* What type of praise have you received for your solution? Once it's been installed, how did this impact productivity? Positive peer testimonials make a huge impression on prospects.

- *Week 5: Send press releases.* Send newsworthy items that have just been released about the market, the industry, the product line, and the company.

- *Week 6: Show where you stand in the competitive climate.* If you rank highly when stacked against your competition, send them the proof. Make sure whatever you send gets right to the point, preferably with graphics.

- *Week 7: Invite them to webinars.* Which of your webinars drew the biggest crowd? Which continues to have high on-demand downloads? Remind them why it will be worthwhile for them to register or download the recorded event.

- *Week 8: Invite them to a roadshow/executive briefing.* Is there a breakfast or luncheon coming up where your prospect might network with other people in their field? Invite them.

- *Week 9: Share your awards.* Has your solution been recognized by the industry or has the analyst community voted it within the top emerging solutions? Let the customer know.

- *Week 10: Send an ROI calculator.* Put the numbers together and let them know why this investment is worth it and it makes sense to sign up.

SALES SKILLS ALIGNMENT

Prospecting takes skill; it is both an art and a science. And, no matter how good your team's prospecting prep is, an unskilled or minimally skilled salesperson will probably do poorly. For managers, this means doing everything you can to build your Superstars' skill set and make sure they keep their skills sharp over time.

The best way for teams to build up skill is to adopt the TeleSmart 10 skills in *Smart Selling on the Phone and Online*,[8] a sourcebook for the essential prospecting skills for new calls. Following is a brief overview of each skill and how it relates to prospecting.

Time Management

Prospecting needs focus, and this begins when salespeople manage their time proactively beforehand, so they are not interrupted or distracted by tasks that should already have been accomplished.

- Make sure that your team members set a nonnegotiable call time. This avoids distractions and keeps the momentum going.

- Guide them to establish a clear call objective prior to each call. Focusing on desired goals and results is essential to earning time with their prospects.

- Be sure that they know how to manage their tools for greater productivity. High tool IQ is the key to their success.

- Remind them never to waste LIVE calls and to aim for meaningful conversations.

Introducing

Many calls are blown at the beginning, when salespeople suddenly fumble for an introduction. Ensure that your team understands that introducing is the customer's first impression of your company.

- Confirm that your team brands and evangelizes the solution through the "Triple Threat": voicemail + email + social. Focus especially on gathering a variety of strong subject lines. Load some fresh email templates in their library.

- Encourage regular and strong social media activity through LinkedIn.

Navigating

Stress the importance of calling deeper and wider into the organization rather than chasing just one contact. Navigating skill is about traveling through an organization, gathering names, and engaging with gatekeepers who can help rather than stand in their way.

- Remind them to avoid No-Po's, who can clog up forecasts and bring the sales cycle to a halt. Early detection of No-Po's will save you lots of time.

- Encourage your team to build org charts and to open their circle of influence by calling deeper and wider and incorporating a 2 × 2 penetration strategy.

Questioning

Many prospecting efforts work backward: they try to quickly disqualify prospects instead of spending time *qualifying them*. Bland and empty qualification criteria like BANT (Budget, Authority, Need, and Timeframe) are popular, but don't get the job done.

- Coach your team to use the Trust Thermometer to uncover needs in the right sequence. This includes the following eight categories:
  1. Current environment
  2. Business needs
  3. Decision-making process
  4. Decision-making criteria
  5. Competition
  6. Timeframe
  7. Budget
  8. Next steps

- Encourage your teams to be brave and ask tough questions early and often on the call, probe deeper to uncover hidden needs, and guide the prospect through the call with a strong plan.

Listening

It's easy to focus on hitting a volume number of calls, but that moves the focus to dialing and loses the human focus. *Listening* to Customer 2.0, paying attention to uncover their pain, is essential: One of the main reasons leads do not move forward is because salespeople are not speaking to the prospect's pain.

- Listen in on your reps' calls: Are they really listening to what the prospect is saying or are they multitasking and waiting for the prospect to stop talking so they can pitch?

- Make sure your team uses more precision questions in their qualification arsenal.

- Educate your team on using the essential of information capture and integration to build urgency on each call and to listen for hidden pain and creating urgency around a solution.

Linking

When salespeople are linking correctly, they are adjusting their conversations to match the needs of the title or roles of the decision-maker they are speaking with. Salespeople must be comfortable talking with all levels of the decision-making process and especially at the highest level.

- Help your team understand the "pain chain" and how various levels sit within the hierarchy of influence.

- Role-play with team members to deliver different messages to different titles.

- Have them observe you making calls. Be sure that they pay attention to the way you adjust your messaging to engage with various titles in the pain chain.

Presenting

Customer 2.0 loves to be entertained and hates to be bored. Delivering presentations must sit at the heart of your prospecting efforts.

- Invest in Web conferencing tools, and encourage your teams to collaborate with prospects. They can use this opportunity to up-sell and cross-sell.

- Make (or have your salesperson make, or acquire from marketing) quick, fun, and colorful four-minute (or less) video demos and presentations to send on the spot.

- Help your team strengthen their position when having competitive discussions.

Handling Objections

According to a Culpepper and Associates compensation survey,[9] 80 percent of salespeople are willing to accept a 90 percent rejection rate. Not acceptable!

- Work hard with your team to anticipate potential objections, and coach them on how not to cause the objection themselves.

- Provide them with ready rebuttals to the toughest objections.

- Encourage them to immediately call prospects when they receive email objections as their quick response time may help salvage the rejection.

Partnering

Partnering in prospecting has never been more important. Today's customers are very socially influenced, and often they will choose to engage based on how many of their peers and friends know of you.

- Have them set expectations and establish agreements to cohesively work together.

- Your team must be aware of the unique value they bring and why they are "partner-worthy."

- Encourage them to be proactive with internal and external partners and to take control instead of letting others control the interactions.

Closing

When prospecting, salespeople must understand the final outcome: What is the hand-off process? Is it appointments? Is it an order?

- Be sure that your team understands how to forecast opportunities and what it takes to build a healthy funnel.

- Encourage your teams to establish a strong forecast momentum that is accurate throughout the quarter.

MANAGING YOUR TEAM FOR PROSPECTING 2.0

Here's what old-style prospecting looked like.

The phone jocks made hundreds of outbound dials and spent hours talking with prospects. They called off their big Rolodex of names, they wrote notes in binders, they faxed prospects spec sheets, they took the time to write VITO letters, and they scheduled on-site appointments for their field partners. Managing them was not easy, but it was more predictable.

Today's Sales Superheroes, by contrast, are operating in a much different universe. They seamlessly juggle among different sales communications methods, from phones, mobile (text), email, and video to social (LinkedIn) and IM. They have a sixth sense about which tool is the most appropriate to use, and they're not afraid to push the connection envelope.

The best salespeople need very little guidance; they are already miles ahead of the curve. But for the most part, your team needs you to help them structure their day correctly and fill it productively.

Now let's watch potent prospecting in action and see what the possibilities are. Here's an outline of what Prospecting 2.0 looks like, complete with the time your salespeople should aim for to complete the tasks. How close is your team to meeting these criteria?

1. *Just as they are getting ready to start their day, they automatically turn on all their tools.*

Sales Productivity Tools

Hardware • Calendaring • Power Dialing • CRM • Communication • Target • Company URL

Sales Intelligence Tools

Communication • Presentation • Marketing Automation • Triggers & Alerts • Research • eSignature

Sales 2.0 Toolkit

LinkedIn • Facebook • Twitter • Blogs • Slideshare

Social Media Tools

FIGURE 4-3 | The Sales Superhero's Toolkit

2. *They set up for success.* They strategically plan and understand their territory and determine the best penetration strategy. They learn their tools and prepare tactics, sales analytics, and intelligence. They make planning a priority by carefully organizing whom to call and never engage in "rapid-fire dialing." *Time estimate: as long as it takes.*

3. *They prepare to make calls.* They prepare their hardware. They sit down at their paperless desk in an open cubicle and check their setup:

- A laptop, an iPad
- Two monitors
- A keyboard
- Phones, landlines, cell phones
- A whiteboard

They open all software tools and leave them open throughout their prospecting efforts: email templates, calendar, CRM, dialers, campaign lists, quoting, web conferencing, sales intelligence, social, email marketing, IM/Chat. *Time estimate: five minutes.*

4. *They prepare while dialing their prospect.* They keep their eyes on their tools and prepare to have a relevant dialogue with their prospect. They glance at alert tools and pull up information about the prospect's company and industry; review sales intelligence to understand the hierarchy; and look at the social tools to see if they have any mutual connections in common. *Time estimate: a matter of seconds.*

5. *When they get a LIVE one, they're ready.* They never waste a call because they understand that call-backs are rare. Sales Superheroes are ready to talk, and they have something intelligent and well thought out to say. They have a strong, live opening statement that includes a strong call objective, so their message gains traction and opens the customer's mind. They use their tools to buy them more time on the call.

    They have already accessed the right information; now they translate this information into messages that engage and persuade. They integrate information while talking with their prospect— glancing at their prospects' URL to confirm details, checking LinkedIn to review their social graph, looking into Salesforce to see if anyone else from their team has called in. They qualify, search, refresh, confirm, and integrate information so they can earn time as a trusted adviser and solutions provider. Datahounds at heart, they capture the information into their CRM database. *Time estimate: one to two minutes.*

6. *They hold their weight on the call.* They flex their razor-sharp questioning skills and immediately begin a preliminary qualification process using their Trust Thermometer (see page 79). They identify the current environment, business need, decision-making process, competition, timeframe, and budget to quickly determine whether this is a qualified opportunity that is ready to close or one that needs to be nurtured for the future. They engage and build trust with the prospect and earn more time than others because of their sharp intelligence that entices their prospect. *Time estimate: one to two minutes.*

7. *Their raw curiosity stretches the call.* They are compelled to know everything about the solution they are selling and the customer they are selling it to. They know what they want, they know how to find it, and they keep asking why until they find out. *Time estimate: three to four minutes.*

8. *Their super listening skills earn them more time.* They pay attention to what people are really saying and are always sensitive to the unspoken alerts and triggers. They listen deeply and take notes, simultaneously integrating information and cross-referencing while they are talking with their prospect. They know how to uncover a potential need and expose it so that the urgency for a solution becomes greater. Their timing is synchronized, their listening is sharp, and they establish excellent rapport. *Time estimate: four to five minutes.*

9. *They finesse an appointment on the spot.* They have their calendar open for a meeting, but they know that no-show rates are climbing up to 50 percent. So they push for a "hot transfer" and ask for additional minutes on the call so they can present value and use collaborating tools to share documents, jump, or web or video conferencing demos immediately. *Time estimate: nine minutes.*

10. *They leave tracks.* After making initial contact and qualifying their prospects, they begin the slow content-nurturing process, preparing them for their upcoming appointment.

PROSPECTING SUPERHEROES: TAKE TWO

When Gina wakes up from her March Madness blitz nightmare, she realizes that her team's issues with blitz dialing are not on them—she didn't plan the blitz well, and she didn't offer them any effective guidance. "My bad," she thinks, and decides to design some new guidelines for herself to ensure success next time.

Here are Gina's seven rules for call blitzing:

1. *Avoid scheduling a call blitz on a Monday. This can be a discouraging time to proactively call on outbound leads.*

2. *Don't schedule a blitz for more than two to three hours. Expecting your team to sustain that high level of momentum for that length of time is unrealistic.*

3. *Coordinate call campaigns with the marketing department by organizing lead sources and developing stronger lists for the teams. Help the team prioritize who to call and make sure they have enough people to call.*

4. *Preload sample voice mail and email templates into CRM so that the team doesn't have to break its momentum to create new ones.*

5. *Schedule a meeting with team members to discuss the campaign, their list, and their messaging and conduct some role-plays before the blitz.*

6. *Design fun, creative incentives that don't rely solely on the team picking up the phone. Instead, create healthy competition and motivation and map the rewards to the right behavior.*

7. *Create high energy with the teams. Put on your cheerleader hat and have fun!*

MANAGEMENT TIPS

- Align with marketing to endorse a consistent marketing message that brands and evangelizes the solution. Help your team craft good introductions based on this message.

- Call your team together before the campaign starts to make sure that they understand the message, that they can articulate it, and that they know what you expect from them. Provide customized multiple-attempt email templates for them to use.

- Make sure your team does not give up if they cannot reach the prospect live. Your watchword should be, "Don't let them get away!" They should immediately send email, leave a voice mail message, and follow up with a LinkedIn invitation.

- Explain that their solution has no boundaries. Make sure that they gather more names and traverse multiple departments—IT, Sales, Marketing, Finance, Engineering, and so on—until they find the right audience.

PART TWO

THE COMPASSIONATE MANAGER 2.0

Your Playbook for Building an Effective Hiring, Training, and Coaching Ecosystem

You walked into your management role wanting to make a difference for your team, and you really are the best person for the job: You know their world, you've sat in their seats, you embrace the company culture, you know the space well, you know how to present the entire product line, you know all the territories, and you are driven to close deals at the highest level. In fact, you can do everyone else's job with your eyes closed.

Oops, did you forget something? Your peeps—your teams, your talent—are the ones you need to develop and nurture every day to their full potential. That means approaching your team members with compassion; taking time to understand their strengths, skill gaps, and motivations; and managing them from the inside out. No smartphone app—not even Siri!—can give you this bond.

Whether you are managing a team of 4 or 186 people on several teams, understanding the human side of sales management is an essential piece to being a Smart Sales Manager. Knowing how to hire, train, coach, and develop your talent, as well as how to listen, watch, observe, learn about, and motivate them: these are the keys to managing your inside sales organization from the inside out.

Think of this section as your Sales 2.0 ecosystem retention strategy playbook. These chapters will guide you through the essential management skills you never learned as an individual contributor and will become the lifeline to your inside sales teams. These will set you apart as the smart and sage inside sales manager; the one who holds deep wisdom and insight when it comes to today's Talent 2.0.

In Chapter 5, you'll meet the new inside sales Superheroes, the reps who will change the face of your entire organization. We dive into the sizzling inside sales job market and help you sort through the vast talent pool with an "always be recruiting" strategy that sends an inviting message to qualified candidates.

In Chapter 6, you'll learn how to build a sustainable training structure that lays the groundwork for your training investment to stick and establishes a comprehensive sales skills system that works long after training has been delivered.

In Chapter 7, you'll be guided in structuring an integrated coaching plan that gets up close and personal in-cube and extends out to call calibrations with managers. We'll provide you with handy call monitoring forms and a winning criteria for stack-ranking your teams.

In Chapter 8, you'll target your coaching to your team members' core character to transform behavior and drive results. You'll learn how to coach from the inside out and meet and learn insightful coaching wisdom when it comes to managing the most classic inside sales personalities

And finally, in Chapter 9, you'll learn why counting calls is a thing of the past and it's time for a metrics makeover, as we will introduce you to the new call metrics of the future that go beyond call volume to embrace the specifics of the sales 2.0 ecosystem.

CHAPTER 5

HIRING SUPERHEROES

The Talent Building Blocks of an Inside Sales Organization

Every week, I get an email or a call from a manager asking me to help in hiring a "real hunter" or a "cold-calling animal" by month's end. Each explains the need to hold off on training until a full headcount is reached. Recently, for example, I heard about Tracy's hiring struggles. She had spent all morning scouring Craigslist for potential new inside sales candidates. They received a new round of funding, she told me, and a new headcount had been approved. Now, she needed to hire 18 new SDRs (Sales Development Reps) within the next four months. This was a victory: she had spent years convincing management of the viability of inside sales. Now they've finally listened and given her a generous headcount—even more than the field organization.

She knew she should be thrilled, but Tracy is exhausted. She explained that she spends hours on recruiting and hiring efforts with very little support: her management doesn't want to pay commissions to external recruiters and HR is clueless when it comes to hiring inside sales talent. The last so-called "rock star" candidate they sent her way worked as a tour guide driving tourists through the city's urban jungle. Then, they sent her a radio disc jockey with no sales experience because he aced his phone interview.

Tracy's skeleton team is overworked and managing large territories, and their field counterparts are screaming for more help. Her inside teams' morale is so low that they can't even get any of their friends excited about interviewing. And when she has some of her team members interview the candidates, their disgruntled faces are instant deal breakers.

Still, she's got jobs to spare—lots more jobs than candidates. Tracy can't figure out why it's so difficult finding talent: Her company's location is central, their comp plan is competitive, their product is quickly growing in popularity, and they are the leaders in the data management space. "In today's job market, why can't I find any good people who are willing to sell data for a $75K package?" she asks in frustration.

* * *

You can structure an inside sales organization all you want with the latest in tools and technology, but the single most important factor in creating a successful team is hiring the right people. If the *people* component is missing, you're not making sales. While hiring as a desperate last-minute measure may net the occasional star, to ensure the best team you need a viable plan and a repeatable process that will work throughout the cycle.

In this chapter, we'll explore how you can take control of the never-ending hiring wheel. You'll meet today's inside sales Superheroes: part social, part virtual, and part authentic human being. You will also learn how to develop a strong recruitment playbook, building your organization from the inside out and replacing tired hiring practices with fresh new idea strategies that work. You'll learn the nine essentials to developing an "always-be-recruiting" ecosystem and get pointed in the right direction when it comes to sourcing candidates, screening talent, establishing a hiring criteria, and identifying the winning competencies for today's Superheroes, the new rulers of the inside sales world.

WHY HIRING IS SO DIFFICULT

Our economy is hampered by a sluggish growth, yet companies are aggressively growing their inside sales organizations—at the rate of 15 percent per year. According to Insidesales.com, in 2012, we were at 1.6 million and estimated to grow to 4.5 million within the next three years.[1] Inside sales has become the alpha dog of today's sales organizations, and the hiring frenzy is in full bloom: everyone needs to hire three-plus this quarter, another six-plus next quarter, and 18 by the end of the year. Yet hiring the *right* people for the job is difficult for many managers.

Hiring is often ranked as one of the top sales initiatives for many executives. They know that building high-performing talent is what will take them to a new level of excellence in the next five years. Yet many sales organization hiring and retention efforts are struggling. According to a Sales Gravy study of 21,000 sales leaders, sales organizations are "ill-equipped to compete in today's market place for top performing sales talent."[2] As companies begin to grow and improve their inside sales organizations, the competition for talent is increasing and the talent pool is shrinking. This scarcity of good inside talent is challenging for several reasons:

- Traditional recruitment, screening, and hiring practices no longer work in today's atmosphere, nor do they provide the results. Managers who came up the old ladder have unrealistic expectations about what the inside sales role entails.

- The inside sales role has changed from what it was just a few years ago, as reflected by Chapter 4's Superhero habits (page 83–86). The skills are more complex and more technically, socially, and virtually robust. In order to hire and retain good inside sales talent, managers must structure well-defined roles and responsibilities and create clear performance expectations.

- The seasoned talent with 15 or more years of sales experience are not only expensive, but a bit dated. Their sales techniques are not 2.0-centric, they are resistant to try new tactics, and they don't have the prospecting mojo they used to have.

- The less experienced and younger talent are tech-savvy and socially networked, but they are mostly young college grads with zero to three years in the field. They are less expensive, but they have little knowledge of basic sales skills and require more ramp-up time.

Today's inside sales organizations invest in building the Sales 2.0 Ecosystem by developing lead nurturing strategies, territory coverage models, outbound call campaign and messaging strategies, and deploying the right tools; yet they lack a consistent recruiting and hiring strategy for bringing in new talent. The costs of a mis-hire can be catastrophic: according to one report, every $10,000 you pay a salesperson who doesn't work out can cost your business $30,000 to $40,000 in loss that doesn't even show up in the P&L.[3]

The solution? Develop a hiring environment that never quits.

NINE ESSENTIALS TO DEVELOPING AN "ALWAYS-BE-RECRUITING" ECOSYSTEM

In Chapter 4, we focused on potent prospecting and the importance of establishing momentum. The same high energy and intention must also power your recruiting efforts. This "always-be-recruiting" mindset will help you find the Superhero, not just at the last possible second but throughout the recruitment process.

Managers traditionally approach hiring more reactively, based on immediate need. Unfortunately, as everyone knows, once these managers get approval on open headcount, they are already feeling the pressure: they don't take time to determine the role requirements for the job functions. Instead, they end up writing empty ads and posting them on sites with thousands of other ads, they screen out too many candidates, they interview too few, and they end up deciding on the wrong ones, who soon leave an empty seat that needs to be filled again. Meanwhile, every day the position isn't filled puts revenue targets in jeopardy.

Smart sales managers build relationships with prequalified candidates *before* they are ready to hire. Their sales staff gets used to this "always-be-recruiting" environment as normal behavior; it is accepted in the culture to always be looking for good talent, widening the pool.

The following are nine essentials to developing a strong "always-be-recruiting" muscle:

1. Learn to recognize inside sales Superheroes when you meet them.

2. Structure inside sales talent by determining the right roles.

3. Establish a "multicareer" ecosystem that entices talent.

4. Work an ACTIVITY not a place.

5. Learn where to source good talent and establish a referral network.

6. Create strong messaging that supports the roles you want to hire.

7. Establish a fun culture that sells.

8. Design a screening process that sticks.

9. Don't be the roadblock to hiring talent.

We'll take a deep dive into each of these in the rest of this chapter.

Learn to Recognize Inside Sales Superheroes When You Meet Them

Sales 2.0 is not one-size-fits all. Not one inside sales organization is structured in the same way as any other. That's because they each have different go-to-market strategies based on their individual product/service, price points, sales cycle, direct/indirect purchase channels, target audience, sales locations, and talents. These living, breathing microbusiness 2.0 ecosystems are constantly in flux. The thing that is the same across the board is the never-ending quest for good talent.

In Chapter 4 you watched the Superhero in potent prospecting action. Now you're probably asking, *"How can I get one of these on my team?"* Well, the key is learning to recognize them when you see them.

Today's inside sales Superheroes' sales buzz is viral, vast, technically potent, and sprinkled with marketing wisdom." And they are culturally different from the previous sales generation. They don't announce their presence with ringing phones—they're jacked into the virtual world. If their fingers are flying, they're making things happen in Sales 2.0. Take a look at their 25 superpowers outlined in the next section and commit them to memory!

The 25 Superpowers of the Inside Sales Superhero

FIGURE 5-1 | Sales Superhero

Is there an inside sales Superhero sitting in front of you right now? Learn to identify the superpowers that help them fly through today's Sales 2.0 ecosystem.

1. *They are intellectually curious.* They are genuinely curious about people, about business, and about filling a need with their solution.

2. *They are hungry.* They are motivated to make calls every day. They have the emotional drive to want to do whatever's necessary.

3. *They write well.* Writing good content is the key to survival. Whether they're crafting a quick proposal, an email blast, a rejection response, or a clever subject heading, their writing abilities clearly and effectively communicate their intelligence and intentions.

4. *Their explanations are clear and succinct.* They have the ability to deliver the message to customers clearly; this is vital. If they can't talk, they can't sell.

5. *They are persuasive.* Their ability to apply logic and knowledge to convince prospects is strong.

6. *They collaborate.* They understand how to present, collaborate, and share their fresh knowledge through web-conferencing tools. They are creative collaborators who can engage customers with entertaining content and relatable conversation.

7. *They understand financial value.* They are not quick to discount but they are very strong when explaining ROI and long-term investments.

8. *They move at the speed of light.* They think fast, learn fast, and move fast. They're confident, bold, impatient (in a good way!), and definitely not shy.

9. *They maintain maximum momentum.* Their pace is consistent, solid, and balanced on a daily, monthly, and quarterly basis.

10. *They have laser focus.* They stay on task and have the ability to focus no matter what distractions are happening around them.

11. *They are tenacious.* They know that their survival depends on their ability to hang in there, so they don't give up. They are persistent and determined to win.

12. *They rebound well from objections.* They bounce back from rejection quickly, and they bravely rely on their creative approaches to respond to objections.

13. *They forge solid partnerships.* Everyone wants this person on their team because they know how to create, manage, and align with partners.

14. *They have strong product and technical knowledge.* They understand the solution from both a technical and business standpoint.

15. *They are coachable.* They are committed to improving themselves and are interested in learning, developing, and growing personally and professionally.

16. *They are competitive.* They know how to engage in friendly competition because their desire to win is strong.

17. *They are resourceful navigators.* They know how to move through the internal and external systems to get answers and complete tasks.

18. *They are professional team players.* They are not just out for themselves. They make choices that benefit the entire team by sharing knowledge and mentoring others.

19. *They have digital influence.* Their social media digital footprint is strong; they have quality contacts and influential followers.

20. *They understand Customer 2.0.* They can read this complex independent customer and meet them on their terms.

21. *They are not shut out by hierarchies.* They are comfortable talking at all levels within the organization and refuse to let anyone shut them out or hold them down.

22. *They have a high tool IQ.* They are comfortable utilizing tools. They have a fast learning curve with new tools and use them throughout the sales cycle.

23. *They are savvy marketers.* They are comfortable using analytics to measure response, and they keep their marketing hat on when they are selling.

24. *They are trustworthy.* They are not pushy or self-serving; they know how to establish a strong level of authentic trust with prospects.

25. *They like winning.* Losing is not an option. They maintain a high level of commitment to bringing the business in.

Structure Inside Sales Talent by Determining the Right Roles

Revising the sales team structure is a top sales effectiveness initiative for many companies.[4] As your inside sales organization continues to evolve and grow more complex, structuring it with a wide assortment of roles and job functions becomes more and more important.

The most critical decisions managers must make involve listening to their customers, deciding what they need, and recruiting the right talent to fill that need. Your first step is to understand the unique requirements of the various roles you are hiring for. Determine the roles you need to fill, what each position entails, and the specific competencies that are required for that role. It is critical to take the time to define the role early—before you start interviewing and hiring: a Sales Development Rep and an Inside Sales Rep are two very different roles, and each has a specific skill set.

The following pages define each role you might find within a B2B inside sales organization and explains the job function and competencies to look for when you are hiring. As you read, always remember this important fact: *The inside sales Superhero has all of these competencies!*

Lead or demand generation team: Most inside sales new hires start in lead generation because it exposes them to the customer and the company from a sales and marketing perspective. This team may sit under the marketing umbrella, as their role primarily focuses on following up from inbound marketing-generated leads, Web leads, webinar invites, trade shows, and whitepaper downloads. This role is transactional and focuses primarily on the front or beginning part of the sales cycle.

Superhero competency requirements: Lead generation requires strong customer service, quick follow-up and response, and strong information capture and documentation skills. Internal knowledge of the company is very important. These individuals are usually the first point of contact, guiding customers through the website and various resources. Product knowledge is not essential for lead generation team members.

Sales development team: Sales development teams usually report under the sales umbrella and may follow up on leads generated from the marketing organization. Their role is exclusively proactive: as they follow up on leads, webinar attendees, or trial eval downloads to schedule meetings and appointments and progress the sale further.

Superhero competency requirements: Sales development is the primary "hunting" group. They must have fearless hunting mojo to navigate through organizations, quickly learn the hierarchy, identify the power players, qualify new opportunities, and move the sale along. More product knowledge is required for these team members, especially to help with deeper qualification and listening for the customer's pain.

Inside sales team: Inside sales teams come in two flavors. They may overlay with the field sales team and geographically manage territories, or they may be fully quota bearing and manage the entire sales process on their own. According to one report, 55 percent of companies are structuring their inside sales organizations independent of the field sales teams.[5]

Superhero competency requirements: The experience requirements for this group are high because they must manage a quota and make things happen. They must have strong product knowledge, exceptional sales skills, good customer relationship skills—in fact, most of the Superhero qualities outlined in this chapter.

Hybrid inside sales team: The scope and dimension of selling has changed significantly, so many organizations no longer have a pure "field selling" role or a pure "telephone selling" role. Hybrid inside sales combines a bit of both. They work on larger, strategic named accounts, spending a few days in the office and visiting prospects when necessary. They approach the sale similar to a field salesperson and a seasoned inside sales rep.

Superhero competency requirements: The hybrid salesperson must be technically, culturally, socially, and skillfully diverse and astute. They may be seasoned field talent who now want to work inside and travel light.

Renewal teams: Renewal is no longer the place where salespeople go when they're put out to pasture. This group has tremendous untapped revenue potential, and many companies are investing more in these teams. They hold tremendous usage knowledge from the existing customer: the valuable information they need in order to renew.

Superhero competency requirements: Renewal talent must be true farmers or account managers. Their ability to build strong, personal relationships with install-based customers encompasses far more than just getting a one- or two-year renewal. They must have strong product, strategic planning, and positioning knowledge. They must approach renewals with up-selling and cross-selling potential and not from a single dimension or goal for renewal.

Government teams: Government procurement cycles are changing and becoming more active; they are not as predictable as they used to be. These teams can no longer afford to be patient with timelines, as more budget sources are being uncovered daily.

Superhero competency requirements: These teams need the ability to figure out the intricacies of the government procurement process and create internal alliances. They also need to be extremely responsive to the "spend it or lose it" tidal wave that hits them when spending freezes open up.

Social selling team: Social selling is a response to today's social Customer 2.0. This group leverages social media, follows online virtual conversations, and creates active nurturing campaigns full of contagious content to generate more inbound quality leads.

Superhero competency requirements: Team members must be socially savvy, technologically competent, and an excellent writer with a distinct "voice" or "style" that engages. They must know how to swim in the social river, how to be chief listening officers, and how to simultaneously juggle multiple social online networks.

Team lead: This position is usually filled by a senior inside salesperson who demonstrates leadership skills and is willing to divide time between being an individual contributor and coaching and mentoring team members.

Superhero competency requirements: Must have good overall leadership skills. They must be extremely knowledgeable in all the various positions, skills, product knowledge, company, customer, and market. They are basically the "go-to" person and must be approachable and understand how to educate and train.

Coach/mentor: This may be a full-time coach, doing call monitoring and providing feedback on calls. They will listen to calls and work with the teams on developing their skills. They will also act as quality assurance to monitor product messaging and customer issues.

Superhero competency requirements: Must have strong product knowledge and exceptional sales skills, plus the ability to listen and teach. They must also have influence with the team because their goal is performance improvement and development. This role will be discussed further in Chapter 8.

Establish a "MultiCareer" Ecosystem That Entices Talent

Talent 2.0 is ambitious and wants *your* job—tomorrow. They are eager to get better and contribute and grow in their jobs in the company and in their long-term careers. Members of this group don't like to pin their identities to just one job. According to DeVry University,

22 percent of Millennials expect to work at six or more different companies during their professional lives.[6]

When hiring talent from this "What's next?" generation, it's important to establish a career progression. Many of them get into inside sales as a steppingstone for field sales or management, so establishing defined roles and responsibilities and timelines for advancement is important. Offering a growth career path up front will help to ensure retention. In my experience, the roles and job functions illustrated in the previous pages show a career progression from lead generation to coach; this takes years, averaging at least 18 to 24 months in each position.

Work an ACTIVITY, Not a Place

According to The Bridge Group metrics report, although more and more sales organizations are starting to decentralize their inside sales teams, less than 10 percent of their teams are working remotely. Nonetheless, the statistics estimate that 41 million corporate employees globally are spending at least one day a week teleworking and another 100 million will work from home at least once a month.[7] So today's sales is not about *where* you work but *how* you work.

Traditionally, inside sales organizations have relied on the synergy of a cohesive team for regular motivation. They learn by osmosis and through general team support and motivation. We are all too familiar with the "contagious" nature of this team; they can "infect" each other with good news or bad news when they are sitting in such close quarters.

Managers have been reluctant to risk the lack of team support, information sharing, and strength in numbers, which is largely why they don't decentralize their teams. But attracting talent has become increasingly more difficult, and trends point to the future of a remote, decentralized workforce. Geographic territories are already being structured differently to accommodate Talent 2.0's desires to work virtually, socially, and interculturally. As increasing numbers of salespeople join the remote workforce, today's "plug-and-play" offices are becoming more mobile and flexible. Next-generation cloud-based and collaboration tools make it extremely easy for team members to work from home, and this trend within inside sales will continue to grow. And this is a good thing: An Edinger 360-degree feedback report found that people who work remotely are actually more engaged, more committed to their work, and rate their leaders higher than those who work from the office.[8]

Managing Remote Talent

Here's the hidden reason that managers are sometimes reluctant to decentralize their inside teams: they are unsure about how to manage them. Here are some tips.

1. *Make sure they have the right qualities to work remotely.* Look for these specific Superhero qualities in any potential remote worker:

    *   *Resourceful:* They can quickly tap into the internal and external information company network and get themselves included in everything from meetings to brown bags.

    *   *Independent:* They can work well in physical isolation from the group.

    *   *Laser focus:* They can easily separate personal from business and transition smoothly from one to the other.

    *   *Motivation:* They can motivate themselves to make calls and hold themselves accountable for results.

2. *Require new remote employees to initially work on-site.* You will be holding them responsible for the same sales metrics, sales productivity tools, and sales responsiveness requirements as your on-site team, so observing their skills firsthand for at least six months will help you determine if they have the basic qualifications to work remotely.

3. *Assign them a "buddy" or "sponsor" who works on-site.* Insist that they be in regular communication. The buddy can act as their corporate lifeline, a collaborative conduit to keep the remote employee in touch and excited about what's happening in the organization.

4. *Review their home office setup.* It's difficult to work from home if your "home office"—wherever it is—isn't properly set up. Work with your IT department to help set up your remote workers. Ask your remote reps to take pictures

or videos of the setup once their workspace is organized. Make sure that they have the same tools and technology that they would have in the office and a separate space to dedicate to your business.

Learn Where to Source Good Talent and Establish a Referral Network

Finding talent isn't just about doing a search for keywords like "phone sales" or "telemarketing" on Craigslist, Monster, or CareerBuilder. Where and how you source talent will determine the type of talent you will get.

Remember: You are on a quest to find inside sales Superheroes. Although there are some Clark Kents hiding out there, you will probably not find the candidates you're looking for in the want ads. This is not a group that scours job boards, mainly because they hear about jobs from friends. A better strategy is to entice the right candidates by actively recruiting. This means putting on your marketing, social, and sales hats and continually feeding and following professional and social networks.

- *Professional networks:* The American Association of Inside Sales Professionals (AA-ISP) is dedicated to advancing the careers of inside sales professionals. This vibrant organization is thriving, with chapters opening up all over the world. Networking at these chapters is a great way to meet potential candidates. LinkedIn specialized groups is another great way. The most vibrant one is Trish Bertuzzi's Inside Sales Experts Group, which has almost 20,000 members who come together to discuss and share job postings.

- *Social networks:* Most employers have a Facebook fan page, a LinkedIn company page, and a Twitter presence. Make sure you advertise through these networks—that's where every candidate searches. Remember to establish a strong digital footprint to show that you engage in the conversation economy. Demonstrate a strong company message and image in their social networks with lots of friends that "like" your page.

- *Industry referrals:* Create a list of industry referral partners that includes content partners, vendors, and internal and external customers. Just as Customer 2.0 depends on peer references, Talent 2.0 will choose a job based on where their friends or their college alumni network.

- *Job or career fairs:* Get yourself out there and expose your organization to the hundreds and thousands of potential candidates who attend job fairs, career fairs, open houses, and the like. Your company may also consider hosting an off-site monthly breakfast or "happy hour" and inviting potential candidates. This is a great way for them to taste your company culture and meet their potential peers in a casual setting.

- *Online search:* Some of the best websites for inside salespeople are Salesladder, LinkedIn, CareerBuilder, and Monster. Learn to use these sites by plugging in key words such as "inside sales representatives" or "social selling reps" or "hybrid inside sales" to narrow your search. Repost regularly to activate the search engines and crawlers.

Create Strong Messaging That Supports the Roles You Want to Hire

Strong messaging is important in finding talent. In essence, you are selling the job to potential candidates. Your messaging embodies everything about your company's culture, what the job is, and the person you want to attract. Today's Talent 2.0 wants to be part of something big, fun, energetic, and with a future. Anywhere you can sell the company—from the "Join Our Team" section of your website to the specific job description—your message about finding talent must be loud and clear, fresh and inviting. Your messaging must:

- Demonstrate your reputation

- Sell candidates on your company values and mission

- Highlight the importance of being part of your company's "transformational vision"

- Emphasize that your organization will nurture their talent and provide opportunities for personal growth

Establish a Fun Culture That Sells

If you think that, as the potential employer, you hold all the cards, think again. Managers often want to hire based solely on the candidate's resume and skills, only to find that the candidate doesn't think much of the company's culture. Talent 2.0 wants to belong to the FUN Club. When they start looking for a job, they first check out the Top 50 Best Companies to work for or follow their college alumni network for the "funnest job." They are looking for more than "just a job": they want a sense of community, camaraderie, and competitive activities, especially when they can win.

More and more companies are investing a lot of time and effort in creating a FUN culture. Often, that starts at the top, with the company's CEO. These high-energy CEOs embody the social spirit that creates an entertaining culture based on working hard and having fun. In fact, they are the ringleaders of the FUN club: their tweets, blogs, videos, and physical presence draw us to their companies.

When it comes to spicing your sales culture with the fun factor, managers must go the extra mile to discover the events, music, food, games, and ideas that pump up the fun volume. If this is not your thing, outsource: nominate a few "fun ambassadors" from your sales organization who are creative, resourceful, and full of motivational energy.

Design a Four-Phase Screening Process That Sticks

Screening sales talent can be tough because salespeople are strong at persuasion. But according to Insidesales.com, limited screening can contribute to a bad hire.[9] The solution is to develop a strong, consistent talent screening program for all candidates that will actually screen *out* those who are inappropriate and allow the Superheroes to get noticed. You can accomplish this through four phases of interviewing and vetting the talent that looks for a perfect storm of three characteristics: the need for achievement, competitive drive, and optimistic outlook.

Phone Screening: First Impressions Count Phone screening gives you your first impression of the candidate. Phone interviews can last anywhere from 3 to 20 minutes. In this initial exploratory phase—sometimes in the first few seconds—you can begin to get a sense of whether or not this is an individual you want representing your company.

Some of the questions you might ask include:

- What attracted you to this job posting?

- What are you looking for in an inside sales position?

- What's your present job, and why do you want to leave?

- What are your career goals? How would this position fit into them?

- What makes a job enjoyable for you?

- Under what conditions do you work best?

- Are you self-motivated?

- How would team members describe you in a team environment?

- How do you approach managing multiple projects and clients?

- How do you use your tools every day?

- How do you organize and prioritize tasks?

- What positive or negative thing would your boss say about you?

- What are your major strengths? Where do you need help?

Face-to-Face or On-Site Interview: Going Deeper The face-to-face interview is the second phase of the process. The candidate has passed the initial screening, so now you can ask more in-depth questions. Find the appropriate environment for this interview: a quiet place with few distractions and no interruptions.

Many managers bring in a panel for this interview, including reps and other managers or peers from other departments. Be careful that everyone doesn't ask questions at once; this will make the candidate feel uncomfortable. Instead, distribute interview questions so everyone can take a turn. This "divide-and-conquer" approach also reduces the chances of repetitive questions. You may want to ask the same questions in the same order every time you conduct an interview, just to keep things simple. Be sure not to overwhelm the candidate with too many questions!

Twenty-Five Questions That Reveal Character

Salespeople are masters at answering the basic questions, like "How would you sell me this pencil?" or "What animal describes you?" If you ask generic questions, you will get generic answers; and you will not get any closer in your search. Real behavioral questions, in contrast, will take a deep dive into the candidate's character. The following 25 behavioral questions are aligned with the inside sales Superhero's qualities:

1. *Intellectual curiosity:* How do you get customers to talk about their business priorities?

2. *Hunger:* Can you describe an instance where you managed to progress a stalled deal? Please explain the personal energy on your part over an extended period of time.

3. *Strong writer:* Give me an example of your messaging on an outbound campaign. What would your email look like—subject line, LinkedIn group follow-up, and Twitter?

4. *Clear and succinct explanations:* Describe how you explain complex issues so that others find them easy to understand. Can I hear an example?

5. *Persuasive:* How do you know a customer is convinced by your line of thought?

6. *Collaboration:* What do you deliberately do to promote a sense of team spirit and encourage collaboration in your current/previous job?

7. *Financial acumen:* Can you talk about a time you successfully pushed through a price increase?

24. *Trustworthy:* What is it about you that your customers trust? How do you establish rapport and trust?

25. *Winning:* If losing an opportunity isn't an option, how do you stay focused and create a win-win strategy?

Role-Play This has become a major part of today's interview process because it demonstrates how potential candidates really sell and how well they think on their feet in a live setting. Set up a mini-sales call where they contact you as though you were the prospect. Listen to them manage the call. Throw objections and questions at them and hear how they rebut and hold their ground. Will they ask for the close at the end of the call?

Go-Do Assignment Go-Do is literally that: you ask the candidate to go and do something concrete. This important part of the interview process tests thinking, listening, and follow-through skills and shows you how a candidate applies skills and aptitude in the real world.

You can assign them anything from putting together a sales presentation or a one-page territory plan assignment. You may decide to give them a writing assignment. You might also ask them to follow up and expand on some of these questions:

- How have you grown since you first started your sales career?

- What do you wish you had known when you first started that you know now?

- What will you do differently going forward?

- How will you determine which accounts to pursue and when?

- How will you generate leads?

- What will be your approach to booking a meeting?

- How will you differentiate our offering from the competition's?

8. *Intrepid, fast-moving:* Describe a time when you had to quickly move something. What did you do?

9. *Momentum:* What's your ideal work environment: one in which you c on several dynamic projects at one time or one in which you can one task at a time through completion?

10. *Laser focus:* How do you personally stay focused while working in a ronment that has many distractions? How can you keep others focus

11. *Tenacity:* Can you tell me about a situation where you pushed yours others to achieve an important goal? What was the outcome?

12. *Objection rebound:* What are your comeback tactics? How do you re from stress?

13. *Solid partnerships:* How do you establish cooperative partnerships for one involved in the sale?

14. *Precise and analytical:* What do you feel is the difference between an an ical approach to problem solving and a creative approach? Do you use approach more than another?

15. *Coachability:* What type of coaching have you received in the past? What the outcome?

16. *Competitive:* Can you give me an example of a time when you were com ing for a job or a deal? How did you gain a competitive advantage?

17. *Navigators:* How do you handle gatekeepers to gain access to busy decis makers? Do they help you or keep you out?

18. *Team players:* What do you think makes a good team player? Would you scribe yourself this way? How do you deal with those who are not?

19. *Digital influence*: What is your method for approaching influencers who a high social clout score? What is your digital engagement strategy?

20. *Customer 2.0-centric:* How do you stay connected to customers who want you to stay away and who regard the phone as a rude interruption

21. *Fearless of hierarchies:* How do you adjust your sales pitch to diffe audiences?

22. *High tool IQ:* What is your tool adoption curve?

23. *Savvy marketers:* What's the extent of your marketing knowledge? At point do you put your marketing hat on?

- What metrics do you use to keep yourself on track?

- What will you do to continually enhance your knowledge and skills?

Personality Test According to one report,[10] 55 percent of companies conduct sales aptitude/competencies assessment testing. There are many personality and assessment tests out there already; some build or buy (then customize) a profile-based structured hiring process.

It's up to you to determine when in the interviewing process you want to use this tool and what you want it to measure. An assessment early in the interview process can quickly weed out bad candidates and save you time in the long run.

The Final Interview: Selling the Job This is the wrap-up phase. You want the candidate, but now you may need to sell your opportunity—there's a lot of competition for the good ones. Be sure to have all your ammunition about why your company is the best and why this job is a great career path for the candidate. The "What's in it for me?" question is a major selling point for young talent.

Evaluating Candidates The evaluation criteria you create for each candidate can be the stack-ranking criteria in Chapter 6. This will allow you to consistently compare inputs from multiple interviewers. Evaluate them on intelligence, personal presence, attitude, energy, and communication skills. Also evaluate candidates on preparation, cultural fit, industry experience, and past sales success. Be sure to leave room for any other comments interviewers might have. Sometimes a candidate who looks great on paper and ticks off all the boxes still won't fit for some less tangible reason.

The competition for A-list inside sales talent is brutal —everyone wants that Superhero on their team. You know, that innovative, disruptive game-changer who will bring your entire team to a new Sales 2.0 level of excellence.

Competition between managers is fierce when it comes to enticing the good talent. Make sure that you are not creating an unintentional turnoff!

Don't be the Roadblock to Finding Good Talent

Pay attention to these 10 ways that managers can unintentionally turn off potential Superheroes:

1. Before the interview, the Superhero will check their potential manager's professional and social media networks. If the manager isn't well positioned or connected, that's a turnoff.

2. During the interview, the Superhero will ask the manager probing questions. Lengthy and evasive answers cause them to immediately drop out of the candidate pool.

3. During an interview with the team, the Superhero is turned off by the team's level of mediocrity. Strong candidates are motivated by having teammates they can learn from.

4. The Superhero has a high tool IQ. If the prospective company does not have state-of-the-art tools that keep them innovating and collaborating with today's Customer 2.0, that's a turnoff.

5. The Superhero has high expectations and a detailed list of requirements that must be met (and deal breakers that must be avoided) before accepting the job.

6. The manager asks the Superhero to engage in a role-play or make a sales presentation, but uses outdated, irrelevant, and uninteresting scenarios that reveal the manager's old sales thinking.

7. The prospective employer is not strong in response time or decision-making capabilities, so good talent gets restless, impatient, and snatched up by a competitor.

8. The Superhero listens to the manager describe the team, but the description lacks insight and time commitment. This signals that the manager may never be available for (or capable of) coaching and training.

9. The prospective manager is biased, judgmental, jumps to conclusions, doesn't understand the value of diversity, and wants to have

a team that looks like him—a turnoff to Superheroes operating in the Sales 2.0 globally wired world.

10. The Superhero asks about sales contests, spiffs, and incentives to motivate behavior and the chance to compete. The sales manager responds, "We expect you to do your job, that's why we pay you." Instant turnoff.

THE RECRUITMENT: TAKE TWO

I coached Tracy and helped her step out of the panic zone. Together, we designed a 21-day playbook to jump-start an "always-be-recruiting" strategy that would match her needs and timelines.

Here's an outline of the steps we took together:

- *We began by designing a Superhero-criteria template. Then we carefully studied her org chart, looking for team members who might possess some of these qualities. She was encouraged to find that several of her salespeople were Superheroes waiting to be revealed.*

- *We continued to examine the talent she had, reviewing their roles and job functions to determine if she could repurpose any of her headcount into different roles. The light went on when she saw that mixing it up a little might make a huge difference.*

- *We then looked at what she could do externally: networking with professional organizations such as AA-ISP, networking with local chapters, and reaching out to managers who might have some good talent they could point her way.*

- *We refreshed her job descriptions to make the position and the organization seem more inviting.*

- *We found that her most spirited rep had tons of extra energy to be the new cheerleader and would come up with fun activities and ideas on a regular basis.*

- *We established a referral network within her organization to include incentives—cash bonuses for internal referrals.*

- *We worked on some targeted messaging to get the word out, and developed a few fun gatherings that could bring in some curious talent.*

MANAGEMENT TIPS

- Don't rely on just-in-time hiring strategies. Develop an "always-be-recruiting" strategy designed to draw inside sales Superheroes.

- Structure your inside sales organization with the right roles and match them with job functions. This is the first step in clearly defining a "multicareer" ecosystem that attracts ambitious talent who are on a career trajectory

- Establish a referral network that includes professional, social, and industry networks to always spread the word that you are hiring for great talent; back it up with fun and enticing messages about your organization that attract talent to you.

- Practice strong screening and interviewing techniques to help qualify Superheroes and ensure you make choices that will stick and grow.

- Shake up individual roles. Can you repurpose talent into roles where they can really shine?

CHAPTER 6

TRAINING THE TALENT

Making Training Stick and Giving It Legs

It's the first day of my two-day training program. Workbooks are arranged neatly on everyone's seat, and some cool background music sets the mood. As I watch the sales teams walk into the large conference room, I see that some are already checking exits, while others take their seats quickly, laughing and joking with friends.

Several salespeople walk over, shake my hand, and introduce themselves. One alerts me that he will need to step out to coordinate a meeting and wants to know when the morning break will be. Another asks if I have an extra pen because he didn't bring one. Two more take seats at the furthest end of the room and giggle together. One opens the workbook and gives a long sigh as he flips through all the pages; another sets her iPad down and explains that her note-taking skills are much faster on her tablet than in a workbook.

Then their manager walks in. "Unfortunately," he says, "I have a few emergencies to take care of so I will be in and out of the training. Will it be okay if I just slip in and out?"

No, I think to myself. No wonder your team is already restless. "Sure," I reply, "happy to have you." Then, I ask if he can introduce me to the group as a way to kick off the training. He agrees.

"Hey, everyone," he starts. "Good morning and thanks for making it here. I'd like to introduce our trainer this morning. I know you are probably wondering WHY you are all here for sales training, and I just want you all to pay attention and just try to learn ONE THING from this two-day session—even if it's basic, these are great REMINDERS for everyone, no matter how senior you are." They all laugh.

"I KNOW this isn't a good time for training," he continues. "We have lots of deals on the table and our trainer will give you guys breaks. But this is important stuff, OK GUYS? I'm gonna try to be here through some of it but want you all to be on your best behavior. Thanks everyone." And with that, he's gone. I'm thinking, Uh-oh. This manager has not set me up for success. I know from experience that I'm going to have my work cut out for me.

I'm right. For the rest of our two days together the team is restless, suspicious, defensive, and ready for battle. They argue every point, they challenge every claim, they discount every new idea. They explain that they've had way too much training, fold their arms across their chests, and stare at the clock.

* * *

You've worked really hard at building an inside sales structure, loading it up with sales productivity tools, partnering up with the marketing organization, establishing a sales process, and recruiting the strongest talent. But onboarding new hires still averages six months. Turnover rates are at 34 percent, and win rates on deals are at 50 percent. "Productivity" generally ranks as number one on the list of inside sales initiatives, and managers are seen as the lynchpin to increased sales rep productivity. But when they dump their teams off at the door, expecting sales trainers to instantly make their teams brilliant, they will watch their talent and training investment rapidly diminish.

It's time for managers to take training seriously and make it a high priority for today's development of hungry talent: the quality of your training will determine the fate of your teams and the entire organization. In this chapter, you will learn how to build a sustainable training program, one that has legs and lives way beyond the training itself, thriving inside the DNA of your inside sales organization.

WHY TRAINING IS LOW ON THE PRIORITY LIST

Inside sales training has changed dramatically over the years. It has evolved from the cringeworthy—hand-me-down field sales training revamped for inside sales, fly-by-night "smile-and-dial" phone etiquette—to the targeted inside sales focus training has today. Nonetheless, this dismal history still has power. According to a study by the Executive Board's Corporate Leadership Council, more than half of sales managers believe that shutting down Learning and Development (the training organization) would have no impact on their teams' performance. Yet a McKinsey Quarterly article titled "Getting More from Your Training Programs"[1] confirms that companies that are *not* investing in training suffer from higher turnover and lower productivity.

According to ES Research Group,[2] these seven pitfalls are the top reasons that sales training initiatives fail:

1. Misunderstanding the customer's underlying needs

2. Letting selling gaps go unnoticed

3. Selecting the wrong training company

4. Inadequate (or nonexistent) underlying sales methodology

5. Inadequate support systems

6. Ineffective coaching/lack of reinforcement

7. No measurement system

According to a Culpepper and Associates compensation survey and services study,[3] 87 percent of all sales managers have had fewer than eight days of formal sales training and 94 of their teams have had fewer than five days of formal sales training. Inside sales managers are overwhelmed with huge pressures—higher quotas, multiple product offerings, increased customer demands, unpredictable sales cycles, and hiring and ramping up new talent. No surprise: training often sits at the bottom of their list of priorities.

BUILDING A SUSTAINABLE TRAINING INFRASTRUCTURE

Most inside sales organizations today are in rapid-ramp mode, and they don't have much budget to spend: According to one source, 64 percent of companies spend under $1,500 per rep on training.[4] So when they do decide to have their inside teams go through sales training, they want that training to stick and to grow as they grow.

The best way to protect your training investment is to build a sustainable training structure that is incorporated into the inside sales organization and designed to support the new sales skills. This organizational commitment means that before you roll out training, you must carefully survey the following four areas: sales process and structure; sales and marketing alignment; sales productivity tools; and team talent and skills. This will secure the reinforcement before, during, and after the training takes place.

Figure 6-1 provides a visual representation of this sustainable structure. Let's break each of these areas down.

Sales Process and Structure

The biggest reason inside sales organizations fail is because either they do not have a defined charter or it has not been communicated throughout the company. Everyone must understand their sales charter, how it is structured, their revenue goals, the competitive landscape, and the customer's engagement strategy.

Use the following questions to identify your structure and process:

- How is the inside sales organization structured?

- What is the inside sales team's charter?

- What are the revenue goals?

- What is their primary focus (e.g., lead generation, appointment setting)?

- What product and/or services are they selling?

- Are they geographically aligned to support the field organization, ratio?

Sales Productivity Tools

- CRM; information capture and documentation
- Outlook email calendaring
- Sales intelligence tools
- Phone systems and call metrics
- Call monitoring forms
- EM and VM templates
- Audio library

Marketing and Sales Alignment

- Lead nurture strategy
- Lead acquisition, distribution, and nurturing, qualification
- Lead conversion
- Outbound strategies
- Call campaign and blitzes
- Marketing campaigns

Training and Development

Sales Process

- Inside sales charter
- Revenue goals
- Inside sales structure
- Sales cycle
- Customer engagement and retention strategies
- Competitive landscape

Talent and Skills

- Managers
- Team leaders
- Training managers
- Coaches
- Sales representatives
- Lead development
- Telesales
- New hires

FIGURE 6-1 | Training Sustainability Diagram

- At what point does the handoff process happen? How well defined is it?

- What is the length of the average sales cycle?

- What is the sales process and strategy?

- How many sales stages are there? What are they?

- What is the typical customer? Titles?

- What are the customer challenges?

- What size companies are they chartered to call? Verticals?

- What is the percentage of installed base versus new customers they are calling? Up-selling and cross-selling?

- What are customers asking for?

Sales and Marketing Alignment

Selling in today's Sales 2.0 ecosystem requires deeper alignment and broader understanding of marketing functions, as discussed in Chapter 4. The sales department must put its marketing hat on and learn how to nurture top prospects with engaging content.

Use the following questions to identify the type of alignment that's in place to support the training goals:

- How does the marketing organization align with the sales organization?

- How are leads generated? Webinars, whitepapers, etc.?

- How many active campaigns do you have in place?

- What type of marketing automation tool is in place? How are salespeople accessing it?

- How are you distributing leads?

- What is your lead nurturing strategy?

- What is the lead qualification process?

- What types of marketing campaigns do you roll out?

- How often are you doing call blitzes?

- How much email marketing is happening? At what level? Rep or marketing?

- What is your lead conversion process?

- What type of lead scoring is in place?

- What type of messaging program is in place?

- What is your go-to-market strategy?

Sales Productivity Tools

Today's sales tools are the fuel that powers the teams, as discussed in Chapter 3. The training curriculum has to address the "must-have" sales productivity, sales intelligence, and social tools that help Superheroes sell.

Use the following questions to help determine the team's Tool IQ and how the tools are being used:

- What type of CRM, SFA do you have installed?

- What type of activity metrics are in place?

- Any call recordings? What system?

- What type of calendaring tools are in place?

- What type of collaboration tools are in place?

- Are you working with any dialers? How are they being used?

- What type of sales intelligence tools are being used?

- What social media tools are your teams using and for what purpose?

- What type of email templates do you have in your library? How often are they being refreshed?

Team Talent and Skills

Buy-in is the most important part of making any talent development goals stick. It's vital to have strong leadership that includes team leads, coaches, quality assurance, managers, and directors who are deeply involved in performance improvement and can reinforce a universal language at all times.

Use the following questions to identify the individual talents, skills, and needs of each team member.

- What is the general talent pool and skill sets within the teams (new hires to seasoned pros)?

- What is the average level of experience?

- How are they performing? What percentage is hitting quota?

- What is the career track?

- What is the general culture within the team environment? Morale issues?

- What are the team's current challenges?

- Do they have dedicated Systems Engineers to help them with product knowledge?

- What is their propensity to change?

- What type of coaching is in place? Who is doing it? How often?

- How do the coaches come together to calibrate on skills?

Figure 6-2 complements the sustainability diagram, focusing exclusively on the talent that gives it legs.

DETERMINING THE APPROPRIATE SALES TRAINING CURRICULUM FOR YOUR TEAM

Once you build your sustainable structure and survey the landscape, it's time to select a curriculum that fits and matches the complex needs of your organization. You may decide to build your own or explore hiring an external service provider. If you take the latter, it's buyer beware: inside sales is hot right now, and the sales training world is becoming more crowded every day. Hundreds of sales training wannabes are making lots of promises and guarantees for greater access to decision-makers, inspiring scripts, and warm and cuddly coaching reinforcement—but only a relative handful of trainers actually deliver the goods.

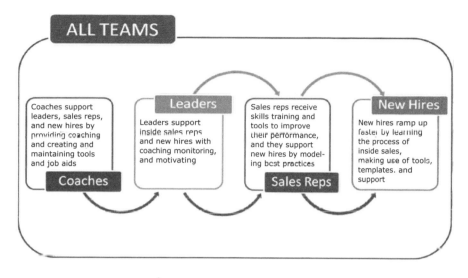

FIGURE 6-2 | Inside Sales Talent: Roles that Reinforce Training

Before developing any training, a good trainer assesses the situation. Today's inside sales organization is a unique mix of people with a wide assortment of job functions and sales skills, as described in Chapter 5. Not one inside sales organization is exactly the same. Not all inside sales organizations will have all of the elements listed below, but the following snapshot of a typical department shows just how complex and diverse inside sales training needs may be:

- Lead Development—reports into marketing

- Lead Generation—partners with field

- Inside Sales—full quota-bearing

- Inside Sales Hybrid Rep—quota bearing and travels out for large opportunities

- Renewals—majority came from Customer Support

- Government—5 percent

- Millennials—60 percent (mostly men)

- Gen Y'ers—40 percent (mostly men)

- Managers—manage team on a 9:1 ratio

- Directors—manage 4+ managers

- New Hires—25 percent

- Decentralized and work remotely—15 percent

- Selling both direct and indirect channels

- SMB and Enterprise teams

- CRM Tool—Salesforce

This example illustrates how different and varied the needs and skills of one organization might be and how important it is for vendors to consider these differences when designing training. It is critical to select a vendor who is tuned in to the unique nuances and complexities of this kind of organization. Their deep understanding of inside sales will help customize a program that will fit your organization, engage your reps, and hold their attention—and make your investment stick.

CHOOSING A VENDOR WHOSE PRIMARY SERVICE OFFERING IS INSIDE SALES TRAINING

Make sure you choose a vendor whose primary service offering is inside sales training. Training vendors must have a deep and wide knowledge and understanding of inside sales, from departmental, team, industry, and end-user perspectives. And they must also understand the various models—inbound, outbound, direct, and channel. A good training vendor will carefully customize a solution that fits your company, your department, and your team.

Use this checklist of questions to ask external vendors before you make your choice:

- Does this vendor have a strong understanding of inside sales from a department and infrastructure perspective?

- Does this vendor understand how to sell from various models: inbound, outbound, direct, and indirect?

- Does this vendor offer a new-hire onboarding training curriculum?

- Does this vendor have a sales training methodology that spans the entire sales cycle, from beginning to close? Does the training target the unique skill requirements for developing inside sales talent?

- Does this vendor design training for maximum skills retention and coaching to accelerate selling effectiveness immediately?

- Does this vendor design training programs for inside sales managers who started as individual contributors and now must drive revenue with their team?

- Does this vendor have a credible track record of being on the front-line of inside sales with an investment of at least 10 years in the field?

- Does this vendor have a client list that includes inside sales training as their primary offering and not field sales or customer service?

- Does this vendor have a client list that demonstrates ROI success in the varied sectors?

- Does this vendor demonstrate the personalized, consultative, professional, and flexible approach?

- Does this vendor have a strong global presence?

- Does this vendor customize curriculum for you and not provide you with off-the-shelf, dated material?

- Has this vendor been recognized by an accredited organization such as AA-ISP (American Association of Inside Sales Professionals), ES research group, or ASTD (American Society of Training and Development)?

SELECTING A VENDOR THAT INCORPORATES THE SALES 2.0 ECOSYSTEM INTO TRAINING

In Part One, we examined some major elements that have transformed the face of inside sales. These must all be taken into consideration when selecting a sales training vendor.

Customer 2.0: This busy, elusive, independent customer is here today and gone tomorrow—and back again a couple of months later. The inside sales training vendor you choose must address how this affects sales strategies. Training must:

- Encourage intelligence and knowledge on each call and crisp, succinct messaging that makes every second count. Time allotments on role-plays and case scenarios should be dramatically shortened to demonstrate the discomfort of working within such a limited framework.

- Remind salespeople to build up small, digestible, engaging bits of content treats that they can feed the prospect to nurture and cultivate the virtual relationship.

- Strengthen authenticity and relationship skills because this customer needs to feel special and heard.

- Build rebuttal skills to handle Customer 2.0's tidal wave of objections and excuses.

- Impress on the customer the importance of calling deeper and wider and not giving up.

Talent 2.0: Holding the attention of this ambitious and vibrant group may be tough, so training should offer shorter training modules that can be delivered in bite-sized pieces with coaching reinforcement on the back end.

- The curriculum design must be fun and include competitive games with break-out team sessions that engage and motivate. Classroom style, "talking head" lecture trainings make this group run out the door.

- Training methods must keep your team's attention. These may include video examples, audio, mobile, web conferencing, and e-learning.

- Talent 2.0 will either ask lots of questions or sit in silence. Trainers must take control by engaging the quiet ones and tempering the boisterous ones.

- They are great multitaskers but also get easily distracted. Trainers must specify "no texting" during the training and allow generous breaks for them to catch up.

- Training must emphasize the importance on increased productivity since this group places such a high value on productivity.

Sales Tools 2.0: Inside sales training *must* be Sales 2.0-centric, so watch out: many traditional sales training providers fall short in the area of sales tools.

- Training curriculum must incorporate the essential sales productivity, sales intelligence, and social tools that help Superheroes sell.

- Training curriculum must demonstrate and support tool adoption and reinforce the importance of a high Tool IQ.

Prospecting 2.0: The training you choose must spark enthusiasm when it comes to prospecting.

- Training must demonstrate the skills, tactics, qualities, and competencies the inside sales Superheroes possess.

- Effective training will play sample calls from your team's blitzing and campaigns to demonstrate desirable or undesirable skills.

The sales skills shown in Figure 6-3 are fundamental and must be learned, practiced, and perfected to Superhero status. Preparing to deliver each skill requires in-depth understanding of where the talent stands on each skill to best diagnose what they need. Effective inside sales training vendors will help your team improve and excel in these areas.

TeleSmart 10: Skill Ranking

Date: **Coach:**

Team Member: **Manager:**
Ranking 1 (lowest)—10 (highest)

1. Time Management	5. Listening
Proactive vs. reactive	Understands Customer 2.0
Planning and preparation	Precision questioning
High Tool IQ	Strong information capture
Sales momentum; nonnegotiable time	note taking
Determining strong call objective	6. Linking
Doesn't waste a LIVE call	Political organizational chart
2. Introduction	Authority/Influence matrix
Messaging = em + vm + social	Power clues and influence clues
Word choice; strong vs. weak words	Questioning up the pain chain
Vocal tone is confident, professional	Levels of buy/sell relationship
Succinct voice mail messaging	7. Presenting
Email template library	Conference call presentation
Strong subject lines	Web conferencing presentations
Social media; LinkedIn	Asks trial closing questions
3. Navigation	Understands competition and product
Calling deeper and wider	Strong value proposition
Building organizational charts with the 2 x 2 rule	8. Handling Objections
Engaging gatekeepers	Objections radar
Recognizing when in the No-Po zone	Why salespeople create objections
Understands how to call around No-Po	Email objections
4. Questioning	Objection rebuttal
Opening probes that engage	Proactively handling objectives
Questioning strategy	9. Closing
Question formulation; closed- vs. opened-ended questions	Funnel analysis
Questioning style and techniques	Closing techniques and approaches
Questioning order; Trust Thermometer	Creating urgency and compelling events
Setting appointments that stick.	Establishing closing momentum throughout the month
	10. Partnering
	Initiates strong partnerships
	Establishing good, supportive partner agreements
	Bringing value to partnerships

FIGURE 6-3 | TeleSmart 10 Inside Sales Skills Breakdown

Onboarding New Talent: An Essential Part of Inside Sales Training

Take a look at your team. How many of them were there three months ago? Six months ago? Last week? I'm betting that a good percentage of your team is composed of new hires. That's why a strong inside training program must include a new-hire component in the mix.

Protecting Your Investment in New Talent

The cost of hiring and onboarding new sales reps is higher than many believe. According to a whitepaper from sales management expert Lee Salz, "Highly successful companies perceive adding headcount to the sales team as an investment in revenue not as hiring salespeople. . . without onboarding, these companies continue to 'churn and burn' salespeople, wait forever for sales performance and incur huge unnecessary costs."[5]

As companies increase headcount and customers demand more, the burden is on inside sales managers to onboard and ramp their new hires as quickly as possible. But often, "quickly" isn't fast enough. One report found 42.5 percent of companies need more than six months to ramp up their new hires.[6] Another report found that ramp-up time may average more than six months.[7]

You are already spread pretty thin. That's why an established structure makes sense. It will help reduce the time you spend with each new rep individually so you can leverage your coaches and the call audio library for their new hires.

Ramp Camp: A Comprehensive Approach to Onboarding

The solution is to have a comprehensive approach to onboarding new hires. This will help increase their confidence and quickly assimilate them into the sales organization. Focus on doing versus knowing to help the new hire retain information faster.

Here's an example of a new hire "ramp camp" that keeps your new hires focused on six critical elements:

1. *Company Branding:* its mission, purpose, history, organizational structure, policies, HR, regulatory, environmental, and other related topics

2. *Service Offerings:* the product, service, solution, value prop, design, attributes, key clients, business partners, thought leaders, case studies

3. *Competitive Landscape:* their offerings, key clients, comparison graphs, sample objection rebuttals

4. *Internal Departments:* all processes internal to sales and any cross-functional process; internal departments such as HR, Technical Support or Sales Engineers, Customer Support and Service, Sales Operations, Finance, Marketing, Channel Partners

5. *Sales Process:* mastering the complete set of steps from beginning to end of the sales cycle, account planning, call scripts, and email templates

6. *Tools and Technology:* CRM, tools, sample calls from audio library, web demo archives, company videos

Camp starts during the interview! If your organization did a great job at "employee branding," then your new hire has already been exposed to your sales and company culture. Send them an employee handbook in the offer letter to start them early.

WHY MANAGERS NEED TO ATTEND TEAM TRAININGS

After I deliver training, I usually meet with managers and debrief them on how things went. I discuss how well their teams participated and give them my observations regarding each of their team members. After 20 years in the business, coaching and training thousands of sales reps and observing them through a training lens, I've developed a good understanding of how salespeople learn best, how to spot where they're getting off track, and how to help the course correct quickly. But this is not a skill unique to me: you can learn from your teams too. Please don't skip out on training!

Training is the perfect opportunity for managers to learn from their teams: to watch, listen, collaborate, role-play, and observe them in action. You may just discover your next Superhero.

Here are just a few of the behaviors you can watch for, observe, and learn from during training:

- *Body language:* Do team members make eye contact? What does their posture tell you? What do you read from their facial expressions? How do they walk into the training? How do they look when they leave the training? How attentive are they during the presentation?

- *Seating arrangements:* Where do they choose to sit—back, front, middle, on the side for a quick exit? Whom do they sit next to?

- *Questions:* Who asks questions? Who doesn't ask any questions? Who interrupts? How intelligent are their questions? How do they formulate questions? Are they really listening to the answers? What do they really mean by what they are asking?

- *Team dynamics:* Are they team players? Who's the loner? How do they interact in a group? Do they take the lead, are they the spokesperson, how are they perceived by the group, whom do they look up to, whom do they ignore, who is high maintenance, who is consistent and predictable?

- *Learning styles:* Do they get the point quickly, nodding in agreement, or do they have a puzzled look on their face? Do they need information repeated before they understand? Does it help them to watch others in action in order to get it? How quickly do they think? How methodical are they? Are they perfectionists? Do they think instinctively and intuitively or methodically?

- *Instructions:* How often do they have to hear instructions repeated? How quickly do they take in the information? Do they take notes?

- *Fears and frustrations:* What are they afraid of? Do they get defensive when they are provided with feedback? Do they walk around with a shield to protect themselves from criticism? How do they role-play? How do they present? Do they resist new ideas? Do they spend more time speculating about issues beyond their control.

- *Motivation:* What motivates them? Recognition? Incentives? Prizes? Money? Career advancement? Is it the "perfect storm" mentioned in Chapter 5? The need for achievement, competitive drive, and optimistic outlook?

Finally, remember that you are your team's manager, which means that you are also their coach, mentor, strategist, and all around cheerleader. If you are attending the training with them, and embody a positive attitude toward all they are learning, you are modeling the behavior that you want to see from them. They will listen, learn, and bring it all back to work for the organization.

THE TRAINING SESSION: TAKE TWO

It's the first day of my two-day training program, and I already know that things are going to go smoothly. Here's why:

A week prior to training, the Director sends out a brief introduction to the upcoming training and explains why it is very important for his team to attend.

The day of the training, the manager is the first one in the room and he's watching the teams as they walk in.

Once we are ready to start, the manager stands up and makes the following announcement:

> *"Good morning, everyone! I'm happy to see all your bright and shiny faces ready to learn and grow in the next few days. It is my pleasure to introduce you to Josiane Feigon, author of the book* Smart Selling on the Phone and Online *and President of TeleSmart.*
>
> *"The training you are about to start has been customized for your needs in your specific roles and designed for your needs as a sharp, sophisticated inside sales team. Management has invested in all of you, and we know that we will not get to a new level of excellence unless you all have the skills you need to meet today's customer on their terms. Josiane brings years of experience in training global inside sales organizations in our section, and will tell us all the 'little*

secrets' that make them successful. She has also invested valuable time in observing our world, collecting data to customize the training, and even listening to your sample call recordings—yes, your calls." (They're laughing with nervous anticipation, a good sign.)

"Based on her findings, she has designed a program that is tailored to our company and for our unique challenges. I have reviewed the content and I'm super excited. And I'm really glad we can learn together. The next two days will be loaded with excellent tips, new ideas, trends, and sharing of best practices. Lots will be coming your way and I want you to take it in with an open mind, digest it, and next week, we will regroup to debrief on how you will put this into practice as you develop your territories."

I look around and see everyone sitting upright ready to take notes, nodding their heads in agreement with a few people saying "great" and "cool" and leaning forward ready to start.

MANAGEMENT TIPS

- Take training seriously. The quality of your training will determine the fate of your teams and the entire organization.

- The best way to protect your training investment is to build a sustainable training structure that is inserted within the inside sales organization and designed to support the new sales skills.

- Before you roll out training, carefully survey the following four areas: sales process and structure; sales and marketing alignment; sales productivity tools; and team talent and skills.

- Make sure you choose a vendor whose primary service offering is inside sales training. Training vendors must have a deep and wide knowledge and understanding of inside sales, from departmental, team, industry, and end-user perspectives. And they must also understand the various models—inbound, outbound, direct, and channel. A good training vendor will carefully customize a solution that fits your company, your department, and your team.

- Choose a vendor that incorporates the Sales 2.0 Ecosystem into its training, particularly addressing the special needs of Customer 2.0 and Talent 2.0 and incorporating Tools 2.0.

- Onboarding training is essential. A strong inside training program must include a new-hire component in the mix.

- Training is the perfect opportunity for managers to learn from their teams: to watch, listen, collaborate, role-play, and observe them in action, without the stress of making sales for a distraction. Especially when the new Superhero is just waiting to make their grand entrance.

CHAPTER 7

READY, SET, COACH!

Building an Integrated Coaching Program

I am on a conference call with three inside sales managers at the same company. As part of my needs assessment, I ask, "How much coaching are you doing with your teams?"

"Not much," says Manager 1, "but that will be changing soon."

"I spend a lot of time with my team," Manager 2 responds. "I meet with each one individually in a weekly 1:1 forecast review, and we meet as a team every two weeks without fail."

Manager 3 is silent. I ask if she is doing any active coaching. She says, "Well, my cubicle is located right next to all my reps so that I can hear all of them on the phone and answer any questions they have—which I do. In fact, I spend most of my time answering one-off questions."

Then I ask about the current team morale and how they would feel about coaching. "My team would get really nervous if anyone sat with them in-cube," Manager 1 responds. "I remember when I was a rep, they used to listen to calls to determine who would stay and who would go. Luckily, I was one of the ones who stayed."

"Yeah, my team has been very suspicious since we had our recent merger," Manager 2 adds. "Coaching would just be a negative dis-

traction that could potentially throw them over the edge. It's not going to happen at this time."

Manager 3 doesn't say a word.

* * *

Coaching is the new game changer. Over the last five years or so, sales organizations have invested more time and effort to improving managers' coaching of reps than they did in the previous 50 years. But even though coaching has become a household word in corporate America, it's easy for managers to ignore it in favor of more pressing management activities. And no wonder: When the average manager-to-team ratio is 9:1 and managers allocate time with their team members to 1:1 forecast reviews, team meetings, team trainings, and one-off interactions throughout the day, time for coaching gets left behind.

Time constraints aside, other issues keep managers from embracing coaching. Most have never received any formal training, don't understand what coaching entails, and feel inadequate to the task. They don't see the difference between coaching and simply listening in on reps' calls and commenting. Often, these managers have trouble determining who really needs coaching on their team: Talent 2.0 constantly seeks approval and guidance, and seasoned reps just want their managers to get out of their way and let them sell. When these managers do attempt coaching, they find themselves repeating the same feedback over and over with no resulting change. Eventually, coaching fatigue settles in, and they put off coaching indefinitely or avoid it altogether.

It's time for managers to rethink coaching. Design an integrated coaching plan that includes every individual in your organization, be distracted, and make that time nonnegotiable: Don't be distracted, or check your email, or talk with other reps while you are coaching. This is their time with you.

In today's digital, social, and highly complex sales environment, coaching is the trust bond that holds top talent and managers together. Talent 2.0 considers coaching as their lifeline to their job, and they're right. Authentic, compassionate coaching can improve quality, productivity, and teamwork and impact the bottom line.

Coaching isn't something you can outsource. Managers must establish a structured plan that maximizes time and gains mileage. Done well, this kind of coaching will actually save you from answering endless one-off questions. You'll see improvement in your core players and the functioning of your team while you grow new inside sales Superheroes and help your current Superheroes soar to greater heights.

"The role of the sales manager," according to Miller Heiman's 2012 Executive Summary on Sales Best Practices Study, "is to drive the action necessary to achieve the results. Their role should be viewed mainly as a conduit to drive action, which is highly dependent on their leadership and coaching skills."[1] In this chapter you'll learn about the value of establishing an integrated coaching plan that works to reinforce training and solidify the bond between reps and managers, infusing new life into old coaching habits

STRUCTURING AN INTEGRATED COACHING PROGRAM

If you still approach coaching as you sitting in the cubicle with the rep, waiting for that rare live call, and madly scribbling notes on what to say, it's time to rethink your approach. Coaching at its best is a personalized, one-to-one relationship between the rep and the coach that uses inquiry, teaching, and personal discovery to build the reps' self-awareness, confidence, and sales skills. This dynamic process helps reps get to their next level of excellence by identifying the fears, obstacles, and skill gaps that are holding them back and helping them to overcome them.

Each coaching session is tailored to address the individual's unique learning style, personal strengths, and areas for needed improvement. Sessions are proactive and responsive to help establish personal goals and address attitudes and behavior. And, of course, your coaching will be aimed at maximizing your team's potential for success as inside sales Superheroes in your own sales organization.

Designing and planning a diverse and integrated coaching program will motivate you to find time to coach more often and with purpose. It involves five basic steps:

1. Committing to creating a safe, trust-based coaching culture throughout your organization and setting up agreements about ground rules with all of your team members.

2. Gathering call recordings.

3. Putting call calibration into play and having all managers come together to agree on baseline skills.

4. Deciding which coaching method (in-cube, group, or remote) best suits each team member and how often individual coaching will occur.

5. Stack-ranking your team as A-B-C players: How much of your coaching time should you devote to which reps?

CREATING A TRUST-BASED COACHING CULTURE

When both manager and team member approach coaching with the freshness, confidence, and curiosity of a new experience, they will walk away with skills that can change the way they work for the better. Both partners in the coaching relationship must both bring something to the table, with trust holding the space for it.

Starting at the Top

Establishing a trust-based coaching culture is most successful when the highest executive level endorses this as an organization-wide initiative. The goal is to create an atmosphere of mutual trust, respect, cooperation, and commitment to self-development. This means building a healthy culture that includes regular coaching, call reviews, and group coaching sessions in which team members are motivated to share their calls and are open to constructive feedback on areas requiring improvement.

I'd like to share this example from one of my clients. Carahsoft, a government reseller with over $1 billion in revenues, has embraced the TeleSmart 10 program. Before our coaches' training for the junior and senior coaches, all participants received this letter from CEO Craig Abod[2]:

> Carahsoft Coaches:
>
> I want to thank you all for clearing your schedules today and dedicating this time to focus on further developing our coaching skills and coaching roadmaps.
>
> Our investment in our people is incredibly important. Our ability to help our sales people learn to sell is a strategic advantage for us. Our ability to find and qualify opportunities for our partners and vendors is what sets us apart from our competitors. It is as important as making sure we understand our vendors' solutions, processes, and customers.
>
> The time you and your coaching peers invest in one-on-one coaching and group coaching is equally critical to our success. And coaching allows us to reinforce the sales skills taught in our Smart Selling classes. With these investments you and your staff will be more successful and help our vendors find quality leads and close more business.
>
> I know it can be difficult to find time, especially during busy season. But please commit to carve out the time and help your team experience a tremendous return on investment

Trust Agreements: Agree on the Ground Rules

It is important to establish and agree on some ground rules before you start. These ground rules will establish an atmosphere of trust, confidentiality, and mutual responsibility in the coaching relationship. This agreement will go a long way in creating an atmosphere in which both team members and managers feel safe in giving feedback and voicing feelings without fear of retribution.

These are the 10 rules of agreement between manager and team member I suggest making before you begin a coaching partnership:

1. *Manager:* I believe coaching is the biggest investment I can make for my people and my organization to ensure we bring the skills and talent to a new level.

2. *Manager:* I want to establish a regular and consistent coaching culture.

3. *Manager:* I will dedicate time to reviewing, organizing, categorizing call recordings.

4. *Manager:* I will schedule individual and group coaching sessions with my teams.

5. *Manager:* I will rely on coaching to give me information about our customers, talent, company, and marketplace.

6. *Team member:* I agree to fully participate in the coaching experience, whether it is in-cube coaching, group coaching, or remote coaching.

7. *Team member:* I agree to be open to constructive feedback without getting defensive.

8. *Team member:* I agree to try new approaches I may never have attempted before, even if they take me out of my comfort zone.

9. *Team member:* I agree to demonstrate the initiative to change, grow, and develop.

10. *Manager/team member:* We will maintain confidentiality, trust, and cooperation throughout this process.

Gathering Call Recordings

Now start gathering samples of recorded calls. Call recordings are used in many coaching situations, as well as for onboarding new hires. They are especially necessary when you have teams investing many hours on outbound calls. Here's why:

• Team members are usually less defensive and more relaxed when their calls are recorded, as opposed to when you are physically listening in on the call.

• Each call can be replayed, paused, saved, and used for demonstration for increased learning improvement.

- Reps and managers can listen to audio samples (by downloading a WAV file or MP3) outside of the workplace in a more casual setting.

- You can use the recordings to start building an audio call library, which includes a variety of calls and best practices.

Call Recording Basics

Most phone systems today have built-in recording capabilities. If you don't want to include IT in setting up, I usually recommend an easy and inexpensive digital recorder by ProLoggers that works with any phone system. Generally, when calls are used for training and coaching purposes, they can be recorded. (Do check the telephone recording laws in your state—some states have restrictions on recording calls.)

Start by giving the team member control of the recording process. Ask each member to record the full call, from beginning to end. Sample calls might include voice mails, first call qualification, follow-up second calls, and presentations. Before the coaching session, ask the team member to select their best or most challenging call (or both) to present for feedback.

Conduct audio call-review sessions for new hires at least two times per month and once a week for remote workers. For the rest of the team, once per month is enough.

Build an Audio Call Library

Once you have an inventory of sample calls, you can start building an audio library. This is one of the best investments you can make for quick ramp-up of your new hires. As mentioned in Chapter 5, your goal is to shorten the ramp-up cycle. Instead of having them sit with team members waiting for a live call, they can maximize their time by downloading sample prerecorded calls and observing skills.

Choosing which calls to include in your library is time consuming but worth the investment. For example, you might include sample first attempt, second attempt, and third attempt calls; request for appointment; lead follow-up; invitations; blitzing call samples; technical calls; product calls; and partner calls, and consider organizing these based on the TeleSmart 10 sales skills listed in Chapter 6.

CALIBRATING CALLS

I'm always surprised that so few managers calibrate on calls together. This simple technique gets managers on the same page in terms of desired outcomes, and it's the best way to establish a baseline for your organization and assure the quality of the calls your teams engage in. A call calibration session, which usually involves the entire management team, sets the standard for what to observe. Calibrating is the great equalizer; the more you can calibrate on calls as a management team, the stronger the unified message will be to your teams.

Here's how it works: Managers come together as a team, meet in a conference room, listen to call recordings, and make notes on desired skills and behaviors. The session may focus on multiple calls and may observe one skill or multiple skills.

A call monitoring form provides a solid framework for observation. Figure 7-1 is one such form, based on the TeleSmart 10 skills. Once managers have monitored the calls, you can calibrate your impressions about each rep.

Call calibration sessions should happen at least on a monthly basis. The best times to calibrate on calls are:

- When there's a new management team or new reps that have started

- When a merger or organizational shift or turnover has taken place

- When a new product is launched

- When it's the end of the month and more customer objections happen

- When a new sales campaign, incentive, contest, or spiff is taking place

TeleSmart 10 Outbound Monitoring Form

Rep's Name: _____   Call Date: _____   Time of Call: _____

Manager's Name: _____   Monitored by: _____   Overall Rating _____
$\hspace{10cm}$ (1–10)

1. Time Management	Strong planning, preparation, and organization of target accounts
	Strong tool IQ, utilizes tools throughout sales cycle
	Strong proactive focus instead of being reactive and scattered
2. Introduction	Uses a volume tone that is approachable and confident
	Effectively earns time to move forward with the call
	Constructs voice mail messages that are brief, clear, and informative
	Has ability to capture attention with an opening statement and opening probe
	Strong call objective immediately establishes cooperation and rapport
3. Navigation	Has ability to establish rapport with the gatekeeper and create an ally
	Builds a robust org chart (2 x 2) that facilitates calling deeper and wider
	Understands how to navigate and stay under the radar
	Identifies the "No-Po" gatekeeper; realizes how No-Pos may keep them out
	Is aggressive about calling high throughout the sales cycle
	Creates value when contacting high-level decision-makers
4. Questioning	Establishes control by asking effective questions early in the call
	Uses effective probing and questioning techniques
	Asks questions in an appropriate order
	Adjusts questions based on the customer's technical level
	Maps questions to a questioning plan
	Probes to uncover details of current and future opportunities
5. Listening	Listens and retains customer communication, avoiding repetition
	Listens realistically and doesn't assume answers or information
	Listens actively by paraphrasing and giving verbal cues
	Displays strong information capture and strong, concise note-taking skills
	Aligns sales tactics based on Customer 2.0 requirements

(continues)

FIGURE 7-1 | Outbound Monitoring Form

6. Linking	Understands the political hierarchy within an organization
	Ability to deliver title-specific messaging
	Fearless when talking at the highest level
	Aligns questions based on the hierarchy of influence
7. Presenting	Has proficient presentation timing—doesn't pitch too soon
	Uses persuasive adjectives when discussing product offerings
	Displays confidence and a positive attitude about product/service
	Asks soft and hard trial closing questions throughout the presentation
8. Handling Objections	Effectively anticipates objections and sells appropriate benefits
	Avoids making negative comments or introducing objections
	Is fluid and confident with rebuttal strategies on various objections
	Responds quickly on email rejections
	Has a strong questioning style that neutralizes objections
9. Closing	Gains commitment before ending calls
	Uses an explanation of product line that includes benefits for the customer
	Creates urgency and compelling events
	Recognizes customer buying and discount signals
	Is creative and resourceful in explaining discount policies
10. Partnering	Strong pro-active partner, shows initiative with strong follow-through
	Brings value, stays current, visible, and resourceful
	Sets partnership agreements and leverages them into the sales cycle
	Demonstrates strong collaborative initiative and establishes trust

Parallel Monitoring (Side-by-Side)

Pre-Call Planning	Pre-call research time is well balanced
	Reviews notes and information prior to making call
	Manages time effectively
	Multitasks effectively
Tools	Has resources/price lists easily accessible
	Uses CRM and tools efficiently
	Tools are well displayed on single or double monitors
Nonverbal Comm.	Ergonomics
	Seating position
	Nervous behavior

FIGURE 7-1 | Outbound Monitoring Form *(continued)*

COMPASSIONATE COACHING THREE WAYS: IN-CUBE, GROUP, AND REMOTE

Whenever I ask managers what they think makes them a good coach, they're more than happy to tell me: "I've done their job for many years; I can feel my reps' pain." Or, "I genuinely care. I want to help them make the most out of each call." Or, "I have strong product knowledge and that's a big help to them." Or, "I used to be part of the Million-Dollar Club when I was a rep, and I miss selling. So if they tee it up for me, I can jump in and close their deals."

But when I ask them what their impact is as a coach, they often don't have a clue: "The numbers show the results, don't they?" Others shake their heads and complain, "They never seem to hear what I'm saying." "I give them hundreds of pointers, and they don't follow any." In response, I sometimes share the following story.

When my daughter was thirteen years old, sitting on our front steps with the sun shining on her face, she looked up at me, and I snapped a picture of her. When I saw the photo, I was startled. I said that I could see exactly how she would be ten years later, as a young woman: it was all there, shining right out of her eyes. Of course, being thirteen, she just rolled her eyes at me and went back in the house. Yet today, at age twenty-three, she has grown right into that same potential I saw so long ago.

I know: You're not their parent, you're their manager. Yet seeing the potential for brilliance in your people is where good coaching starts. Every team member, even a C player, has at least one Superhero quality. You hold onto that insight and use it to start understanding what they are capable of, what motivates them, what their true potential is, what they need to learn. And then you work with them to motivate them to open up, learn new skills, and achieve all that they are capable of becoming.

Compassionate coaching involves making insightful observations about how your team members do their jobs and then delivering non-threatening feedback that motivates new behavior (more about this in Chapters 8, 9, and 10).

Choose from the following three coaching structures methods, depending on the individual: in-cube, remote, or group coaching. One might be the most suitable for a particular individual, or you may combine methods from time to time. Try them all and see what works best for you and your reps.

Before coaching begins, have each team member evaluate his or her skills with the self-assessment form in Figure 7-2. As you coach them, you can track your own evaluation of their skills (see Figure 8-1 for more on how this might work). This will give you a basis for real discussion and change).

In-Cube Coaching

In-cube coaching is just what it sounds like: you sit in the rep's cubicle as they make calls and observe them in action. This is your chance to get a real picture of how they work and who they are, so pay attention to everything (see the in-cube observations below for ideas).

You will sit side-by-side with your rep and wear a training headset or Y adapter that lets you hear both sides of the call. Pay attention to everything: how they begin the call, how they listen and respond to what the customer is saying, how they handle objections. Again, respect your nonnegotiable coaching time. This is their time with you.

Managers usually choose their lower-performing reps or new hires for in-cube coaching in the mistaken belief that their seasoned teams do not need it. *This sends the wrong message throughout your organization.* In-cube coaching is vital for all team members, regardless of their skill level or tenure. New reps should get in-cube coaching weekly or biweekly, and seasoned reps on a bimonthly basis.

Begin giving feedback in real time, right after the call. That way it's fresh and meaningful, and you can observe as they immediately implement the feedback you are giving them on the next call.

TeleSmart 10 Skill Self-Evaluation

Please refer to the descriptions page. Rate your skills in each skill.
Add comments on how applicable the skill is to what you do, or on your
particular strengths and challenges in each area.

1. Time Management
  1   2   3   4   5
  Disorganized   Efficient
	Comments:

2. Introducing
  1   2   3   4   5
  Inarticulate   Influential
	Comments:

3. Navigating
  1   2   3   4   5
  Shut out   Intrepid
	Comments:

4. Questioning
  1   2   3   4   5
  Interrogative   Relational
	Comments:

5. Listening
  1   2   3   4   5
  Inattentive   Inviting
	Comments:

6. Linking
  1   2   3   4   5
  Fears authority   Strategic
	Comments:

7. Presenting
  1   2   3   4   5
  Confusing   Persuasive
	Comments:

8. Handling Objections
  1   2   3   4   5
  Apprehensive Courageous
	Comments:

9. Closing
  1   2   3   4   5
  Careless   Convincing
	Comments:

10. Partnering
  1   2   3   4   5
  Conflicting   Symbiotic
	Comments:

FIGURE 7-2 | Skill Self-Assessment Form

In-Cube Coaching Observations: Stop, Look, and Listen

As noted in Chapter 6, you can learn a lot about your team members just by observing them in a sales training environment. The same is true of their work environment. Before you step in to coach a team member, take some time to
observe—*really* observe.

One of the most revealing aspects of a salesperson's character, behavior, habits, and work styles is *where* they work: their cubicle. This is a very personal and intimate space. Stepping into someone's cubicle is personal and intimate— like stepping into their living room—so it should be respected.

When you walk by or into your reps' cubicles, take a mental snapshot of the visuals surrounding that person—their tools, their desk toys, their family photos. Are they messy? Organized? Watch them work—notice their work style, pace, momentum, habits, body language.

In Chapter 4, we watched the Superhero in prospecting action and observed their tools, momentum, and work style. Look for those and these other more visual clues:

- *Body language:* Are they sitting up straight and leaning forward on calls? Are they slumping, distracted, laughing, smiling, energetic?

- *Seating arrangements:* Where do they sit? Whom do they sit next to? What is their influence: positive or negative? How is the ergonomic set-up? Are they wearing headsets?

- *Organization:* Is their space messy or neat? Do they have all of their tools open and ready to go, or are they looking for things they need during the call? Do they have visual reminders or products, messaging, and pricing surrounding them for easy access?

- *Work style:* How's their momentum? Are they slow, methodical, quick, intuitive, disorganized, organized, erratic? How are their keyboard skills? Do they take notes on each call and quickly document the call? Do they get up every 20 minutes to walk around or do they sit for hours without taking a bio break? What stress relievers do they reach for? Are they focused on calls or shouting to friends over the cube wall?

- *Goal-oriented:* Do they have whiteboards, post-it notes? What about personal motivation and competitiveness—self-improvement quotes or photos of family, friends, sports, and pets?

Group Coaching

Group coaching resonates with collaborative Talent 2.0 since they are easily influenced by peers and enjoy group dynamics and the sharing of best practices. These sessions may include a blend of managers, peers, coaches, and technical advisers, but limit the group to eight people total.

The goal is to get a healthy discussion going on sales skills, using sample calls to provide real-life examples. Set up the session as you would a sales meeting, with an agenda, time constraints, and so on. Ask everyone to bring a sample call for review and discussion. Everyone listens to the call recordings and provides feedback from their unique perspective. The manager facilitates the meeting, controlling the outcome and setting the tone.

Here's an example of when group coaching is a good idea. A manager may notice that four people on his team are receiving appointment cancellations more than most. He sets up a group coaching session and asks the four reps to bring in one sample recorded call where they set up a meeting or an appointment. During the session, everyone listens to the calls. The feedback focuses on predicting whether the appointment will eventually get cancelled based on what they heard on the calls. In this example, the manager has increased awareness of a sales challenge; created a safe environment to discuss it; encouraged the participants to contribute new ideas, examples, and tips; and motivated the reps to improve this skill.

Remote Coaching

Remote coaching is an option any time that you and your team member cannot be in the same location. The numbers of remote reps are increasing all the time, so it's especially important to find ways to include them in your coaching program.

Remote coaching—by phone, video, or Skype—is much like in-cube coaching. Have your rep send you a call recording, listen to it before the coaching session, and be prepared to discuss your observations. Coach remote workers once a week.

Ten Qualities of a Compassionate Coach

The following 10 qualities make a compassionate coach.

1. *Be a good listener.* Use the same active listening skills that make you a good salesperson. Give the rep your full attention, and listen without interrupting. Be empathetic and compassionate, and don't get defensive.

2. *Be observant.* You can learn so much about your team members just by paying attention to the way they present themselves, the objects they choose to have around them, the friends they hang out with, whether they speak up during meetings, how they listen when you talk, how they interact with others . . . the list goes on and on....

3. *Be patient.* Some people are quick studies, but not everyone. Behaviors can change; everyone has his or her own unique rhythm. Give them time to develop.

4. *Be supportive.* Make sure that even the least skilled know that you believe they have what it takes to improve and get ahead. Some team members may just be waiting for permission to be seen as the top dog on the team. Treat them as if they deserve to be in that spotlight.

5. *Be flexible.* Change can be effected in a number of ways. If one approach fails, try something else. Be creative. Keep an open mind, and become sensitive to differences and different ways of doing things.

6. *Be interested and aware.* Take time to get to know the salesperson you are coaching. What do they like? How do they live? This will give you insight into what motivates them.

7. *Be perceptive.* When your intuition kicks in—and it will!—trust it.

8. *Be energetic.* A good coach has energy that is contagious and persuasive. Model the kind of positive energy you want to see.

9. *Be focused.* As a coach you must detach yourself from your own pressures and focus on the person you are coaching.

10. *Be trustworthy.* Above all, coaching must take place in an atmosphere of safety and trust. Your team must trust that you are working in their best interests. Your team members are your potential Superheroes. Treat them with respect and confidence.

WHO GETS COACHING? STACK-RANKING YOUR TEAM

One of the toughest decisions time-crunched managers struggle with is deciding which team members warrant their coaching time. Choosing *who* to coach is just as important as *how* to coach.

A *Harvard Business Review* article entitled "The Dirty Secret of Effective Sales Coaching"[3] says that sales managers often skew their coaching efforts dramatically toward the "tails"—the very best and the very worst reps on their teams. They engage with poor reps because they feel they must in order to meet territory goals, and they work with their best reps because it's fun. But coaching is almost worthless when it targets the wrong rep.

Start identifying who needs coaching by stack-ranking your team as A, B, or C performers:

* *A players* are the Superstars who regularly exceed expectations. They are always improving and get involved in projects.

* *B players* are the solid performers who usually meet and sometimes exceed expectations. They usually come in at 80 percent of quota, show promise, and have a good attitude. These are your core performers.

* *C players* come in two flavors: new hires who need to be onboarded and the poor performers who rarely meet expectations. They cannot perform their current tasks adequately and cannot handle taking on new projects. They usually come in at 75 percent of quota. They are inconsistent. They may be new to the organization, or they may have been there too long and have become complacent.

Your objective is to create a culture where winning and being the best is the goal. But that doesn't mean that everyone on your team has to be perfect. The *real* pay-off from your coaching efforts is in that 60 percent you may have been overlooking—your core performers, the Bs. For this group, coaching improves performance by 15 percent!

Paradoxically, most managers dedicate 95 percent of coaching time to their A players (who probably don't need it), 5 percent to B players (who benefit greatly), and no time at all to C players (most in need of coaching). A far better strategy is to give the A players 20 percent of your coaching time to keep them motivated, B players 60 percent to sharpen their game, and C players 20 percent to see if you can bring them up to speed or need to cut them loose.

To figure out which players are on your teams, make a spreadsheet for each rep and rank them on the following criteria (see Figure 7-3) as A, B, or C:

Name			
Strength Areas	**A**	**B**	**C**
Strong and healthy activity with call volume and funnel activity, # of appointments/meetings			
Deliverables, results, sales performance, paperwork/administrative, expense mgmt			
Track record of sales success; consistency			
General momentum, productivity, and efficiency			
Product and technical knowledge			
Strong partner relationships; customer satisfaction			
High Tool IQ			
Social media score; high digital influence			
Attitude and motivation			
Coachability			
Team player; ability to work with others			
Office presence			
Trustworthy			
Personal initiative			
Communication			
Phone skills			
Corporate citizen			
Independent, self-motivated, self-disciplined			
Price and margin management			
Other Superhero qualities [see pages 96–98]			
Total Ranking Score			

FIGURE 7-3 | Stack-Ranking Criteria Worksheet

READY, SET ... BUILD YOUR COACHING PLAN

Ready to commit to coaching? Figure 7-4 is a worksheet that will help you set up your plan. Carefully think through the types of teams and the outstanding issues and challenges you want to observe. Then monitor your team members, decide on your goals, and build your coaching plan to support those goals.

Method	How Often
Call Recording Coaching	
[team member]	[weekly, biweekly, monthly]
Call Calibration Coaching	
[team member]	[weekly, biweekly, monthly]
In-the-Cube Coaching	
[team member]	[weekly, biweekly, monthly]
Group Coaching	
[team member]	[weekly, biweekly, monthly]
Remote Coaching	
[team member]	[weekly, biweekly, monthly]
Special Notes	

FIGURE 7-4 | Coaching Plan Worksheet

THE COACHING DILEMMA: TAKE TWO

It was clear to me that Managers 1, 2, and 3 were confusing coaching with many other management activities and letting their own biases get in the way. I suggested that we build an integrated coaching plan.

First, we identified a few challenges they were having with their teams:

1. *Stronger and crisper introductions*

2. *Aligning with the right people and stronger navigating to find them*

3. *Quicker rebuttals from common objections*

These would be the areas that their coaching would focus on. We talked about the practicalities of coaching—the 10 Rules of Agreement, call recordings, call calibration, observation, and the rest. Manager 3 said, "Wow, that's totally different from listening to their calls from my cube." The other two laughed in agreement.

"Yeah," said Manager 1, "and it won't make them feel creeped out that we're spying on them."

"We've got our work cut out for us here," said Manager 2, " but I have to say I'm feeling excited about the possibilities for change."

Then we agreed that they would take the following steps in rolling out this integrated coaching plan:

1. *They announced to their teams their goals for coaching and introduced the 10 Rules of Agreement.*

2. *They researched call recording software and asked reps to record their calls.*

3. *They came together as a management team for several call calibration sessions to get on the same page.*

4. *They scheduled every other Friday for group coaching sessions and asked reps to share their calls.*

5. *They also scheduled in-cube monthly coaching sessions with their teams.*

6. *They came back together to debrief on these sessions to learn and keep up with the coaching taking place.*

MANAGEMENT TIPS

- Coaching at its best is a personalized, one-to-one relationship between the rep and the coach that uses inquiry, teaching, and personal discovery to build the reps' self-awareness, confidence, and sales skills.

- Building a trust-based integrated coaching program involves five basic steps: committing to a safe coaching culture, gathering call recordings, calibrating calls, deciding which coaching method suits each team member, and stack-ranking your team as A-B-C players.

- Regularly implemented coaching can improve quality, productivity, and teamwork and impact the bottom line.

- Observe the TeleSmart 10 Sales Skills in action. Coach in bite-sized pieces—one skill at a time. Just adding one of these skills to a salesperson's toolkit can have exponential and immediate positive results.

- Make time to coach by establishing a coaching time budget for yourself.

CHAPTER 8

YOU'RE THE COACH

Listening, Learning, and Giving Feedback

Ryan is distracted by his manager, Chuck, who is sitting only a few inches away furiously scribbling post-it notes with one hand and holding his tuna sandwich in the other. He takes a bite and passes Ryan a handful of notes—suggestions about what Ryan should say, questions he should ask, and products to pitch.

When Ryan gets off the phone, Chuck asks, "How do you think you did on that call?"

"Pretty good," replies Ryan. Then he adds, emphatically, "I got an appointment out of it."

"Yes you did. And your tone was good on the call. But—"

"What?" Ryan's tone is defensive, and he can feel himself tensing up for the attack.

"Well, I felt that you could have done a lot more. You left too much behind. Your opening was weak. They didn't even know who you were. You also asked closed-ended questions, so all he could answer was yes or no. And when he mentioned his group of managers, you could have asked who they were and gotten their names."

"Yeah, but—"

"Also," Ryan continues, "most of your questions were technical. You didn't get much information about their pains. And your description of our company was very confusing, which is why he wanted to get you off the phone. He didn't understand what you were saying. I wished you had mentioned to him that we are offering a new program and the discount ends this week. Does he know they used to buy from us six years ago? It was in your CRM, but you didn't review your notes before calling or during your call so you didn't earn any value. And, when you ended the call, you didn't mention any action step so he doesn't know what to do. Oh, and I counted about 38 'ums,' way too many nonwords. Otherwise, it was a good call. You got a live one, they answered their phone, it's all good, isn't it?"

Ryan is completely confused by the barrage of information and mixed messages Chuck just dumped on him. And the aroma from the tuna salad is making him nauseous.

Chuck perks up and says, "Hey, you're in luck. Why don't we switch places and have you watch me make calls so I can show what I used to do when I was a rep?"

Now Ryan feels like Chuck is invading his space, but what can he do? He rolls his eyes and sinks down into his chair. "Yeah, sure, fine. Let's hear how you became the star player when you were a rep, boss."

* * *

The heart and soul of your influence as a manager is your ability to observe, recognize, inquire, listen, decide, and motivate change with your teams through coaching and effective feedback. This chapter focuses on the human component of coaching: how and when to deliver insightful feedback that acknowledges your teams' essence. It provides strategies you can use to move change toward results.

As coach *and* manager, your sales experience and expertise is vital. But as a coach, you will be more than a sales manager. You will be a change agent—a wise guide whose goal is to uncover and enhance your team's best qualities, change unproductive behavior, and make sure that they have the skills they need to succeed.

Coaching is all about using your intuition, insight, and ability to read your team members. In Chapter 6, you observed them in training action. In Chapter 7, you observed them in sales action. Now you will learn to use what you have observed to instigate behavioral change through insightful observations and compassionate feedback. Once you understand your team members as human beings, you will know how to frame your feedback so that they listen, take it to heart, and put it into action.

YOUR TEAM IN THE FOUR ZONES OF LISTENING AND LEARNING

Have you ever stepped back from your people during a team meeting and noticed how differently each person is listening? Erin is attentive, Daniel is taking notes. Becca looks upset. Aaron is on a texting triage with his field partners. Patrick is nodding off.

Before you start coaching or motivating your teams, you must first check the pulse on the team morale. Each of your team members—depending on their basic personality, their mood, how their work is going, what's happening in their personal life, and their general level of satisfaction—will fall into one of Four Zones that influence the way they listen and learn. Even your dependable A and B players can slip to C sometimes, and Cs can surprise you by suddenly coming alive. Coaching your team requires you to know which zone each person is currently living in and to have a strategy for coaching and influencing change.

Identifying the Four Zones

Understanding the way your various team members listen and learn determines where you will spend your energy. The zone they are in will influence how they receive your feedback, so the first step is figuring out where they are right now.

1. *The Dead Zone:* People in this zone have checked out. Basically, they just don't care. These folks are probably your low-to-medium performers. They've plateaued and have no desire to advance further.

2. *The Comfort Zone:* People in this zone are sitting comfortably in their own little world. They are complacent; they resist any change that is happening around them. These average performers will do just enough to get by and won't show initiative for anything else.

3. *The Panic Zone:* People in this zone feel anxious, nervous, frazzled, and overwhelmed. They care a lot—a bit too much. They are ambitious, perfectionist, and take on a lot.

4. *The Stretch Zone:* People in this zone are excited (but not overexcited), enthusiastic, and ambitious; they have new goals, ideas, and strategies. They care a lot and want to do things differently. These are probably your top performers.

The Four Zones Are Fluid, Not Fixed

No one stays in the same zone forever. A new hire may begin in the Stretch Zone, ready to learn and grow, but once they discover what exactly is involved in the job and find themselves unprepared, they may jump to the Panic Zone. As time passes and they get to know their job really well, they go on automatic pilot—the Comfort Zone. If they've been passed up for a promotion or they have a lousy territory, they may start caring less and less and end up in the Dead Zone.

Ideally, your team should be well balanced. This should be your goal, but it is rarely the case. Left alone, your team is at the mercy of many internal and external factors that influence the zone they are in from day to day and week to week.

Your team is likely to be heavy in one zone depending on its structure, their seniority, and the time of the sales quarter. When you have a lot of senior team members, for example, the majority of them may sit in the Comfort Zone. If you have lots of new hires, they may all sit in the Stretch Zone or the Panic Zone. If you are experiencing big organizational changes, most of your team may be in the Dead Zone or Panic Zone.

What Zone Are You In?

This is the beginning of your coaching journey. It's important to understand what zone you are in when you are coaching because coaching is a two-way street: you get out of it exactly what you brought into it. If you are sitting in the Dead Zone, you will be useless to any team members that you are trying to coach. Find ways to energize yourself by working with your peer managers, colleagues, or another coach to keep you motivated. The Manager Diagnostics in Part Three— 18 motivational questions on team meetings, 1:1 forecast reviews, team motivation, and employee interventions—are designed to get you in the Stretch Zone at a moment's notice.

COACHING IN THE FOUR ZONES

Once you have monitored your team members and know which of the Four Zones each individual is in, you can devise a practical strategy for coaching and influencing change. If you see them drifting into the Dead Zone or the Panic Zone for more than a couple of days, step in quickly! If they have spent too long in the Comfort Zone, shake them up.

Remember, the Four Zones are fluid, not fixed. People spend time in all these zones at different times of the day, week, month, year, and entire career. Before you coach, do a zone reality check to decide which team members may need rebooting and tailor your coaching to meet individual needs. Here are some pointers.

Coaching in the Dead Zone

The Dead Zone is dangerous. Salespeople who are working in this zone are barely working at all. They no longer care, they are resistant to trying anything new, and they are very close to leaving the organization.

Many managers fail to recognize when someone is in the Dead Zone, mistaking it for a passing phase. They want to solve the problem fast. If it's a seasoned salesperson, for example, they may give them new hires to mentor to help them feel "needed" and get them out of their "funk." Big mistake! The negativity and gloom of the Dead Zone can easily infect your new hires and drive out the seasoned rep altogether.

Your first step is to find out what got them into the Dead Zone in the first place. Let them know that you've noticed that something seems off about their approach to calls, that they seem to have lost interest in the job, and that you wondered if something was wrong. Be probing and concerned but respect their boundaries. The issue might be anything from a bad breakup to conflict with a colleague, to frustration with their job, or a combination of factors. Often, just knowing that you have noticed can make a difference, and they will open up.

If it is a job issue, you'll need to have that tough talk. Some people in the Dead Zone are simply done with the organization but do not know how to move on; others are just doing a job they are not suited for. Ask them if they think they are in the right role; evaluate your own observations on this. You may need to help them learn new tools or skills, or you may want to encourage them to move into a different role or department. In the worst case, you may need to cut them loose.

Coaching in the Comfort Zone

Salespeople who have been part of the old sales regimen may sink slowly into the Comfort Zone. They're stuck. They work only at the level they are at ease in and are low risk about adopting new ideas. Be careful! A person in the Comfort Zone who is allowed to stay there may soon end up in the Dead Zone, where it might be too late for change. But take heart. These salespeople are very coachable because they really care. They just need some help to wake up and take charge.

When you coach someone in the Comfort Zone, you have to shake them up in some way: change their routine, their territory, their product responsibilities, or perhaps their vertical. You might want to put them on a new project to manage or give them the opportunity for recognition and reward. Try sitting your Comfort Zone rep next to someone in the Stretch Zone—they just may share some energy and get a breath of fresh air.

Coaching in the Panic Zone

Salespeople in the Panic Zone may be new hires who have finally figured out what's expected of them and are running scared or they may be senior team members who are overachievers with low self-esteem who panic at the end of the month when they try to hit their numbers. Be gentle. The last thing they need is more pressure from you; they are putting enough pressure on themselves.

Let them know that you understand how overwhelmed they feel, but that panic isn't the answer. Be supportive and stick with them. Help them slow down, sort through, and organize what's in front of them. Prioritize with them: separate the tasks that really need their attention from those that can wait. They probably need work on their time management skills, and they may need to learn how to use their sales tools properly.

Coaching in the Stretch Zone

We wish that all of our team members could be in the Stretch Zone! Coaching reps in this zone is delicate, though. You don't want to be overbearing and potentially kill their spirit; you just want to keep them on task and energetic. People in the Stretch Zone are ambitious and always looking to improve, develop, and change—sometimes too much so. Coaching them here requires focus: encourage them to stay enthusiastic but ensure that they follow up on their great ideas.

POORLY DELIVERED FEEDBACK DOES NOT GET HEARD

Today's Talent 2.0 is starved for feedback all the time. Bring it on! Today's social culture of "likes" and "followers" has created a work culture where salespeople continually want to know how they rate and where they rank. Managers must create a healthy feedback and reinforcement culture that reassures team members that is safe to be open to criticism and constructive feedback.

Your ability to deliver feedback can make a tremendous difference on how your team members receive it. But be warned: Delivering constructive feedback is a delicate job; poorly delivered feedback can actually do more harm than good. Feedback perceived as hypercritical or judgmental or hurtful or angry can threaten your credibility, impact your team's productivity, and result in loss of trust. Worse, your team will automatically tune out the feedback, missing out on valuable learning opportunities.

Unfortunately, reps hear a lot of poorly delivered feedback, especially when it comes to their skills and performance. Here are their biggest complaints:

- *Not enough.* Managers are erratic. They send a barrage of mixed messages and then go silent for weeks.

- *Too much to understand.* This is very common in after-call coaching because managers are tempted to throw in every wrong thing they observed.

- *Focused only on the negative.* Feedback that begins with "You should have" or "Next time remember to" or "I can't believe you forgot to ask" or "You always seem to do" sends a negative message that makes the person get defensive and stop listening.

- *Focused only on the positives.* Feedback that consists of "Yeah, it's all good" or "Everything is fine" or "You're doing great" or "Keep doing what you are doing" or "I'll let you know when something is up" is the opposite of helpful and makes them feel like you're not paying attention.

- *Lacks relevance.* This feedback is misinformed or not tied to specific objectives, hence useless.

- *Too vague.* Feedback like "Every time you ask questions, you need to engage them" isn't specific enough to be helpful.

- *Too rushed.* Feedback like "I've got to step into a meeting. I just wanted to tell you it was a good call" doesn't leave them any time to ask why you thought it was good or to learn anything at all.

- *Too late.* "I want to talk with you about that call you made last week." Really? Which of a hundred calls was that?

- *Loaded with cliché phrases.* "We want this to be a win-win" or "Let's look at this outside of the box" or "Let's punch it out" is meaningless. Say what you mean without jargon.

Constructive Live Coaching Feedback

This feedback model is designed specifically to help you, the inside sales manager/coach, to provide real-time live coaching on the fly. Remember, your coaching will be "sandwiched": the negative is the nutritious filling between two slices of delicious positive, before and after.

Move through each of the following six steps in order when delivering your feedback.

1. *Ask them how they think they did on their call. Example: "Judy, what did you think of this call?"* Their answer will tell you exactly how you can frame your feedback. Listen for their signals. If their response is extremely detailed, that is your lead to give them detailed feedback. If their response is self-critical and they are tough on themselves, your lead is to be easy on them with your feedback. If they respond with just a quick "I thought it was fine" or "It wasn't my best," that's your clue that they may need to be educated.

2. *Ask them what their objective was for the call. Examples: "What was your objective for that call?" "What did you want to accomplish from that call?"* Their answer will help you understand how focused and ambitious they are on each call. Their response will also indicate how much they feel they accomplished on the call.

3. *Lead with the positives. Examples: "A for effort." "Practice makes perfect." "Hey, you got them live on the phone." "You picked up the phone." "You moved the call along." "I thought you said that really well." "That question you asked at the beginning was extremely strong."* Start with the positive because that will make the negative easier to digest. Many times, however, you will wonder where the positives are. No matter how bad the call was, however, you can always find something positive to say about it.

4. *Identify their unique genius. Example: "Judy, you have such a wonderful ability to be friendly with customers! You can use that to your advantage when you want to ask very pointed questions."* Everyone has a unique characteristic that you can use to preface your feedback—e.g., being detail-oriented, assertive, friendly, professional. For example, you have a very social person who loves talking with peers, but it somehow doesn't make it into their phone skills. You want to take their unique characteristic and channel it into your feedback.

5. *Areas of improvement. Example: "Judy, what would you like to do differently next time?" Or "How will you change this next time?" Or "What will get in your way from making this happen?"* Ask what they feel they can improve on and what they will do differently next time. The way you ask them this question will motivate them to change.

6. *Accountability. Example: "Judy, go ahead and try that during the next week; then check in with me to see how it is working for you."* Provide an action plan for how the individual can make these improvements and how to use the positives more strongly, then hold them accountable. Make a plan with them to check back within a reasonable amount of time to see that she is implementing these actions.

COACHING THE CLASSIC INSIDE SALES PERSONALITIES

No matter where I go to deliver sales trainings—East Coast, West Coast, Midwest, South, or even globally—I meet salespeople who share traits with many others I have met: classic inside sales personalities. I bet you have more than one—maybe even all of them—on your team.

Can't-Make-a-Call Carl

What? You're in inside sales, and you hate the phone? Yes, Carl will find any excuse not to get on the phone and make calls. This is common these days, especially with Millennial talent who don't like the phone and see no need to use it. They are getting much more traction with email, and they are more comfortable with nonverbal communication.

Coaching recommendations: Work with Carl to help him understand the importance of the Dynamic Duo (vm + em = response) or the Triple Threat (vm + em + social = response). Explain that all of these components work together to increase response. It is essential for prospects to hear a vocal presence. Encourage Carl to set a nonnegotiable calling time of a few hours at the time of day when he has his most energetic voice to make calls.

Big-Talkin' Bob

Bob always has an exaggerated story that he blows up—and it's a long one. He is busy making lots of calls and having drawn-out conversations. His presentations are involved explanations with lots of slides. The problem is that Bob is all talk and weak in his follow-through efforts, which never amount to much.

Coaching recommendations: The more concise you can be with him, the better. If you have an open-ended discussion on goals and objectives, he will run with that. . . and keep going.

Send him quick emails asking him to tell you the top three objectives he will focus on. When you coach him, say upfront what you want to discuss and stay the course.

Work with Bob on his listening skills. He's not qualifying well because he is more interested in hearing himself talk than asking questions. Have him listen to his calls and make sure he sticks to the 80/20 rule: 80 percent listening, 20 percent talking and asking questions.

Service-Oriented Sam

Sam is a really nice guy. Customers like him because he will do everything for them. Perhaps he came from a service or technical position and believes the best way to sell is to service. But he is just not cutting it when it comes to selling.

Coaching recommendations: Thank Sam for his dedication to the customer and always going the extra mile for them. Then help him understand the difference between a sales call and a service call: one is revenue generating and the other isn't. Work with him to remove any deep-rooted assumptions that salespeople are too pushy, aggressive, slimy, or untrustworthy. Explain that a service mentality can be the launching point for selling but cannot replace it. Ask him to set a strong call objective and to make sure it's one that moves him along the sales cycle.

Fast-Crankin' Freddie

Freddie is super fast and impatient. He blows through leads, opportunities, and inquiries like lightning. He always complains he doesn't have enough leads, that marketing isn't giving him anything in his territory. And when he gets a campaign, he complains that the leads are low quality.

Coaching recommendations: The last thing you want to do with Freddie is scramble to give him more leads. Empty some of his lead bucket and suggest that he focus on fewer leads. Freddie has let his prospecting muscle soften up, and he has lost trust in the lead process. He is impatient, perhaps a bit panicked, and is not fully qualifying leads.

Help redirect his energy into a focused hunting mentality. Is he asking good questions? Can he actually recognize a good opportunity if it is staring at him? Develop his navigating skills; he's got to learn how to dig deeper and wider.

Push-Back Paula

It happens at every team meeting or when something new is implemented: Paula shakes her head, claiming it will not work. Her favorite phrases are "That's not a good idea," "I don't agree," and "I prefer the old way of doing it."

Coaching recommendations: Paula is probably resisting out of fear of change and insecurity. But she can overcome her trepidation once she gains confidence. Counteract Paula's resistance with a positive spin. If she says "I don't like that idea," respond with, "Great, we could use some constructive feedback. What do you think won't work, and what do you think will?" If she says, "That's not my job," respond, "There are other ways you can contribute. What are you best at?"

Guide Paula to focus on what she wants to achieve in the long run. Show her how change can help her reach her goals. She may just be looking for more attention and leadership.

Know-It-All Nick

Nick is self-absorbed. He believes that there's nothing more for him to learn because he already knows everything. Nick may also be a bit of a control freak who closely guards his knowledge. His know-it-all attitude keeps him from learning anything new, and it shows in his performance.

Coaching recommendations: Nick is probably suffering from low self-esteem, and his know-it-all behavior is a great defense mechanism. Do not let him continue to keep new knowledge out.

It's important to help Nick understand the value of developing himself, so give him new challenges and stretch goals. He needs the opportunity to make mistakes because that will force him to reevaluate himself. Just because he thinks he knows it all doesn't mean he really does.

Erratic Elizabeth

Elizabeth is unpredictable. She tends to bounce from extreme highs to extreme lows and back again. Although she often has the spirit and the energy you want from her, she is inconsistent and easily distracted, and you cannot count on her performance to meet your bottom line.

Coaching recommendations: Elizabeth is motivated by fear and needs to be closely managed. If left to her own devices, she will spiral out of control and you will have to reel her back in.

She needs help focusing, so give Elizabeth a specific task, such as reviewing her hourly and daily plan. Keep her on top of time management issues: make sure she always plans her calls, keeps a nonnegotiable calling time, and has a clear call objective.

Needy Nora

Who is always in your office? Who checks in with you for everything? Nora! She demands constant recognition on how she is doing, where she is going, and how she ranks compared to others.

Coaching recommendations: Nora needs some boundaries. Give her a challenge or a stretch goal to help her build her self-confidence, but limit the amount of time and supervision you give her. It's a good idea to schedule weekly check-ins with her to let her know you're there for her, but not at her beck and call.

If she gets behind, don't jump in and rescue her. Help her become more independent by guiding her to solve her own problems. When she comes seeking answers, give her questions: "What do you think you should do?" "What do you think the client wants?" "What do you need to find out?"

Hitting-His-Numbers Hal

Everyone wants Hal's crown but they can't hold a candle to his sales success. He is top dog and exceeds every goal. Hal is charming, smart, and very well liked by his team. But all this comes at a cost: he refuses to do any of the grunt work and, since he is always top in his game, everyone lets him get away with it.

Coaching recommendations: Hal is making you money, but his prima donna quality sets a bad example for your team. You may want to stay out of his way and just let him sell, but this will disrupt the cohesiveness of your group.

Instead, give Hal a coaching and mentoring role to force him to share his knowledge and expertise. Make him aware of others by giving him responsibility for giving constructive feedback. Focus on building his partnering skills to help him realize that his accomplishments depend on others.

Long-Winded Leslie

Leslie is a chatterbox who insists on giving you blow-by-blow details—over and over again—of everything she had to do to win the deal. Once she starts talking everyone around her scatters. Worse, instead of making recommendations, she confuses the customer with long explanations of the product.

Coaching recommendations: This is a tough personality to coach simply because we instinctively tend to avoid her, hoping we won't get caught in her verbal web. Your goal is to help Leslie become aware of her behavior.

Have her record her calls and listen to them. Interrupt her politely by asking her closed-ended questions. Get her to focus by asking her precision questions. Help her formulate short succinct qualification questions so that she doesn't ask long, leading, and rambling questions. Focus on developing her listening skills and get her to stick to the 80/20 rule.

Greta the Gossiper

Greta is the team gossiper and usually exaggerates the gravity of certain issues. Her behavior is bad for morale because she spreads rumors and wastes time. She creates distractions. If the team is goofing off, Greta is likely to be in the middle of it.

Coaching recommendations: You need to crack down on Greta's unprofessional behavior. Rumors and gossip are ways that people deal with fear of uncertainty. She is making up stories to explain situations she doesn't understand.

It is critical for Greta to stay focused on things she can control and move away from what she cannot control. Set clear expectations and hold her responsible for the consequences. Shine a light on her behavior and let her know that she is not operating in the shadows. Address the rumors openly and counteract them with the facts. Be transparent, so that others won't get wrapped up in Greta's speculations.

Entitled Erica

Erica believes that she should get a raise or promotion anytime she does something well, especially when beating a milestone quota. She wants to get everyone else fired up when she doesn't get what she believes she deserves, no matter how unrealistic it is. When you don't promote her, she says she will start looking around. In fact, she really does believe that the grass is greener everywhere else.

Coaching recommendations: Be very clear about career paths with Erica. Set clear expectations about what is required of her job and what is truly exceptional. Help her understand that leadership isn't about telling people what to do and being in charge. Work on her partnership skills and help her recognize how much she depends on others to succeed. Get her involved in team-building activities and encourage her to work as hard for others as she does for herself.

* * *

In Chapter 7 we provided a skill self-evaluation form for team members. Figure 8-1 shows how managers can use the same form to evaluate skills during the coaching session to use as a basis for constructive feedback.

COACHING FEEDBACK: TAKE TWO

Chuck was surprised to see that Ryan's performance declined after his coaching, and decided it might be time to get some coaching himself on his feedback delivery techniques. Once he got up to speed, he quickly did a reboot on all of his efforts. He took the following steps:

1. *He started by designing a coaching schedule for his team and communicating it well in advance so they could prepare.*

2. *He asked his team members to identify three sales challenges they would like to explore during their coaching session.*

3. *He took time to prepare for each session by reviewing their call metrics, stats, and forecast prior to the session.*

The next time Chuck walked into Ryan's cubicle—an in-cube session that he had set up in advance—he took steps to make his presence small, turning off his cell phone and asking Ryan to drive the session.

Prior to each call, he asked Ryan, "What is your call objective for this call?" Then, once the call was in progress, Chuck focused his entire attention on listening to Ryan's technique. When it came time to debrief and evaluate the call, Chuck spent time asking questions rather than jumping to conclusions or offering to make calls himself. These questions included:

- *"How do you think you did on that call?"*

- *"What do you think you did well?"*

- *"What could you improve on?"*

- *"Anything that stood out for you as good or bad?"*

- *"Anything you would change on future calls?"*

These questions helped Ryan come up with the answers on his own. They ended their coaching session with action steps, with Chuck asking Ryan:

- *"What are you going to do next?"*

- *"When are you going to do it?"*

- *"Will this action meet your goal?"*

- *"What might get in the way?"*

- *"How can I support you in reaching your goal?"*

1. Time Management 1 2 3 4 5 Disorganized Efficient	*Comments:* You seem organized, methodical, analytical, and detailed. Pace is very fast and must include more strategy and call focus.
2. Introducing 1 2 3 4 5 Inarticulate Influential	*Comments:* You are energetic, enthusiastic, and have a personable demeanor. Your pace is strong as you capture attention, create urgency, and maintain authority and confidence in your calls. Your voice mail messages need more organization and pace may be too fast.
3. Navigating 1 2 3 4 5 Shut out Intrepid	*Comments:* Your opening statements could include more pre-call research and demonstrate knowledge about your prospect. You engage well at the gatekeeper level, your pace is strong, and you establish good rapport.
4. Questioning 1 2 3 4 5 Interrogative Relational	*Comments:* Your questioning pace is extremely strong and direct and immediately engages your prospect. You must listen to the answers before formulating your next question and relate your next question to their response. Watch that your questioning efforts do not sound too closed-ended, too broad, or too robotic. Take the time to probe deeper and move away from your "rapid questioning mode." Trust your intuition.
5. Listening 1 2 3 4 5 Inattentive Inviting	*Comments:* You demonstrate strong empathetic listening but must be patient with their answers, not interrupt or formulate a new question without acknowledging the answer. Active listening and paraphrasing will help build trust and establish rapport. Paraphrasing will buy you extra time and help you focus on what your prospect is saying.
6. Linking 1 2 3 4 5 Fears authority Strategic	*Comments:* Listen to your responses as they indicate the type of decision-maker you are speaking with and learn to align with their unique "pains." Remember to listen to customer needs, focus on being in their world, and link the appropriate solution to their needs.
7. Presenting 1 2 3 4 5 Confusing Persuasive	*Comments:* Pace may be too fast, and you tend to present prematurely without thoroughly identifying needs. Remember to ask what their familiarity is with your organization.
8. Handling Objections 1 2 3 4 5 Apprehensive Courageous	*Comments:* You are brave in your questioning efforts after hearing potential objections and maintain great momentum.
9. Closing 1 2 3 4 5	*Comments:* Great work at taking control of call and gaining commitment on next steps.
10. Partnering 1 2 3 4 5 Conflicting Symbiotic	*Comments:* Make sure your partnership with your resellers and Field partners has a stronger distribution of responsibilities by setting expectations. Be careful not to move into a service/support role but instead take more sales control. Field partners but most take more control versus being too service oriented for them.

FIGURE 8-1 | Coaching Feedback and Evaluation on the TeleSmart 10 Skills

Ryan left the session feeling listened to, heard, and inspired. He was excited about the session and came away with many new ideas. Chuck left the session feeling like he'd gotten to understand Ryan's potential for success in a whole new, and constructive, way. He was excited about what this new coaching effort would mean for his team as a whole.

MANAGEMENT TIPS

- Seeing the potential for brilliance in your people is where good coaching starts. Hold onto that insight and use it to start understanding what they are capable of, what motivates them, what their true potential is, and what they need to learn. Then work with them to motivate them to open up, learn new skills, and achieve all that they are capable of becoming.

- As a coach, you will be more than a sales manager; you will be a change agent—a wise guide whose goal is to discover and enhance your team's best qualities, change unproductive behavior, and make sure that they have the skills they need to succeed.

- Determine which zone your team members are in—the Dead Zone, Panic Zone, Comfort Zone, or Stretch Zone—before coaching, and tailor your feedback to their needs.

- Your ability to deliver feedback can make a tremendous difference on how your team members receive it. Remember to "sandwich" your coaching feedback: the negative is the nutritious filling between two slices of delicious positive, before and after.

CHAPTER 9

METRICS 2.0

Call Activity Gets a Makeover

*An all-hands meeting has been announced for the entire sales organ-
ization. Peter walks over to Building 5 with his Inside Sales team,
joining a few hundred salespeople gathered in a large room that is
decorated with Formula 1 race cars and Grand Prix pictures. What's
up with the cars?*

*The VPs of Sales start the meeting. The first one begins, "Hey,
guys, welcome everyone. This year has been off to a sluggish start,
but we caught up midyear, and with our new product launch we are
optimistic for Q4. Here's how our sales are tracking to date and the
numbers we are looking for by end of year."*

*The other VPs provide a status review of the revenue numbers,
new accounts, and big wins for the year. Everyone claps.*

*"Since we are moving into Q4, we want a final push to get us over
the top," he continues. "That's why we are excited to announce our
'Winter Warriors on Wheels' Incentive program, designed to rev up
the engines throughout our entire sales organization!"*

*Everyone looks around in anticipation and excitement. Peter's
team is happy to be included in this sales incentive and curious to find
out more about the program.*

"Okay, ready? Here are the details and rules:

"Any rep who brings in over $500K in revenues per month will get a $5,000 cash bonus.

"Any rep who exceeds pipeline and bookings by 150 percent will get a $2,500 cash bonus.

"Any rep who brings in a minimum of five new logos will get a $250 Amex card.

"Any rep who sells our new product with an order minimum of $100K gets a $500 Amex card.

"The final winners will be announced at the end of the quarter and will get to go to Presidents Club, and guess where it will be held next year? That's right: Monaco, for the Grand Prix!"

Everyone is clapping and people are whispering. Peter hears one of his reps, Rita, say "Yeah, right," under her breath. A few field reps ask the VPs about specifics, but your inside team looks discouraged and frustrated. No surprise there, thinks Peter. Out of 46 people on his team, maybe two or three stand a chance of winning—and it's mostly because their field partners are on fire in their territory. But the rest of the team won't even come close to winning any of these in-centives. Rita is now clearly upset.

"What were they thinking when they designed this incentive? That women love European auto racing?" she gripes. "Do they even KNOW what we do every day? Who makes up these rules, anyway?"

The whole team is now staring at Peter, who shares their dissatis-faction. WHY didn't these VPs even think to discuss this program with me before making this announcement? Do they even know how much power inside sales has in the organization? But it's too late now, the damage is done. Their high-octane motivator just demotivated 46 people.

* * *

Inside sales today has a deeper involvement throughout the entire sales cycle: These teams have their hands on the tools and they're driving and dominating the growth in most sales organizations. All eyes are on this group. The pressure to drive new business and increase company revenues has never weighed so heavily on inside sales organizations and individual salespeople. Yet most people at the top—and even managers in the trenches—are holding on to outdated stereotypes of how to measure their success and motivate them to *more* success.

Some managers watch their outbound calls and activities metrics dashboard and complain that "It's awfully quiet out there. Where are the ringing phones?" But the new productivity is quiet: it's based on social, virtual, and mobile connections. Today's sales rules have changed dramatically. The old metrics are not measuring what really matters; insisting on measuring activities is not going to give you the results you want nor will it motivate anyone.

It's time for a metrics makeover. This chapter gives you the playbook on meaningful Sales 2.0 metrics that will stimulate productivity and motivate your teams to drive revenues.

WHEN SALES METRICS GO BAD

Every day your salespeople are hit with a demotivating emotional cocktail served up by busy, distracted, independent Customer 2.0. Reps desperately make outbound dials to "call-me-maybe" prospects who see the phone as a rude annoyance and a disruptive interruption. So they send emails. But customers routinely reject them without reading as "too long"; far too often, the subject line doesn't even make it out of their spam filters.

When reps finally get a live call, they beg for just a few seconds: 47 seconds on a call is a good call. And then, sweet! They are lucky enough to actually have a meaningful conversation with the rare prospect who is generous, cooperative, friendly, and smart . . . and once again they turn out to be a nondecision-maker, a No-Po. The rep leaves work feeling betrayed and used.

The next day:

- Reps have to deal with prospects who were fully on board yesterday and then mysteriously vanish.

- Another client returns after nine months of radio silence demanding to buy NOW.

- A qualified lead is passed on to the rep's field or channel partner, who never follows up on it.

- Reps respond to the pressure to continue making hundreds of calls per day with the occasional help of a robo-dialer that magically does all the dialing for them, and when they pick up the rare live call they forget their introduction.

Despite the heat being generated by inside sales, salesperson voluntary turnover is high[1] and the average length that an inside salesperson stays in their role is about two years.[2] Reps selling into the challenging conditions of Sales 2.0 require daily motivation.

In the end, salespeople are only as good as their last lead or deal they closed. And then it all starts all over again next month, next quarter. . . . Where's the fun?

Welcome to the 125-day, three-to-six conversations, 1.4-to-2.5 appointments per day club! For many inside sales organizations, these are the standard sales metrics that have defined their teams' daily, weekly, monthly, and quarterly existence. If your idea of motivation is to keep repeating the same mantra, "It's a numbers game, get your numbers up or get out," reps will quickly get bored and look for the next shiny object—fast. Metrics like these, which focus on numbers and do not acknowledge inside teams' unique sales challenges, fail to motivate and can actually drive reps straight to the Dead Zone.

Managers who don't carefully plan their approach to metrics are liable to make mistakes. They rush to set metrics based on numbers; they fail to acknowledge the various needs of their groups; they believe that everyone is motivated solely by money. When metrics are not aligned with a strategy, the motivational system backfires. They drive the wrong behavior and sometimes drive team members to "game" the system.

When Well-Intentioned Metrics Go Bad

The following few real-life examples prove how well-intentioned metrics can go bad:

- *The Phone Booth Hour:* Bill learns that his teams could not coordinate any time for outbound prospecting, choosing to make prospecting calls when it fit into their busy days. So he decides to impose a "phone-booth hour," requiring team members to go into a conference room for a solid hour three days a week to make their outbound calls. This causes the teams to view prospecting as a punishment relegated to phone booth time and to avoid doing any proactive prospecting during the week.

- *How (Not) to Create a Shorter Sales Cycle:* Toni tells her team members that she wants them to shorten the sales cycle. In response, they work the opportunities on Excel spreadsheets. Then, at the last minute, when the deal is about to close, they create an opportunity in the CRM so it looks like they just started working on it. Voila! A shorter sales cycle.

- *Cash for Appointment Setting:* Phil is so desperate for his teams to set appointments that he offers a $250 cash incentive for every appointment they set each day. Woohoo! Appointment activity quadruples instantly—but weeks later, the appointments get canceled or the wrong people show up on the appointment. Some even set appointments as Part 1 (fifteen minutes) and Part 2 (another fifteen minutes) with the same prospects so that they will win two cash bonuses for the same prospect.

- *Pushing Products:* Larry wants to increase sales in specific new products and creates an incentive program. His teams responds by pushing new products. Great? No. They neglect the products with weaker incentives or the ones that may actually have been a better match for the customer.

A METRICS MAKEOVER FOR THE NEW NORMAL

Once upon a time the success of your inside organization was apparent in the loud buzz you could hear every day from six in the morning to about two in the afternoon (PST). You'd walk down the sales aisles and hear ringing phones, bells, whistles, horns, and cackling sounds from team members high-fiving each other after a successful call. You loved these sounds because they validated that your team was generating some call activity. You could substantiate their value by measuring the number of qualified leads that converted to sales and the number of appointments they sent to the field.

But, as we've seen throughout this book, Sales 2.0 brings a New Normal: outreach efforts are different, response rate is different, follow-up efforts are different, *and* messaging is different. Educated, independent prospects insist on engagement, collaboration, education, and mobilization. Holding on to the old familiar metrics just discourages the progressive activity of Sales 2.0 and drives potential Superheroes out the door.

How to Measure the Sounds of Silence

It's hard not to worry: When you walk down the sales aisles and team members are texting, IMing, and socially surfing on Facebook or on the Tweetdeck—with one earbud in one ear and half a headset in the other, you can't help but think that nothing is happening. You just want to scream, "Can everyone just get on the phones and make some calls?" Because that's the familiar lever you pull when you want to see some action you can measure.

But that was yesterday. In a 2011 report, The Bridge Group[3] found that "call metrics as an inside sales KPI is falling out of favor." Not surprisingly, however, they also found companies were having a hard time letting go of the old metrics:

- 48 percent do not track email activities.

- 66 percent do not track social media activity.

- 34 percent do not track daily rep conversations.

- 37 percent do not track number of presentations.

- 48 percent do not track number of proposals.

- 30 percent are unable to clearly identify revenue generated by inside sales.

- 64 percent could not identify the percent of qualified leads that convert to demo.

It can be hard to wrap your head around social media in terms of metrics. How do you measure it? Where's the tangible return? There is a way: It means considering a metrics makeover designed specifically for Talent 2.0, Customer 2.0, Tools 2.0, Prospecting 2.0, and Teams. These metrics seem outside the box, but they make sense in-the-cube.

Metrics That Make Sense for Talent 2.0

Your digitally astute team members know in their guts that metrics today have nothing to do with babysitting a robo-dialer. As Penelope Trunk, CEO and founder of Brazen Careerist says, "[Gen Y] is the most productive generation that has ever graced the planet; they can run circles around all of us when it comes to productivity."[4]

Because this group puts such a high value on productivity, members need to understand the WHY behind the metrics you ask for. What activities will get them there? How many meetings does it take to close a sale? How many dials a day are required to reach their sales goals? If you walk them through this thought process and the activity requirements and explain the rules of engagement, you will encourage them to approach their proactive efforts with precision and patience and focus on productivity.

But focused as they are on the work, they also need FUN: this is their way of feeling acknowledged and getting feedback. These competitive inside salespeople need to be motivated *all the time*. The sales incentive business is a $40 billion industry for a very simple reason: salespeople need regular kudos and acknowledgment. And they love public displays of fun—just look at all the happy, shiny people that show up in their Facebook pictures and Twitter activities. For more on motivating with FUN, see Chapter 12.

Metrics That Matter for Customer 2.0

Customer 2.0 does not respond well to robo-stalking. They want you to know them personally, connect with them socially, know their friends, and engage in an intelligent conversation. And they are elusive: team members need to call around to make sure they are speaking with the person who actually has the power:

- *Number of multiple contacts within the same organization:* This metric will encourage teams to call deeper and wider into the target company and build org charts.

- *Number of live meaningful conversations with prospects and partners:* Even the most slippery prospects crave a deep, meaningful, honest conversation—especially the power buyer. Encourage more LIVE conversations that are not wasted.

- *Number of collaborative conversations:* Customers may not come back twice, so incentivize teams to have meaningful live conversations that include collaborating with web conference or video presentations while they have the customer on the call.

- *Number of triple-threat introductions:* The phone can no longer fly solo in today's Sales 2.0 environment. It needs a little help from its friends: phone + email + social media friends. Send out at least 25 new intros per day.

- *Number of new LinkedIn contacts per week:* Motivate your people to engage socially (Twitter, LinkedIn, Facebook, as starters) and listen for the live conversation feed. Remember, this customer likes to feel heard and is still hungry for relationships.

- *Number of inbound calls per day:* The goal is to generate enough interest from content lead-nurturing email marketing campaigns that you receive inbound requests from your prospects. Why? Because they have self-educated and they're ready to talk.

- *Number of meetings and appointments that didn't get cancelled:* Since Customer 2.0 likes to back out of appointments at the last minute, consider using metrics that incent appointments to stick.

- *Number of web-conferencing iPad presentations:* Video is king. Reserve a web presentation and prep your (very short and visually enhanced!) PowerPoint slide deck for an eight-minute presentation.

- *Number of mobile messaging campaigns:* A growing number of organizations are utilizing mobile messaging in their blitzing efforts.

Metrics that Matter for Tools 2.0

Your organization may be ripping out landlines in exchange for Skype or VOIP and using smartphones, iPads, and social tools in prospecting efforts. But don't get carried away accumulating as many shiny tools as possible. Tools metrics focus on *quality*, not quantity:

- *Quality of their CRM:* Everything lives in the CRM, and tracking sales metrics can all happen from the CRM plus the quality of their information capture and data can be monitored. How clean is the data? How updated is it?

- *Quality of active campaigns utilizing Dialers:* Tools such as dialers will create an uptick and spike in the outbound numbers. Dialers should not be used as a crutch but more strategically.

- *Quality of lists that translate to quality conversions:* List building is key. Old lists in particular should get resurrected, because Customer 2.0 comes back.

- *Quality of email templates stocked in their library:* Building a robust selection of email templates for multiple attempts and content nurturing strategies is also effective. Customer 2.0 loves content and will pay attention to your well-designed ten-week nurture campaign.

- *Quality of LinkedIn profile:* Cultivate more and more connections with high influencers.

- *Quality of LinkedIn discussions per week:* Write such thought-provoking, insightful, fresh content about your space that you earn credibility and become involved in the inner circle of prospects listening for trigger events.

- *Quality of sales pipelines:* Your pipeline should be clear and flowing, not clogged up with No-Po's.

Metrics that Matter for Prospecting 2.0

In Chapter 4, we watched potent prospecting in action and observed an intelligent strategy that includes leads, messaging, qualification, email/voice mail, social media, and quality versus quantity. Prospecting 2.0 metrics focus on outbound activities:

- *Master Prospecting Plan:* A well-designed territory plan that includes Top 25 target accounts is essential as this is the best way to focus on preparation.

- *Visual proof:* How prepared are they to make calls; are all their tools open and ready to go?

- *Setting nonnegotiable time for prospecting:* Prospecting still requires uninterrupted time and sticking with that several times a week will increase productivity.

- *Qualified leads:* Smart prospecting efforts involve qualifying prospects to keep them in or out of the sales funnel.

Metrics That Matter for Your Teams

Setting effective metrics in the Sales 2.0 Ecosystem requires careful thought, strategy, and attention. It also means tailoring those metrics to the needs of the people who use them.

The metrics that will work for your team must work for their specific roles and job functions. Clearly identify the sales activities and behaviors you want to observe, measure, and compensate, and make sure the metrics you use are job specific.

Look at your sales team as a portfolio of investments that require different levels and kinds of attention. Lead Gen, Sales Development, and Inside Sales teams (as outlined in Chapter 5) each have their own needs. The metrics you choose must recognize each team's unique sales charter and match the measurement goals of each role. Here's an assortment of metrics to measure for each group:

- *Lead or Demand Generation Team:* Metrics that focus on triple-threat intros, more inbound response metrics, webinar registrations

- *Sales Development Team:* Metrics that focus on calling deeper/wider into an organization to uncover the committee of decision-makers, triple-threat intros, setting appointments

- *Inside Sales Team:* Metrics that focus on meaningful conversations with decision-makers, more collaborative selling opportunities, LinkedIn contacts, converting appointments into meetings, presentations, and proposals.

- *Hybrid Inside Sales Team:* Metrics that focus on collaborative sales opportunities, LinkedIn contacts, on-site appointments, presentations, proposals

- *Renewals Team:* Metrics that focus on LinkedIn contacts with existing accounts

- *Government Team:* Metrics that focus on triple threat, multiple contacts within the agency, appointments

- *Social Selling Team:* Metrics that focus on following their digital social footprint, such as LinkedIn, Facebook, Slidesharer, YouTube, blogs

ALL-HANDS TEAM MEETING: TAKE TWO

After the meeting ends, Peter tells his teams to hang on just a little longer—he has some ideas that might work. Before the VPs of Sales can even leave the room, he sets up a meeting for the next day. He plans to build a case for getting additional spiff/contest dollars for his own team.

At the meeting, he provides activity reports, quarterly sales forecasts, and realistic projections to what they can bring in for Q4. The

VPs are surprised: They did not realize that the Inside Sales team would not benefit from the incentive they designed. They give Peter approval for additional funding for contests, and he adds a few creative incentives. Now Peter is motivated!

He sends a follow-up email to his teams that afternoon to announce that there is a new feature of the "Superheroes on Wheels" program designed exclusively for the inside sales organization.

Subject: Superheroes on Wheels

Today we kicked off our sales contest for the entire sales organization and here's an additional plan specifically customized for the inside sales organization. The goal is to create some October fun around beating our bookings goals for Q4. Here are some specifics:

Incentive Starts: 10/1/12

Incentive Ends: 10/31/12

How to Win: The winning team will have the highest percentage of bookings to their target for October. All percentages and goals are tracked within Salesforce.com.

Contest Prizes: The winning team will be eligible for Presidents Club and will get a team lunch (and bragging rights). Approx value $250.

Keeping Track of the Standings: I will send leaderboard updates via email twice a week. You can also see up-to-the-minute results by going to our leaderboard report here.

If you have any questions about the contest, let me know. And good luck!

Within seconds of sending the email, Peter gets a few initial positive responses. He watches the people working nearby and sees their faces transform from apathetic to excited, from frustrated to energized. He knows he is on track.

Peter's team is completely on board now. They ask questions, suggest sample scenarios, and even commit to new business they have in the pipeline. As they go back to their cubes they are smiling and talking about the possibilities, even challenging each other to duels about who's going to do better. They feel seen and heard, no longer misunderstood or forgotten.

MANAGEMENT TIPS

- Metrics that are not aligned with a carefully constructed strategy, or that are aligned with sales strategies that are no longer relevant, are demotivating. Worse, they drive the wrong behavior and sometimes cause team members to "game" the system just to make their metrics.

- Metrics that matter for Talent 2.0 focus on the WHY behind the metrics you ask for. What activities will get them there? How many meetings does it take to close a sale? How many dials a day are required to reach their sales goals?

- Metrics that matter for Customer 2.0 focus on making human connections and feeding their curious brains.

- Metrics that matter for Tools 2.0 focus on the quality of the tool and how well it is utilized, not on how many tools are available.

- Metrics that matter for Prospecting 2.0 focus on outbound activities, such as call blitzing, lead nuturing, and the triple threat.

- The metrics that will work for your team must work for their specific roles and job functions. Clearly identify the sales activities and behaviors you want to observe, measure, and compensate, and make sure the metrics you use are job specific.

MOTIVATE FAST!

Smart Sales Manager 2.0

Part One gave you an overview of the basic building blocks of the New Normal Sales 2.0 Ecosystem: Customer 2.0, Talent 2.0, and Prospecting 2.0; Part Two gave you the playbook on hiring, training, retaining, and coaching today's inside sales Superhero. In Part Three, we turn the light on you: Manager 2.0—leader, motivator, Fun Meister, and the one who has to make the tough decisions.

These four final chapters are quick references for your daily life as a manager. Each one starts with a Manager Diagnostic—18 questions that will help you check whether you are in the STRETCH ZONE, and what you need to fine tune. Read these chapters to get an overview, and pick them up anytime for quick reference on everything from planning and leading team meetings to motivating with fun. These how-to strategies, tips, and tricks will get you ready to impact your teams right now or anytime.

In this part:

- Team meetings are your place of influence—a real power center for motivation. Chapter 10 is all about owning your space as manager and *being* the behavior you want to see.

- Those moment-of-truth 1:1 forecast reviews can be great opportunities for motivation. Chapter 11 is filled with tips on making
forecasts count and getting realistic predictions from reps.

- Nothing motivates more than F-U-N and prizes, right? Chapter
12 is all about planning contests and spiffs that invigorate your
teams and inject the happiness factor to boost the bottom line.
There is a special bonus section on motiving your Millennial talent
with texts timed for just the right moment in the day or the
month. All the motivation in the world won't help a person who
just isn't cut out to be a salesperson. Chapter 13 helps motivate
you: to intervene with difficult conversations, set consequences,
and have those seriously tough conversations that determine if
your team member stays or goes.

CHAPTER 10

FLEX YOUR INFLUENCE!

Smart Strategies for Team Meetings

Your weekly meeting is about to begin. Before you walk into that conference room, you need a little, tiny ATTITUDE ADJUSTMENT. That's right, no matter how many things are on your mind and how much pressure you are feeling about your team not making its numbers, how you feel will SERIOUSLY affect the mood of the team members. Take this Manager Diagnostic first, to make sure you are in the STRETCH ZONE right from the start.

Answer these 18 motivational questions.

1. *Do I start and end my team meetings in an organized and prepared manner?*

2. *Am I disciplined to stay on task and move myself and my team in the direction of my goals?*

3. *Do I model strong time management behavior and delegate effectively?*

4. *Have I taught my team the basics—how to dress, how to talk to customers, and how to act in public?*

5. *Am I consciously diligent about my focus?*

6. *How much trust am I granting others?*

7. *Does my team know what is expected of them?*

8. *Am I finding new ways to challenge my team to think, be resourceful, and work smart?*

9. *Do I present relevant information that influences and has impact?*

10. *Am I responsive during team meetings and do I encourage healthy discussion?*

11. *Do I always check for understanding and reinforce skills with my team?*

12. *Do I take responsibility on issues requiring management involvement?*

13. *Am I worth following? Am I someone whom my salespeople should follow and allow to lead them?*

14. *Do I enforce the value of my company's belief system and culture?*

15. *Have I provided a culture and belief system about what it means to be part of the organization?*

16. *Am I working at building a high-performing team that is deeply committed to the success of my organization?*

17. *Have I been able to raise my team's viability throughout the company as a powerful force that is respected?*

18. *Can I move my team forward on important issues and get consensus?*

* * *

Are you in the STRETCH ZONE? Because if you're not, you might want to think about rescheduling your team meeting to a time when you feel prepared and powerful.

Salespeople know that every nanosecond spent away from sales-related activities impacts their ability to meet their revenue targets. You can't just stumble into your next team meeting unprepared. At the same time, you should not think meetings ought to give everyone that kumbaya-getting-cozy feeling where everyone gets together to share success stories and daily challenges. Good salespeople are good because they are productive. They live and breathe quota attainment. When their daily activity flow is interrupted by needless meetings that are lifeless and dull, they will shut down.

Here's the deal: only call a team meeting when you have something REALLY IMPORTANT to say. Otherwise, just email your team and call it a day. Used wisely, team meetings can be a source of enormous influence for managers. Talent 2.0 is all about group dynamics, career advancement, acknowledgment, and breaking news updates. Use your meetings to send a unified message, make a statement, set the tone, and deliver your message loud and clear.

This chapter is loaded with quick, practical ideas for reinventing sales meetings in your own best image. It's got lots of new ideas for agendas, topics, organization, and flow to keep your teams engaged and ensure that you make a strong motivational impact.

START STRONG, STAY STRONG

"Our meetings are usually pretty casual. I just want to hear what's happening out there." Uh-uh. I've heard this excuse from managers loads of times. Let's get this straight: YOU are in control of your sales meeting—and all eyes are on you. Your role is to facilitate healthy dialogue, inform your team, present new ideas, and encourage buy-in from team members. It all starts with you. Be prepared; don't wing it.

The behavior you model speaks volumes about you and what you expect from your team. Modeling positive, professional, productive behavior is what leadership presence is all about.

Before your meeting, send an email to the team and set the tone and expectations by being clear about the following:

- On-time start

- Active participation

- Attentive, receptive listening

- Willingness to entertain differing opinions

- Appropriate, professional behavior

- Set boundaries and context

USE THE WHOLE MEETING SPACE

For the entire duration of your meeting, remember: YOU OWN THAT CONFERENCE ROOM! Don't let anyone kick you out, and don't get tagged "You're out" when it gets double booked. Just say MINE, and use the room for whatever time you have in it.

- Erase the whiteboard. This is your meeting, not someone else's leftovers.

- Straighten the chairs. Make sure the seating arrangement is circular so that everyone can see each other.

- Throw out empty cups, water bottles, Red Bull cans, and plates.

- Grab the dry-erase markers and write something on the whiteboard.

- Conference your remote people in, and put the phone in the center.

WATCH YOUR BODY LANGUAGE

Body language—nonverbal communication—can speak much louder than words. It can make you look uncomfortable, stressed, distant, stiff, or stale. No matter what you say and what you want them to do, your body language may be screaming, "Hella, I'm done with this! I'm outta here!"

Take a breath, be calm, and begin by doing the following:

- Walk in like you own the room—you do. Stand tall!

- Dress appropriately and professionally. You're the team's boss, not their best bud.

- Make eye contact. Be friendly and inviting, not intimidating.

- Speak clearly, get to the point, and be confident about what you ask team members to do.

LET YOUR TONE SET THE MOOD

The last thing you want to be is BORING and put your salespeople to sleep. If your tone is too serious, you can throw your team into the Panic Zone and prevent them from hearing what you're saying. If your tone is too light, they may not take you seriously.

Set your voice tone for the result you want to achieve:

- Creating urgency

- Motivating the team

- Sharing best practices

- Creating excitement

- Educating

- Learning and sharing

- Acknowledging successes

MAKE IT ALL ABOUT THE MEETING AGENDA

The more organized your agenda is, the better your chances for cre-ating a healthy discussion and getting your people to talk. Distribute an agenda in advance so that your team comes prepared, and ask team members to vote on a few ideas to help prioritize the flow. The more you can educate and reinforce concepts in your discussions, the more you demonstrate the desired behavior, the more it will sink in.

Be sure to group topics so that they flow easily. Change up the data and include a variety of VISUAL tools to communicate your message.

Here are a few ideas:

- Use the whiteboard for commit numbers.

- Play a motivational video to inspire.

- Give out swag for the best story or call recording.

Agenda Items That Create Inside Sales Superheroes

You got the scoop on the Sales 2.0 Ecosystem in Part One. Why not share the wealth with your team? The following agenda items speak to the Sales 2.0 Ecosystem and today's Talent 2.0 (you don't have to have EVERYTHING on this agenda at one meeting!):

Customer 2.0: You have smart, elusive customers who come to you on their own terms. If you've been able to capture them virtually and socially, that's something to celebrate. Hooray!

- What subject lines are getting response?

- What has one of your "happy customers" said about your solution?

- Tell us about a call that lasted more than four minutes. How did the conversation unfold?

- Let's celebrate your success stories and recent sales victories.

Talent 2.0: Make sure team meetings are interactive. Moderate all those opinions.

- Always provide insight on the bigger picture to help team members understand how they fit in.

- For every project, assign committees and give everyone roles and responsibilities. This works well with Millennials, who like to collaborate, appreciate team dynamics, and enjoy project-driven work.

Tools 2.0: It's not just about purchasing the tool but adopting the tool, so talk about tools in your team meeting.

- Pick a team member who is an expert on a tool and have them share with the team how they utilize it.

- Invite a tools vendor to do a quick demo and get the team excited about "shopping for tools."

- Don't forget social tools. Ask team members to share social, professional conversations that have paid off for them.

Prospecting 2.0: Give Superheroes life in your team meetings.

- If you don't have a Superhero, recognize and reinforce the Superhero qualities in everyone. For example, "Alex, I heard you on the phone yesterday. You incorporated all the pre-call research into your opening, and it sounded so clear. That was Superhero behavior."

- Give kudos to any trace of "potent prospecting" you see taking place. Acknowledge it, and encourage lots more of it

* * *

In Part Two you learned about recruiting, training, coaching, and setting metrics with your team. Share your observations about what you are noticing in general, and get some buy-in.

Hiring: You may have found that your best source of candidates are coming from college grads who were leaders—grads who were president of their fraternity, coached the soccer team, organized concerts. Communicate what the ideal candidate profile should look like and then get the word out to these people for more referrals.

Training: Tackle each part of the sales process. Pick one skill per week from the TeleSmart 10 sales training system, dissect it in depth, and do some role-playing. Consider cross-training by inviting internal partners within other departments for a "lunch and learn" with your team.

Coaching: Perhaps you have been listening to call recordings and found a winner. Bring it in and play it for the group as an example of a good call. Make sure you create a safe environment around call monitoring discussions.

Metrics: It's all about the numbers and discussing metrics in team meetings is a delicate operation. Be careful when committing to the numbers in a public forum: everyone wants to look good, EVERYONE IS WATCHING, and you may not always get the whole truth.

Some managers want to share numbers to help motivate their team, while others want to share numbers to understand where they need to be by next week. The whiteboard is a good visual that can support metrics, but think about your motivations and what you want from your team before you start writing. For example, you can post results and rankings and praise top performers—as long as the rest of the team understands what they did to be top performers.

Remember the following:

- Communicate your present and future sales goals.

- Be sensitive to how you request commitment and when you do it—the end of the meeting is best.

- Hold them accountable for hitting their commit numbers by asking them to help you understand how they plan to get there.

CREATE COHESIVE TEAM DYNAMICS

The life force of a team is so much stronger than each individual. The more you value their worth, the more they will outperform your expectations. Lift them up and hold high standards when it comes to creating a cohesive team dynamic:

- Create a safe atmosphere in which everyone can discuss issues and role-play problems.

- Remind them of their significant value and contribution to the entire organization.

- Discourage the "negativity virus" that can spread quickly through a team when they run into objections they can't handle. Encourage solutions for every complaint.

- Hold participants accountable to results.

- Challenge team members and manage the side conversations.

- Negotiate strongly differing opinions to balance the team's power as a unified force.

ASK COMPELLING QUESTIONS

"Any questions?"

Forget that. Questioning and qualifying sits at the heart of all their sales efforts, so you must model master questioning skills. The more compelling the questions you ask, the more you will encourage richer discussion and exchange of ideas. Solicit everyone's input by asking open-ended questions, but stay away from deep, broad questions that require reflective contemplation.

Keep the conversation going by asking some of these questions:

- What do you all think about that?

- What suggestions can you make on improving this?

- How can we come together on these ideas?

- Who would like to take the lead on this?

- When can we review this together as a team?

- Who else feels the same way about this issue?

- How can we win together?

Here are more points to remember:

- When formulating a question, try to preface it with the type of answer you are looking for. This will focus the responses and keep people from wandering off track.

- Take your time before answering questions, especially when you are put on the hot seat for a solution. If you need a minute to reflect, ask what the others think of the same question before you present your response.

- Ask for their input and get their ideas. Write them down; show them you value their ideas. Ask follow-up and clarifying questions (not questions that are seen as critical or belittling).

LISTEN FROM THE OBSERVATION DECK

"Let me stop you right there, I know where you're going on this one."

This manager just turned off the brains and ears of every rep in the room. If you want to build trust and commitment:

- Model active listening skills. Listen to team members, don't interrupt, and take notes on major points and suggestions.

- Make sure you really listen to the issue they are presenting and ask questions to clarify if needed. Make resolution your top priority.

- Listen to facts, not complaints, and learn to neutralize potential gripe sessions that catch like wildfire in a team setting.

- When providing answers or explanations, make them benefits focused.

SET LATE PENALTIES THAT STING

"If you can't make the meeting on time, the door will be closed and you can't come in."

Don't you wish you could say that? But it's actually not the best strategy. Instead, try preventing it by setting the ground rules: Be ON TIME. It's definitely NOT OKAY to roll in five or ten minutes after the meeting starts with an excuse about not being able to end a call. Make sure everyone knows the ground rules beforehand so they have no extra excuses.

If you still have a few people who are consistently late for team meetings, you'll need to institute some penalties that set the tone for accountability. Your penalties should include procedures for how actionable steps will be "owned."

Here are some samples of penalties that sting:

- Put $1.00 in the pot for every minute you are late.

- Put all the chairs away after the meeting.

- Collect information from the group.

- Sing a nursery rhyme in front of the group.

INVITE COMPELLING SPEAKERS

"I invited our channel partner to come and speak to my team but he went over by 25 minutes and completely derailed the meeting. My team was *furious*."

Guest speakers should empower your team, not bore them or make them angry, so choose carefully. If your team doesn't like the speaker or if they are boring or off track, it will reflect poorly on you. A great speaker shares power with you and helps you glow.

Make sure that your invited speakers understand your groups' charter and knows their world. Ask them to keep their remarks short and benefits focused. You can help ensure this by giving them a seven-minute time limit to help them organize their presentation:

- The information must be relevant to your team's selling environments.

- The content must be organized into a meaningful format.

- Include a "What's in it for me?"

- Encourage participation from your team.

CLOSE WITH ENERGY

"All righty, it's time to end our meeting." Look down at your laptop, put your papers in order. Oops, wrong move.

No matter how good your meeting is, if you don't close with positive energy you will inevitably lose some of the enthusiasm you worked hard to generate. Participants should leave the room with more focus, enthusiasm, and understanding than when they came in.

Here are some end-of-meeting closers that send them out focused and ready:

- Define follow-through steps, assign volunteers, and take action to ensure action items are "owned."

- Have a clear conclusion. Summarize what you've all learned and decided, recap what the next steps are, and state follow-up expectations.

- Make sure your voice reflects energy and enthusiasm that motivates your people to get right back on the phones.

MANAGEMENT TIPS

- You are in charge, so model the behavior you want to see in everything you do: arrive early, be organized, dress professionally, be motivating, listen, hold team members accountable, set action steps, and make sure your team leaves the room on a positive note.

- A clear agenda, shared ahead of time, sets the tone for your entire meeting and everything you want to accomplish. Asking for input from your team beforehand and folding that response into the agenda ensures their participation.

- Your nonverbal communication speaks volumes about you. Take time beforehand for a mental and physical check-in, especially on the motivational front.

- Creating a cohesive team that shares your values and managing the team dynamics is a key part of your leadership arsenal.

- Never underestimate the importance of a sales meeting in setting a unified tone with your team.

CHAPTER **11**

TOTAL TRANSPARENCY

Smart Strategies for 1:1 Forecast Reviews

You are about to enter into that full disclosure zone: the 1:1 sales forecast review. You brace yourself for the usual questions: "What's your commit number?" or "What's the upside?" or "What's the best-case scenario?" You also brace yourself for the tidal wave of opinions, wild guesses, estimates, and stories of lost deals and new deals that you're sure to hear.

Take this Manager Diagnostic and answer the 18 questions that follow. Reflect on your approachability and determine how prepared you are for your forecasting review with your team. Your goal is to create a space for your teams to be honest and realistic about their forecast. The point here is not to collect points for every answer you get "right"— there are no right answers. Just think about which questions you need to work on. Coming up to speed on these questions will put you in the STRETCH ZONE when it comes to 1:1 forecast reviews that give you real information instead of happy ears.

1. *Do I hold regular goal-setting and development meetings with members of my team?*

2. *Have I communicated our forecasting criteria to my reps and helped them understand the real issues impacting their forecast?*

3. Do I provide regular team coaching or mentoring and give constructive feedback?

4. Am I always available and approachable to my team?

5. Does my team members understand how our sales process impacts their opportunities to move forward?

6. Am I too focused on closing metrics and not focused enough on opening metrics?

7. Have I armed my team members with everything they need to be able to effectively differentiate themselves and our offerings in a crowded marketplace?

8. Am I holding my salespeople accountable for their results and to their commitments?

9. Do I remove the roadblocks to my salespeople's success?

10. Am I intentionally looking for what people are doing right?

11. Does my team understand what they must do to map their opportunities at each stage of the sales cycle?

12. Am I listening for a hidden agenda of what lies behind the answer I receive?

13. Have I clearly demonstrated how the results we generate are directly tied to the actions we take because we believe what we believe?

14. What needs to get going? What needs a push?

15. Do I encourage people to set their goals high and give them achievement measurements that challenge them fairly?

16. Do I have a good system in place that helps me translate my team's forecast to senior management?

17. Does my team understand funnel health, funnel movement, and the daily actions required for a strong funnel?

18. Am I encouraging my team members to think for themselves?

Answering the questions in the Manager Diagnostic has probably made you think about how difficult it is for your team members to be realistic during their 1:1 forecasts. Think about it: Everyone wants to be seen in the best light possible. Most of us run the other way when it's time to step on the scale—we just want to move that number a couple of notches beforehand. Salespeople experience similar feelings when the MOMENT OF TRUTH arrives to reveal the truth about their sales pipeline: some are shy, some are proud, and some are downright delusional. Your role is to help them look at what's really behind the numbers, identify potential gaps that may have thrown them off track, and help them move forward. Sort through all this before you present *your* forecast.

This chapter provides strategies to help you encourage your teams to be totally transparent by diving into their sales pipeline, analyzing current and future activity, and diagnosing skill gaps where you can step in and help out.

MANAGERS STRIVE FOR TOTAL FORECAST ACCURACY

According to the 2011 Inside Sales Performance Optimization Report,[1] managers who conduct regular win/loss meetings with their teams experience greater forecast accuracy. Forecast accuracy is one area that keeps managers up at night. Both internal and external factors influence the health of your forecast or pipeline.

Your CRM

Your CRM is the guiding light that gives you visibility into your teams' forecasts and creates a dashboard view. For example, a CRM such as Salesforce will give you a mathematical calculation from which you must make an informed decision. The more data you have to work with, the better you will be able to forecast. You can also monitor changes in your dashboard from deals that were added or removed week to week and observe your reps' forecasting patterns and habits.

Your Team Data

The more you know about your team members' personalities, habits, and motivators, the better you can make an informed decision about their forecast—which, of course, impacts *your* forecast.

New hires, for instance, can throw your forecast visibility off because they are new to the product, the sales cycle, and the customer commitments. Team members who suffer from "happy ears" believe everything they are saying; if they give you their forecast for $100K, you can take their fudge factor into account and work with $60K. Reps who haven't made their number in a few quarters and are low risk and low confidence may "sandbag" their deals, so when they're forecasting $100K, you might instead work with $120K.

CONDUCT A PIPELINE INSPECTION BASED ON THE TELESMART 10 SKILLS

A sales funnel is a living, breathing sales microsystem that changes minute by minute. Every forecasting opportunity has a life or death in that funnel. At any time, deals in the funnel can get stuck, can quickly move forward or out, can lag for months and finally close, or can come from nowhere and close immediately.

The variable is always going to be the unpredictable buyer behavior of Customer 2.0—but you can close the gap on pipeline inspection by tying it to the TeleSmart 10 skills. If your team members are stuck on a particular skill or set of skills, this can easily explain why their funnel is not moving forward and growing.

The following pipeline inspection, based on the TeleSmart 10 skills and activities, will help you determine funnel health and figure out how to get a stuck funnel flowing.

Time Management

You can always diagnose the momentum a salesperson has on his or her funnel: Are deals moving from day to day? Are new ones being added in and older ones closing or moving out? A salesperson's funnel will change depending on the time of the month or quarter, and the cyclical activities that align with that particular time.

Early in the month/quarter: This is the time for lots of proactive activity. It's a great opportunity to invest time in territory planning, preparation, strategy, and researching more target accounts.

Your team should be planting seeds by doing the following:

- Proactive call campaigns

- Blitzing

- Following up on leads

- Making more introductory calls to prospects

- Requesting appointments

- Learning new tools and determining how they will be used

- Expanding their reach with internal and external partners by building alliances

- Learning the purchase process and procurement cycle

- Building their social media digital footprint

Middle of the month/quarter: Members of your sales team should be working on the activities and campaigns they created earlier in the quarter. This includes:

- More call campaigns and blitzing

- Following up on their first call and focusing on the second to fifth calls

- Delivering demos and presentations

- Converting appointments into meetings

- Generating quotes, proposals, and RFPs

- Expanding their digital footprint

End of the month: At this stage, teams need to expect most of their efforts to materialize. Customer 2.0 sometimes comes ready to buy NOW, so teams must be prepared.

By this time, they should:

- Have built out their org charts and identified all the power buyers in the committee

- Have a good understanding of the status of their deals

- Be more reactive, because they have generated enough activity that comes through

- Be ready for the close and reduce any chances of being blindsided

- Be ready when they get the "We want it NOW" call from their prospects

- Continue to expand their digital footprint

Introducing

Introducing is like the "speed-dating" part of funnel building. Without this first effort, nothing happens. This is the fuel you need to get the engine running.

- Add at least fifteen new qualified opportunities to your pipeline each week. Your pipeline should have at least 40 percent new business opportunities each month.

- Encourage more LIVE meaningful discussions with prospects.

- Encourage social engagement.

Navigating

That Call-Me-Maybe Customer who strings your reps along can create serious damage in forecasts. Funnel health sits stagnant or keeps getting delayed month after month because of these non-decision-makers. Your salespeople tend to hear "maybe" in the sales cycle. They jump, spin, chase, and beg—and often, they chase the wrong people, including No-Po's, gatekeepers with no power and no potential who generate false hope.

- Time for No-Po rehab? If your people just can't get away from hanging out in the No-Po nation, you need to quickly sniff that out and get them to move out fast. The longer they stick with them, the harder it will be to get away from them. And the more this will mess up your sales forecast and make everyone CRAZY. Big Deals = Big People.

- Break the No-Po logjam by practicing the 2 × 2 rule—call deeper and wider; call up, around, and across.

Questioning

If there is any movement in a sales funnel, it is because of reps' qualification efforts. This is where they can move something up, down, or out of the funnel. Questioning will move the funnel forward.

- Your team must ALWAYS qualify and confirm and requalify and reconfirm using the Trust Thermometer, mentioned in Chapter 4.

- When there are so many leads clogging up the funnel, reps tend to focus more on qualifying something out rather than qualifying them *deeper.*

Listening and Linking

Knowledge of two main areas in the Trust Thermometer will move opportunities through the funnel: (1) pain and (2) power.

- Encourage information capture. Incomplete data is one of the biggest causes for inaccurate forecasting.

- Encourage reps to listen for the business needs and ask about compelling events.

- Make sure reps are aligned with the power buyer and understand the political hierarchy in their target organization.

- Watch that your team is not listening with "happy ears." Listening to what they want to hear instead of what is really being said will distort their funnel.

Presenting

Good presentations are one of the fastest ways to convert leads and opportunities. They create major strides in moving the funnel forward. Deals will move through the funnel faster if your reps are delivering more presentations and they are being understood.

- Have your team add more virtual Web collaboration, and video presentations to their toolkits.

- Encourage them to keep their presentations short, short, short—four minutes max.

- Make sure they present to the right people and do not waste time presenting to technical buyers who lack influence.

Handling Objections

Managers must make sure their teams don't let go and don't give up when they're rejected, because being in inside sales is like handling rejections on steroids. Watch for sudden jumps out of the funnel because reps may have succumbed to objections or accepted a "no" from someone who was not qualified to say "yes." Reps who are constantly being rejected and have no skills to counter objections will quickly succumb to stress, and that can severely impact their self-esteem.

- Help them balance between not taking it personally and being self-reflective enough to understand what their part was in distancing their prospect or making them mad as hell.

- Give them some ready comebacks to common objections.

- Encourage them to learn more about the competitive landscape and to expect new players to come into the picture.

- Reinforce the need for them to immediately pick up the phone to counterattack any email objections they receive.

Partnering

There's power in leveraging internal partners. They may not always understand what an inside sales team does, but you and your team can educate them. Partnering will help opportunities hold longer in the funnel because there is a double effort taking place.

- Forecasted deals can stick longer if an integrated team has ownership, so the divide-and-conquer approach pays off.

- Encourage teams to work together— you can even assign mentor buddies.

Closing

Forget showing off your rescue tactics. Saving your team will only hold them back from learning. Instead, spend more time listening to their strategy and making sure they understand HOW to close deals. If your team is doing everything right, the close evolves as a natural process. If they are rushed, sloppy, and there is no guarantee of anything sticking for long, deals can suddenly unravel at the final hour.

- Coach reps to carefully grow their existing opportunities and move them through the funnel with better qualifying, talking with the power buyers, and managing objections.

- Make sure your team aligns your sales cycle with the customer's buying cycle.

- Encourage your team to say yes to small deals; they are the building blocks of solid salesmanship.

1:1 Forecast Reviews That Create Inside Sales Superheroes

Be sure to incorporate your knowledge of the Sales 2.0 Ecosystem into your forecast reviews. Always remember that customers, talent, and prospecting are different in the New Normal. Pipeline issues are always going to revolve around reps getting up to speed on Customer 2.0 and Prospecting 2.0 and on your getting in sync with the needs and abilities of Talent 2.0.

Customer 2.0: These customers are unpredictable. Even after they've said yes, they vanish for months. When they do come back to buy, it is generally at the last minute—and they want it NOW.

* Make sure reps continue to drip information and "visual bling" their way so that they are always thinking of your solution.

* Encourage your reps to chase and revive old opportunities: Customer 2.0 has been known to come back after a long slumber and remind you that they still need a solution, even after more than six months of silence.

* Today's pipelines must be larger than life. Always encourage your teams to build the pipeline five times larger early in the quarter and three times larger later in the quarter, to allow for fallout.

* This customer will listen to their social networks before anything so encourage your teams to socially solidify opportunities.

Talent 2.0: This "What's next?" generation is addicted to the chase, but they sometimes run so fast they zoom right past something essential and miss it. They also tend to take things at face value.

* They may see no reason for calling prospects who don't answer their phones and don't want to talk with them. Help them see the value of calling and making connections with prospects.

* They may believe that the No-Po is genuinely interested. If the No-Po says yes, they say "cool" and add it to their forecast. If the No-Po says jump, they ask "how high." Your role is to intervene and help your team get away from these professional funnel cloggers.

* Many Millennials do not analyze information; they just want answers. To help them become independent thinkers, stop giving them fast answers and finishing their work for them.

* They are comfortable swimming in the social river, so encourage them to expand their digital footprint.

Tools 2.0: Sales forecasting is part art and part science. The right tools, dashboards, data, and analytics contribute to the sophistication of forecasting. The more you learn these tools, the better you can track the life of an opportunity and accurately make future predictions.

- Your role is to make sure that your teams understand their tools and what they can provide in terms of their sales forecasts: Are they inputting data? Do they understand the analytics? Do they understand how to forecast opportunities?

- Get them to be honest and realistic in their forecasting regardless of how much pressure they are under.

Prospecting 2.0: The funnel is an activity magnet, and prospecting is the only way to build pipe and create activity.

- The more your teams prospect, the more activity they will generate. Whether it happens through call blitzing or content nurturing, they are creating activity.

- The inside sales Superhero understands that prospects need to be heard more than ever. Build quality relationships because these will prevent your funnel from clogging up.

- Superheroes know how to build realistic and healthy pipelines that have life and substance.

ARE YOU FEELING THE SIRI EFFECT?

The number one piece of information to remember in 1:1 forecast meetings is this: You really want to teach your team to think for themselves. Building healthy funnels is the proof that your teams are self-disciplined and have the intelligence and knowledge to sell. It is not about you doing all the thinking for them.

You might be feeling the Siri effect. In today's search-driven, quick response, high-pressure digital and social Sales 2.0 environment, your team just wants the answers fast. But you are not a search engine or a robotic smartphone "friend." You do not have to have all the answers.

You want to build a team of disruptive inside sales warriors who know how to think, analyze, create, engage, and close opps. But are you training them to think for themselves? Talent 2.0 wants your answers delivered to their inbox now. Be on high alert when it comes to rescuing them—especially when they ask questions that they already have answers to, or that they could answer easily with a little thinking.

When you get asked that same question over and over again, don't just give them the answer. Tell them once if you have to, and then help your reps think for themselves.

- *"Hey, what's my log-in?"* Really? I don't care how little time they've been on your team, they should know their log-in cold or have a system for figuring it out.

- *"Do you know what list I should call on today?"* When you build a culture of reactive call blitzers, their prospecting efforts focus more on contacts versus companies. Get them back on track by encouraging them to build a Top 40 list.

- *"I've been here about four months now. Can I get promoted?"* Again? Really? Be clear with your new hires about the career advancement process and set high expectations.

- *"When are you going to send me the new email templates you just loaded into Salesforce?"* Your reps need to take responsibility for their own email template library and stop waiting on marketing or you to spoon-feed them what they should be sending out.

- *"They sent me an email saying it was not in their budget for the quarter. Should I call them back?"* YES! Train your salespeople to immediately pick up the phone when they get an objection. They should not have to ask you this question more than once.

- *"My field rep said that I couldn't call into his accounts. Should I call them anyway?"* Make sure that you are building a collaborative sales culture where everyone is sharing accounts and working with each other, not in conflict.

- *"I sent them five emails and left voice mails. Should I send them an appointment request?"* Help your team members develop a strong outreach strategy that includes emails, voice mails, and social media used strategically.

- *"So what's the difference between a best case and commit again?"* Make sure your team has a good understanding of the various sales stages and how to accurately forecast their deals.

- *"Do you think I should call their boss if they haven't responded to my email?"* Encouraging your team to call high is important, but they should not call high just because they are not getting a response. Remind them that they need to bring value when calling high.

- *"Can I wear a hat when I'm on video if I have a bad hair day?"* Dress codes are changing in inside sales, especially because video requires you to look good from the waist up.

MANAGEMENT TIPS

- During your 1:1 forecast review, get full disclosure from your team on what they've really got. Then identify potential gaps that may have thrown them off track and help them move forward.

- Understanding where deals are stuck in the pipeline is more important than guessing when they will close. Inspect these pipelines based on the TeleSmart 10 skills to gain insight into how to get stuck funnels moving.

- Remember that customers, talent, and prospecting are different in the New Normal, and these new influencers can affect your funnel in ways you might not be looking for.

- Find the tools to build dashboards that provide you with greater visibility into your teams' funnel and your funnel. The more sophisticated the tool, the more accurate your forecast.

- Teach your teams to think, react, and take action. Slow down on jumping in and rescuing them or giving them all the answers. Your role is not to channel Siri.

CHAPTER 12

CONTESTS, SPIFFS, AND TEXTS

Smart Strategies for Motivational Makeovers

Are you having fun yet? You've just been nominated as the Fun Meister. That's right, your inside sales team members want to have FUN and they want it NOW. And by fun, of course, I mean motivation— and that's your job.

Take this Manager Diagnostic and answer the 18 questions that follow. This will lift your head out of your data-driven day and pump up your motivational volume. The point is not to collect points for every answer you get "right"—there are no right answers. Just think about which questions you need to work on.

Coming up to speed on these questions will put you in the STRETCH ZONE when it comes to motivating your teams:

1. *Are the rewards and discipline I use clearly linked to performance and defined behavioral objectives?*

2. *Do I structure work so that it is interesting and challenging and allows for appropriate autonomy?*

3. *When I give a reward, do I make sure it is one that the recipient values?*

4. *Do I try to understand what motivates each individual member of my team?*

5. *In order to be fair, do I use the same rewards for everyone when recognizing good performance?*

6. *How motivated do I appear to my team?*

7. *What does the company need to provide me with so I can motivate my team?*

8. *How do I communicate my personal motivation to my team?*

9. *Am I doing everything I can to recognize and reward individual contributors?*

10. *Are my metrics motivating the right behavior?*

11. *Am I ready to monitor, maintain, and measure the success of my motivational system?*

12. *Can I delegate the Fun Meister role to someone else in my organization?*

13. *Are my teams engaged? Do I always try to create excitement about goals?*

14. *Am I developing my own skills in sales, management, and leadership or simply doing my job?*

15. *Do I know what drives each of my reps to success?*

16. *Do I know what the internal and external motivators are that determine what it takes to make them happy?*

17. *Do I have the energy and excitement required to constantly be cheering for my team?*

18. *Can I be diligent in focusing on the big picture activity goal and not lose sight because of contest distractions?*

The sheer range of these questions should make it clear: In today's "What have you done for me lately?" culture, it's not enough to simply hire, coach, train, and set metrics for your team. If you want to build a culture where talent and teamwork are highly esteemed, where everyone is encouraged to reach their potential and given opportunities for advancement, and where you receive loyalty and commitment for your efforts, you must go the extra mile to motivate your teams in meaningful ways.

This chapter is the Cliffs Notes version of a motivation playbook. It includes individual motivational strategies for your A-B-C performers and team motivational makeovers with a high F-U-N factor. It's also filled with ideas for visual public displays of fun and personalized timely texts designed to squeeze more out of your teams.

WHAT DRIVES MOTIVATION?

Cash is king. Everyone likes to be well paid for their work, and no one will turn down a bonus. But it's not all about money when you are motivating your inside sales teams for success. Inside salespeople need more than tangible financial rewards to maintain daily morale and stay invested in their company's success.

You've observed your team in their cubicles and watched them in team meetings and sales training. You know who the sports enthusiasts are, who the family-oriented team members are, and which ones can't wait for Happy Hour. You've learned, up close and personal, that every single soul on your sales team is unique. Some personalities may be more disruptive than others, some may be looking for praise, some may be quietly taking notes, and some may be sitting in the Dead Zone.

Now it's motivation time! But how do you get the members of this diverse group on the same page and working together?

Although team members are not always motivated by the same things, for most people, it's one of these:

- *Achievement Driven:* These people have a strong need to set and accomplish challenging goals. They take calculated risks and like to receive regular feedback, praise, and recognition on their progress and achievements. They enjoy solving problems, and they often prefer to work alone.

- *Affiliation Driven:* These people want to belong to a group, be liked, and feel useful. They will often go along with whatever the rest of the group wants to do. They prefer to collaborate instead of compete and they don't like high risk or uncertainty. They value relationships above anything else.

- *Power Driven:* These people want to control and influence others. They enjoy competing and like to win at all costs. They enjoy status and recognition. They want to be in charge.

WHAT MOTIVATES YOUR A-B-C PERFORMERS?

In Chapter 7 you learned how to stack-rank your team and divided them into A-B-C performers. Now you can apply that understanding to motivation. For example, A players may stop working if a ceiling is imposed. C players need a lot of prodding to make their numbers. And your biggest group—B players, the core performers—need perhaps the most motivational attention because their contribution is vital to your bottom line.

Clearly, a one-size-fits-all motivational strategy is not going to work here! As you design your strategy, consider the type of motivation required not only for each individual player, as noted above, but for each type of performer.

Motivating A Performers

These performers are your Superheroes. They are ambitious, have large egos, or are very likely beyond your capacity to mentor (or think they are). But they will stay loyal if they feel that they are learning and making a difference to both the company's success and to their personal success. They are generally driven by achievement or power, or both.

Spend 20 percent of your coaching time budget on developing, growing, and mentoring your star performers. The priority is for them to sustain their A-performance status.

- Keep them accountable for their MBOs and revenue goals. Their target goals should always be visible and consistently reviewed so they don't lose focus on the job at hand.

- Ask them to present their success secrets to the team or upper management. This will encourage them to identify their key strengths, expose members to management, and inspire them.

- Give them a mentoring role with new hires.

- Assign them strategic projects that take them into other parts of the organization.

- Allow them to go outside of the department and work with or shadow other senior-level sales reps. This will help begin to identify the gaps they need to fill in order to be considered for the next step.

- Provide ongoing feedback, praise, and recognition.

Motivating B Performers

Most of your team has a real opportunity for meaningful improvement—but only if they get *more* of your attention, not less. Ongoing recognition and consistency in delivering feedback are the keys to keeping these core players moving toward their A game. Most B Players are driven by affiliation, but your Superheroes hiding in this group will also need motivation through achievement and power. Spend 60 percent of your coaching time budget developing, growing, and mentoring individuals you would not consider Superheroes—yet.

- Conduct a review process of their typical day to assess their time management skills, activity level, and desire to succeed. Also conduct a four- to six-week assessment on actual activity levels.

- Revise their typical day slightly. Have them report back to you every Friday, via email or in a meeting, on what worked this week and what didn't. This will help you see a pattern and pinpoint areas where you can help them improve.

- Commit to more coaching time with them—it will pay off.

- Try to understand what makes them tick. Take them to lunch, begin to get to know them. Determine where they get their motivation. Is it from certain perks or recognition? Use what you learn to help motivate them to become Superheroes.

- Expect 10 to 30 percent more out of them, and let them know. A good portion of them will step up to the plate and show you they can do it.

- Assign training initiatives to individual members so they become the subject-matter expert.

Motivating C Performers and New Hires

These underperformers need your help to grow. They may have some raw talent or just need targeted help in basic areas. For some, of course, no amount of coaching will help. They may just be in the wrong job. Get to know them as individuals to learn what drives them: achievement, affiliation, or power.

Spend 20 percent of your coaching time budget developing, growing, and mentoring C players and new hires.

- Make sure new hires have a clear understanding of their responsibilities and your expectations, from time management to achieving MBOs or revenue goals

- Ask them to provide a daily update to their manager and sales director highlighting activity stats, training snapshots, best customer conversations, obstacles overcome, and open questions or problems.

- Ask each individual to provide you with a 30/60/90 plan to support their territory and MBO objectives. Then manage them to that plan.

- Assign them a friendly A player mentor so that you can get a second opinion on their strengths and weaknesses.

DESIGNING CONTESTS AND SPIFFS

Once you have the right people in place, it's crucial to provide an environment that your reps enjoy being in every day. The last thing you want is a negativity virus—it spreads fast and infects the entire team. Morale is the invisible fabric that holds your teams together. Teams with high, positive morale can withstand the stresses they encounter in their fast-paced, high-pressure sales environment.

The first step in your motivational plan is to identify what part of the sales funnel needs a jump start and, then, figure out what specific activities will influence it. For example, generating more leads and building pipeline will influence the top of the funnel; getting sales dollars booked and orders shipped will influence the bottom of the funnel.

Creating regular team contests or spiffs is a great way to improve morale, stir up some friendly competition, break up the daily routine, and infuse some positive fun. A contest is more strategically organized and lasts over a longer period of time; a spiff is generally used when you want to create a spike in sales activity.

Remember: A successful contest incentivizes everyone to improve their performance and productivity and will help your organization meet and exceed its revenue targets. A contest will fail if it is aimed only at the top people, and the rest of the team watches the same people win all the time.

Strategies for Contests and Spiffs

Contests should be fun, be winnable, and create a boost in both morale and metrics. But you can't just come up with any old idea and expect it to work. Think your contest through carefully, and plan, plan, plan.

Base Your Contests on RAM (Reasonable, Attainable, and Measurable): According to Sales Contestology,[1] managers set their salespeople to succeed when planning sales contests based on their RAM essentials. Salespeople should feel confident that:

- What's being asked is *reasonable:* they have the know-how, the proper tools and resources, and so on.

- The goal is *attainable*: not excessive or extreme.

- The performance is *measurable*: typically, a metric they are already familiar with.

Determine the Duration: The best way to rally your team and get the members focused on your motivational program is to keep the time length short—but not so short it won't achieve your goals! The timeframe should align with your contest objective and overall sales department objectives. Setting a specific timeframe also helps sales performers perceive the contest as fair, which in turn boosts morale and improves efficiency.

Choose FUN Rewards and Prizes that Incentivize Everyone: Contests have to be fun from the very beginning for them to work. A contest theme should incorporate a fun name that resonates with your salespeople and include memorable visuals that will be used in your contest communication. When you consider the rewards and prizes for your team, remember what you know about Talent 2.0. They are not into buying lots of toys for themselves, and they are pretty bare bones when it comes to owning anything. For them it's all about access, not about possession. They are more interested in paying Netflix for videos or Kindle for books than in collecting physical piles of items that just create clutter.

Consider the following when deciding on a prize:

- The budget and contest ROI

- The size or value of the prizes in comparison with your sales team's incentive or commission plan

- Whether to use cash or noncash prizes

Here are some creative themed ideas for rewards and prizes that identity teams are likely to remember:

- Lunch with the boss: Once a month, the CEO or manager has lunch with select employees.

- Half-day reward: Reps can go home early on Friday, come in late to work, and take a longer lunch.

- Parking space for the month: One parking space is dedicated to your group.

- Gift certificates: Amazon, Netflix, AmEx—anything that gives access.

- Time off in the field: This could be to attend a conference or tradeshow or to spend the day with a rep visiting clients.

- Sporting events: Get season passes to basketball, baseball, hockey events.

- Massage therapist: Hire a massage therapist to give a chair massage in the office.

- Tiki hut: Many sales organizations set up a tiki hut in the office and have a happy hour.

- Cubicle toys: Fun stress-reduction toys—such as stress balls, Slinky, Etch-a-Sketch—that they can squeeze or bounce or play with during calls (but not video calls!).

- Traveling World Cup: Get a big giant trophy and refill it with a snack every time someone wins custody of it. Remember, the trophy doesn't have to look great. It's being able to have the trophy to display in your cubicle.

- Treasure chest: Remember going to the dentist when you were a kid, and you were allowed to pick a prize out of the treasure chest? Same concept. Just remember to load it with more than lollipops! IPod Nanos, headphones, Bluetooth, and other such prizes are always popular.

- Significant others: Often an employee may work long hours to achieve a goal, neglecting family in the process. Offer a prize they can share with their significant other, like tickets to a game, a show, a concert, or a weekend at a resort or spa.

Communicate the Strategy and Rules: Decide how you will describe the contest. Your message should include an overview of all the contest design components: the sales contest objectives, the measurements of success, and the earning criteria, including timing and prizes. Send it out in an email to the whole team. Here's an example:

> **Subject:** Mad Men in March
>
> We are kicking off this incentive to add *net new* business into the pipeline for this last quarter. For anyone who brings in a signed purchase order from a new company or new logo this month will receive an Amex gift certificate of $250 *plus* they will be eligible for the Grand Prize, the latest iPad with all the bells and whistles. Winners will be announced at our Mad Men cocktail party, where we will be serving up the drinks seen on *Mad Men*, including Martinis, Blue Hawaiians, and Old Fashioneds. *Pssst!* The grand prize is driving in the car that Don Draper drives . . . Can you guess?
>
> > *Contest starts:* 3/1/12
> > *Contest ends:* 3/30/12
>
> *How to Win:*
>
> The winner will have the highest percentage of bookings to their target for March. All percentages and goals are tracked with Salesforce.com.
>
> *Contest Prizes:*
>
> The winner will get a $250 Amex card and be eligible for the Grand Prize.
>
> *Who Is Eligible:*
>
> The contest is exclusively for the inside sales organizations. A complete list of participants is attached.
>
> *Keeping Track of the Standings:*
>
> Leaderboard updates will be sent out twice a week. If you want to see the up-to-the-minute results, go to our leaderboard report here.

Publish Results and Announce the Winners: Who's winning? Who stands a chance? Who's dropped behind? Your team needs this information all the time to stay motivated, stay competitive, and be able to strategize on displacing their opponents. Any successful contest requires *daily and ongoing* communication and reinforcement to maintain momentum. That is the only way your teams will stay engaged and not get bored.

Your team is motivated by winning and being recognized, so make sure you are communicating the standings on a regular basis. Keep reminding them how the contest works and about the rewards and the timing. Make progress visible by posting performance attainment and standings. Clearly identify what it takes to keep moving up and forward. Send daily updates via email, weekly updates in team meetings, and even last-minute motivational texts (see the end of this chapter) to keep it top of mind.

When announcing the winners and performance results, make it an event. Reserve a conference room, invite senior management, have food and prizes, make it special and memorable.

Strategies from the TeleSmart 10 System

Keep the contest you choose simple by selecting one or two actions you want the team focused on. The following activity strategies are based on the TeleSmart 10 system, so you can mix and match them with the entire sales cycle.

Time management:

- To encourage high outbound call volume, run a spiff.

- Reward high call activity to increase talk time.

- Randomly monitor sales productivity tools and cleanup.

Introducing:

- Have all team members submit their "best" email based on response rate, formatting, word choice, etc. Have everyone vote for the best one.

- Create a spiff to increase phone activity. Initiate a "new prospects" call blitz, where team members provide strong introductory calls and emails.

- Run a contest based on the most thorough LinkedIn profile.

Navigating:

- Initiate a "gaining access" call blitz where team members compete on who can gather more information from the same company.

- Create a spiff for calling deeper and wider and building the 2 × 2 org chart

Questioning:

- Initiate a first-call questioning criteria competition.

- Conduct a team competition on who generates the most quotes and proposals per month.

Listening:

- Have team members submit sample scenarios where poor listening impacted a sale.

- Randomly check notes in CRM for proper information capture and documentation.

Linking:

- Run a contest to create new messaging at various levels (CEO, VP, Manager, Ops).

- Have a 2 × 2 contest to encourage calling deeper and wider into prospective accounts.

Presenting:

- Hold a contest for the best online demo or presentation.

- Create a spiff to launch a new product line.

- Get different groups to compete on cross-selling and up-selling.

Handling Objections:

- Hold a contest of quick comebacks and rebuttals for the top 10 objections.

- Create a spiff for win-back business.

Partnering:

- Provide a spiff to increase the number of new partnerships the teams initiate. Have fun with this and use a marriage theme.

Closing:

- Gives spiffs for most deals closed during the month.

- Create a contest for the largest order size.

- Give spiffs for the most deals closed by product, by territory, by team, and so on.

- Give spiffs for a healthy pipeline.

MOTIVATIONAL TEXTING 1-2-3

Panic time! You only have a few days left before closing one of the most important quarters in a long time. Whether sales are lagging or you are actually above quota, this is not the time to slack off. This is the best time to squeeze more out of your team than ever before. And, in a crunch time like this, when time is of the essence, the perfect tool is texting.

Mobile messaging is one of the best ways managers can get team members' attention, generate quick response, and make a statement. Here's how to get started:

1. Make sure you have your entire team's cell phone numbers.

2. Outline a motivational text strategy to include morning texts (motivational, confident, and energetic) and end-of-day texts (grateful, rewarding, and acknowledging).

3. Send out two texts per day—one in the morning to keep your team focused and one at the end of the day to keep them energized. You can create them yourself or use the ones below.

The following list includes motivational texts you can send your team throughout the sales year—beginning of month; end of quarter; in the morning; or end of day to build confidence, create competitive energy, show your gratitude, or reward and acknowledge your team for their impressive work!

Morning Texts

- Today is the start of three huge deals. Knock 'em dead!

- Say NO to distractions and YES to selling.

- Walk into work and strike your BEST sales pose.

- Give MORE today than you did yesterday and you will be that much CLOSER to your goal.

- Let's not be conventional; let's be DISRUPTIVE.

- Strive for excellence, not perfection.

- Let's kick some major butt today! I have a good feeling about today!

- Give it your all today. I PROMISE it'll be worthwhile.

End-of-the-Day Texts

- Thx for moving mountains today—we're WINNING.

- AMAZING work today. The hardest is over. FINAL STRETCH!

- Falling down is how we grow. Staying down is how we crumble.

- You are what you repeatedly do. Excellence is not an event—it's a habit.

Good-Luck Texts

- If you're going to be a champion, you must be willing to pay a greater price than your opponent.

- There is no satisfaction in settling for average—keep pushing for excellence!

- You are not defined by falling flat on your back; you're defined by what you do to get back up on your feet.

- Successful people don't do extraordinary things. They do ordinary things in an extraordinary way.

- If you miss an opportunity, don't close your eyes with tears; keep your vision clear so that you will not miss the next one.

- To be a top performer you have to be passionately committed to what you're doing and insanely confident about your ability.

- Obstacles are only opportunities to succeed or fail; how we handle them determines what will happen.

- Set out on your road to victory and never lose sight of your destination; give it your all everyday.

- The world can only be grasped by action, not contemplation.

Congrats Texts

- WOW! WOW! WOW! YOU DID IT, YOU DID IT!

- Woohoo! Congrats!

- Yahoo! We have a winner!

- Can someone say BONUS?!!?!!?!

Motivational Texts

- Figure out what you want and, if you want it badly enough, you WILL find a way to get it.

- Learn how to separate the majors and the minors; a lot of people don't do well simply because they major in minor things.

- Nothing will ever be attempted if all possible objections haven't already been overcome.

- The journey of a thousand miles begins with a single step.

- If you're going to be a champion, you must be willing to pay a greater price than your opponent.

- There is no satisfaction in settling for average; keep pushing for the top!

- The most important requirement in success is learning to overcome failure.

Texts That Say "I Feel So Lucky to Have Such a Killer Team—THX!"

People need to know how they are doing, they need to feel appreciated, and they absolutely want to receive as much praise as possible. Here are just a few of the many quick ways to say thank you with a text.

- Great Job!

- Nice Work!

- Way to Go!

- We couldn't have done it without you!

- You're a winner!

- You are what this team needs.

- You are one of a kind.

- HOT DAMN!

- The time you put in really shows.

- Your contribution is important.

- Outstanding!

- You are truly appreciated.

TEAM OUTINGS

Let's get some Modern Family community going here. Like team contests, team outings are another great way to get your culture vultures together. The key here is to create such a great culture on a day-to-day basis that your team will truly enjoy each other's company during team outings, not only as colleagues but as friends. They'll see it as a reward for all their hard work rather than a forced field trip or a day away from sales calls. Be sure to take plenty of photos and post them in the office and on your team web page.

SPREADING THE WORD = PUBLIC DISPLAYS OF FUN

Today's Talent 2.0 requires constant feedback and acknowledgment for their efforts. They always want to know where they stand, and they love public and visual displays of recognition. They want mental and emotional "swag" and visual displays of F-U-N.

Any program you design must be supported with visual displays of fun and motivation. This will solidify and reinforce the commitment to the goal. Here are some categories that really work.

Sales Boards

Most sales organizations have a big sales board located in a central area that displays a stack-ranking of the team. Everyone walks by the sales board. They study the numbers, they point to it, they glance at it, they bring their calculator to it. Managers hold team huddles next to it. There are lots of motivational opportunities here for something extra you can write, including new thoughts, goals, reminders, and winners to announce.

TV Sales Monitors

Most inbound and outbound call centers invest in TV sales monitors for real-time results, but how much motivational content is in full display on these monitors? Don't ignore this area of possibility—there is room to make a huge impact here because this lives in the sales aisles.

Consider including the following:

- Daily motivational quotes and tips

- A fun "rep-of-the-week" bio with photo

- Contest results and standings with motivational quotes

- Announcements, such as "breaking news" of "this just in"

- New hire welcomes

- Company-wide "chatter" or tweets with regular updates

- Post activity metrics and rankings

Boast-and-Brag Wall

The boast-and-brag wall is another space dedicated to promoting the contributions of inside salespeople in the organization. This might include:

- Happy customer emails complementing a team member

- New account big wins that inside sales initially uncovered

- Photos of team outings, parties, events, etc.

Wall of Shame

Some sales organizations have found that posting a wall of shame is enough fear to motivate the bottom performers. This is a risky move but if your sales culture is tough, competitive, and motivated by fear, it works well.

Team Landing Page or Video on Company Website

As mentioned in Chapter 5, having a landing page on the company website or Facebook page is a great way to display the fun culture of the team. Betts Recruiting, a San Francisco–based company, publishes some great energizing videos on fun topics, including those called "Workin' for a Living" or "Call Me Maybe" or "S*** Not to Say in an Interview." This is a perfect sales tool for potential prospects who want to know if you are a company worth doing business with.

Swag

Swag praises salespeople's accomplishments and gives them something they can share with their family and friends. For example:

* Trophies, plaques, and achievement certificates

* Personalized thank-you notes written by managers to each team member

Salespeople often treasure these notes, certificates, and plaques for many years, and proudly display them in their work space.

Sales Cheers

Group cheers create and boost team spirit. This company cheer from PeopleMatter is mandatory company-wide every Monday afternoon:

Brought to you by:
"A Bunch of Crunked-Up Rock Stars"
(inside joke)

Q: Are there any PEOPLE in the house?
(Yea)

Q: I said: Are there any PEOPLE in the house?
(YEA)

Q: What do we do?
We Innovate!

Q: How do we do it?
We Create!

Q: What does that do?
It Stimulates!

Q: Then what do we do?
We Celebrate!!!

Who Rocks the house?
PeopleMatter Rocks the house!!

Who Rocks the house?
PeopleMatter Rocks the house!![2]

MANAGEMENT TIPS

- Your team needs an ambassador of FUN when it comes to regular motivation. You may decide to take on this role yourself, or you may assign one of your team members to be the Culture Architect of Fun. But do include this vital element: it's important to the longevity and loyalty of your team.

- Designing regular motivational programs will increase the productivity of your organization and create healthy team competition. Designing the right program—the program that motivates everyone on your team, not just top performers—is essential.

- Creating public visual displays of motivation reinforce your message and capture the energy of your teams.

- Sending motivational texts to team members when they need a push, or thanking them for work done well, sends the message that you care about them and know they are doing their best for the team.

CHAPTER 13

TOUGH TALKS

Smart Strategies and Interventions for
Low Performers and Problem Personalities

*Ready to do some damage control? You are about to confront one of
the toughest parts of your job as a manager: dealing seriously with
your low performers and problem personalities.*

*Take this Manager Diagnostic and answer the 18 questions that
follow. Reflect on your readiness for this challenge. Your goal is to
set real consequences for expected behaviors and be ready to talk re-
alistically with team members who are not ever going to meet expectations. Coming up to speed on these questions will put you in the
STRETCH ZONE when it comes to having these tough talks.*

1. *Can I keep my emotions in check while I have a tough talk with
   my rep?*

2. *Can I hold off on any judgment and emotional history that may
   cloud my thinking?*

3. *Can I stay calm if they try to push my buttons?*

4. *Have I laid the groundwork and expectations for this discussion
   ahead of time?*

5. *Do I have supporting documentation and facts about their behavior?*

6. *Have I been fair and consistent with this sales rep?*

7. *Have I tracked this sales rep's previous performance?*

8. *Am I certain that poor performance is the result of the sales rep's deficiencies and not my own management missteps?*

9. *Have I thought about the short-term or long-term implications of letting this person go?*

10. *Have I sufficiently coached and worked with the sales rep?*

11. *Have I considered how this person's behavior impacts the team?*

12. *Have I considered how this person's loss will impact the team?*

13. *Am I intervening promptly, or did I procrastinate too long before having this talk?*

14. *Is there a neutral space that I can use for this discussion?*

15. *Can I look at this situation objectively?*

16. *Can I listen to this rep and try to understand what's motivating the unwanted behavior? Am I ready to help this rep change the behavior?*

17. *Can I take action to defuse the sales rep's shock and anger constructively?*

18. *When faced with a performance problem, do I take care to establish whether it is caused by lack of resources, lack of motivation, or lack of skills?*

* * *

"Can you step into my office, please? We need to have a talk." No salesperson wants to hear these words from their manager, and no manager wants to say them. But sometimes these tough talks are inevitable. Despite all your best efforts at interviewing and hiring the right people and coaching them through the low spots, there will al-

ways be low performers and problem personalities that make it necessary for you to intervene in situations that threaten to erode your
teams' morale and hold down your revenue numbers.

   This chapter is about asserting your authority as a leader, taking
control, and finishing what you started. It offers strategies for con-
fronting difficult situations and parting ways with low performers so
that it benefits both of you.

TOUGH TALKS WITH LOW PERFORMERS

Managing a high-functioning inside sales organization— where your
happy teams are harmonious and everyone flawlessly hits their revenue numbers—is what every manager strives for. So when chronically
low performers throw a wrench into your well-oiled team, you need
to step in quickly before they throw everyone off their game.

Measure Performance Standards

You can always spot low performers because they are not meeting
your team standards. Have clear standards of performance in place
so that team members always know where they stand. Post them if
necessary, but make sure everyone is on the same page when it comes
to performance expectations.

   The standards you use are up to you. The stack-ranking criteria
on page 152 provides a set of standards against which you can measure your inside sales team. Some managers develop their own criteria
and review them regularly.

   Here's an example of one called Q-W-A-A-T:

* **Q:** Is this rep consistently hitting quota?

* **W:** How is the rep's work ethic? Does the rep come in late, leave
  early, etc.?

* **A:** How's the rep's attitude? Is the person grouchy, grumpy,
  moody, snarky, or positive and happy?

- **A:** How's the rep's ability? Has the person received training and coaching; is the person knowledgeable?

- **T:** How's the rep's tenure? Has the rep put in time? Does the rep have a track record of good performance?

Step in NOW

Low performers are like lights growing dimmer and dimmer. They ignore or forget to turn in sales reports, they show up late for meetings, they continually forget to update notes into their CRM, they miss sales targets, they are disruptive in sales meetings, they fail to acknowledge your requests and take their time responding to your email or voice mail, and they just don't look too happy.

Most low performers are truly performing at the bottom of the curve. Others, however, can fool you: they are hitting their numbers but only operating at a fraction of their potential, making you hesitant to confront them. But these occasional behavioral and performance slips are red flags that alert you that it's time to intervene, find out what's causing this behavior, and follow up with coaching or training or a simple warning.

No one likes to confront problem performance or behavior, but if you avoid it, you are sending a message that it is acceptable. Worse, your credibility will be visibly weakened in the eyes of your team. When you see that red flag waving, do not procrastinate, avoid, or minimize the behavior. Step in, and do some damage control.

Act promptly, but calmly. Review your own attitude and make sure you are not feeling angry or frustrated when you talk to them. You should be the calm rock because they are likely to be shell shocked, angry, and defensive.

Giving Feedback to Fragile Talent 2.0

Today's talent tends to get alarmed when managers want to have a difficult conversation with them. They imagine the worst, they move into the PANIC zone, and they have to be calmed down. This can make an already difficult situation more difficult.

Although the following issues don't describe every member of the Millennial generation, they do fit a surprising number. You would be wise to remember these general qualities and frame your conversation (and your own emotional responses) accordingly.

* They get defensive and don't take feedback well.

* They are not loyal to the organization—they plan to hold on to their jobs for two years at most.

* They are impatient.

* They are not introspective—they just want the answers.

* They see things in black and white.

Approach the rep when he or she is most likely to be receptive. Confront the rep privately; making a scene will only make things harder. Call the person into your office quietly, pull the person aside, or email the rep with the message that you need to talk.

Talk the Talk

Your discussion will go better if you set the stage carefully. Invite the rep into your office or a private space, where you will not be overheard or interrupted. A cubicle is not the proper venue for a difficult discussion about work performance. Be respectful to the salesperson, regardless of his or her behavior.

Let the rep know that you want to have a constructive discussion. State the facts clearly and succinctly. Listen to the other person, acknowledge that person's point of view, and avoid being judgmental. Keep your emotions in check.

When you state your issues, focus on behavior. Don't belittle or blame the rep, don't talk down to the rep, don't attack the rep personally. Frame your concern in a positive way and keep your feedback short. If possible, just focus on two problem areas and be very specific.

Ask the reps to provide you with daily activity metrics and a short-term territory plan to check their strategy.

Make sure the rep understands what he or she is being measured against to determine poor performance, and clearly communicate your expectations regarding behavior.

Allow your message to sink in and give the rep space to digest it and respond. Encourage the rep to come up with a solution to the problem, and tweak it if you need to.

At the end of the discussion, review action steps and goals. Have a clear game plan, write it down, and make sure you both have copies. Get their commitment to change, but put time parameters in place. Set clear time limits for change, and let the person know you will put them on a performance plan (discussed later in this chapter).

End on a positive note and stay friendly. Don't let the rep think you are watching every move!

Finally, document your discussions, and get up to date on your organization's policies for dismissing problem employees. Be sure the person understands that the ultimate consequence for poor behavior is dismissal.

Not every manager-employee interaction ends on a positive note, and you want to make sure you have done everything possible to help your rep *and* protect yourself from future problems.

INTERVENTIONS FOR PROBLEM PERSONALITIES

Low performers are C players, or former A or B players who dropped to C and are hovering near or in the Dead Zone. Problem personalities are something else altogether—they are people in need of special handling that goes beyond a friendly nudge in the right direction. And they may take you by surprise.

After all, you interviewed them, you hired them, you watched them in your team meetings, you watched them in team trainings, you coached them . . . and they seemed just GREAT. But sooner or later, some people will reveal themselves as TOXIC to your organization, even going out of their way to push your buttons and upset your team's equilibrium. They really make you angry!

You wonder, how can ONE PERSON do so much damage? If any of the following uber-annoying personalities are on your team, don't avoid, procrastinate, or minimize their impact: take control NOW.

The Latecomer

They are always late for everything. They come in late in the morning, walk in late to meetings, and turn their reports in late. And they don't seem to care.

Intervention Tips: As far as they are concerned, their lateness is all about them. They may habitually rebel against rules and standards; they may just be bad at estimating time; they may want to say they'll be there to please you, even when they know it won't happen. Help them understand the bigger picture. Let them know how important they are to the group. Explain that you work as a team, and show them exactly how they impact the group when they are late.

The Argumentative

Argumentative people never agree with anything and rarely trust new information. They resist change and always have an excuse or argument.

Intervention Tips: Usually, their argumentative style is a way of asking for more attention; they probably feel like you're not paying attention to their input. Begin your interactions by really listening to what they have to say. Then steer them toward the facts, which are usually much less negative than they believe. When they want to continue arguing (and they will), tell them that for every argument they make, they must come up with a solution.

The Drama Queen/King

They need to be the center of attention, so they create chaos and drama all around them. They hold themselves up as special—as experts who know more than others on every subject. They always know the facts, and use them to show superiority, alarming everyone.

Intervention Tips: Stay calm, neutral, and help get them back on track. It's not acceptable to create drama that gets the team off track. Because you cannot "fake it" with them, make sure you have the facts. You can also capitalize on what they know by asking questions. They love to show off and have others appreciate their knowledge, so give them praise but use their knowledge strategically.

The Cheater

Cheaters are usually creative, resourceful, and very quick to think of ways to beat the system. They tend to make false promises and yet can be so convincing.

Intervention Tips: Ask for details and hard facts. Let them know that cheating the system is immediate grounds for termination and will not be tolerated. Randomly monitor their calls and CRM activity.

The Deadbeat

The Deadbeat is clearly in the Dead Zone. They may not show up for work or they may call in sick, take time off, or give you below-standard work. They are always walking on the edge between succeeding and failing. They are doing enough to stay employed but are not growing professionally nor contributing as an equal team member. Worse, they don't seem to care at all.

Intervention Tips: Figure out what went wrong—personal tragedy, conflicts with coworkers, boredom, and so on. Once you know, you can help do something about it, but they must own the responsibility for their actions and reactions.

Help them see what's in it for them to succeed and improve. Assure them that you have faith in their ability to succeed. Help them

set several short-term achievable goals. Identify something they like
to do every day.

The Troublemaker

Hardcore troublemakers are hostile, abusive, and intimidating. They
always have to be right and will charge like angry bulls if you challenge or cross them.

Intervention Tips: Build up team accountability. Assign them a buddy
with a strong positive attitude. Take a deep breath. Let them blow off
steam and express their anger and frustration, but draw the line at
abuse. Address them by name to maintain control. Then state your position clearly and avoid the temptation to argue. You won't win a battle
with them, especially in a public forum. Set your boundaries early on.

The Chronic Complainer

Chronic complainers have usually been at the company a few years
longer than they expected. The chief effect of the complainer is a general lowering of morale and a reluctance to initiate constructive dialogue with "the enemy"—which is you.

Intervention Tips: The best way to handle chronic complainers is to
keep their views in perspective and not get lost in their negative tone.
Steer them toward the facts concerning the issues involved and discourage regular whining.

The Passive-Aggressive

Passive-aggressive personality types take potshots. They undercut
your authority in devious ways by using sarcasm, which they often
disguise as a joke. They are never direct with their criticism. They
don't reveal their true motives, and you end up in a guessing game
trying to find out what makes them tick.

Intervention Tips: Try to turn their attention and comments to the issues rather than the personalities involved. Once they realize that you won't put up with their sniping, they usually stop. They do not want to be center stage, so they tend to avoid open confrontation.

PUT PROBLEM SALESPEOPLE ON A PERFORMANCE IMPROVEMENT PLAN

If incessant poor performance continues or other behaviors crop up that demonstrate disrespect for the sales manager and other members of the sales team, including outright rudeness or dismissive behavior, you have grounds for putting the rep on a Performance Improvement Plan.

The decision to put your team member on a performance plan usually follows hours of coaching and meetings, when you are at the end of your rope. You see the daily decline, watch the revenues plummet, and feel exhausted with warnings that go unheeded. Figure 13-1 is a typical Performance Improvement Plan.

WHO STAYS AND WHO GOES?

The general rule of thumb is "Salvage first, replace second." For example, if you've set reasonable sales targets and some of your people aren't meeting them, try first to correct the problem through coaching or training. If that doesn't work, then you have to consider replacing them. This is always a difficult decision, and it's a tough conversation. Do everything you can to make it work but, in the end, you have to do what is right for both the person and the company and assist them in getting a new career.

Here are 10 questions that can help you identify whether team members on a performance plan should stay a little while longer, or they have reached their sell-by date and need to go. Pull out your stack-ranking criteria and your call monitoring forms from Chapter 7 to help determine objectively how their actions, behavior, and performance size up.

To: *(Employee Name)*

From: *(Manager Name)*

Date: *(Date)*

cc: Human Resources
           (Employee's file)

Reference: Performance Action Plan

Since your original hire date *[Date]*, it has become increasingly evident to your team, to management, and to me that you have not been performing your assigned work in accordance with what is expected of a *[role/title]*.

On *[Date]*, you were counseled about this unacceptable performance. *[Name of Company]* values you as an employee, and it is your leadership team's intent to make you fully aware of this situation and to assist you in improving your work performance. However, it is important that you realize that the responsibility to improve is yours alone.

You are being placed on a written action plan for the next 90 days: *[Start Date–End Date]*. Your work will be closely monitored by your leadership team.

You must demonstrate immediate improvement in the following areas:

[Identify areas of improvement. Be specific about what needs to be improved and, if possible, list objectives with specific deadlines.]

You must meet these specific performance objectives. *[Objectives should be specific, measurable, achievable, relevant, and time oriented.]*

> Objective 1
> ACTION:
> RESULTS:
> DEADLINE:
> MEASUREMENT OF RESULTS:
>
> Objective 2
> ACTION:
> RESULTS:
> DEADLINE:
> MEASUREMENT OF RESULTS:

FIGURE 13-1 | Performance Improvement Plan

(2)

[Manager Name] will review your progress on each of the above items requiring improvement by each established deadline. We trust that in so doing, we can guide you in creating success at [Name of Company].

Improvement must occur immediately and must be maintained. If any portion of this action plan is violated at any time during the specified timeframe, disciplinary action up to and including termination from [Name of Company] may occur. A decrease in performance after successfully completing the action plan may result in being dismissed from [Name of Company] without the issuance of another warning or action plan.

As always, the Open Door Policy is available for you to discuss any concerns.

Your signature acknowledges this discussion and does not indicate agreement or disagreement with this plan.

_____   _____
Team Member Signature   Date

_____   _____
Manager Signature   Date

_____   _____
HR Signature   Date

1. *Are they coachable?* If they can be coached and if are they open to changing, give them a chance to prove it. No matter how much potential they have, if they are not open to changing and developing themselves, you must cut your losses.

2. *Is there a job match?* It's amazing how many salespeople got into sales by accident. They don't see themselves in a sales role and would rather be in marketing, operations, management, technical support, product development—anywhere else. Do not try to hold on to people who don't want to be in sales and don't have the talent to pull it off.

3. *Do they overcomplicate things?* Reps who are trying too hard tend to distance and confuse their prospects. It is very difficult to coach people out of this habit. Asking them to simplify something is like asking them to walk around with one shoe all day; it is awkward, and they really don't get it. Generally, you will be better off without them.

4. *Do they avoid confrontation?* Some salespeople just can't get to the close. They are very service oriented but lack the focus and urgency to move prospects along. This stems from low self-esteem, lack of confidence, and simply not having the courage to ask and step it up. Coaching, training, and role-playing can often do the trick. But if it has become clear that they will never understand how the game is played, cut them loose.

5. *Are they too robotic?* Good salespeople have depth. They connect with customers on a person-to-person level by being naturally curious and asking real questions. Salespeople who approach sales as a generic and mechanical skill, who never get off script, and who don't have that drive to ask one more question to dig deeper probably do not belong in sales.

6. *Are they good listeners?* Many salespeople ask really good questions but fail to understand and hear the response. Today's customers just won't stand for that—they want to feel heard and they

want a relationship. Role-playing and training around this issue can often get them over the hump. But if they continue to demonstrate a lack of understanding even when they are genuinely listening, it's time to go.

7. *What jobs did they have prior to being in sales?* You may have overlooked the importance of this question during the hiring stage, but it has a lot to do with future performance—especially if they were good at their former jobs. If they were a gatekeeper for a CEO of a company just fielding calls from vendors all day, they are probably not going to make the cut when it comes to outbound prospecting because they feel as though they are annoying people. If they were chasing down fraudulent claims, their militant tone will never establish trust on a call. Training and coaching is a must, but if they continue to be a bad fit with sales, move on.

8. *What is happening in their personal life?* If they are going through a divorce and their self-esteem has been shot, or if they owe tons on their house that is being threatened with foreclosure, their desperation and low self-esteem will cause discomfort with our frazzled Customer 2.0.

9. *Are they motivated by fear?* Many reps do not have the self-motivation to maintain a steady daily momentum. When their activity slips, their momentum plummets. Once they receive a warning and get put on a Performance Improvement Plan, however, that may be all the motivation they need to wake up. If they are still down, it's time to go.

10. *Do customers like them?* Are they well liked by their internal and external partners? Do they make people feel comfortable? Are they approachable? No to any of these questions is a HUGE red flag. Unlikable people DO NOT belong in sales!

MANAGEMENT TIPS

- Despite all your best efforts at interviewing and hiring the right people, and coaching them through the low spots, there will always be problem behaviors and difficult personalities that make it necessary for you to intervene in situations that threaten to erode your teams' morale and hold down your revenue numbers. Do not procrastinate.

- Act promptly, but calmly. Review your own attitude and make sure you are not feeling angry or frustrated when you talk to them. You should be the calm rock because they are likely to be shell-shocked, angry, and defensive.

- Approach the rep when they are most likely to be receptive. Confront them privately—making a scene will only make things harder. Call them into your office quietly, pull them aside, or email them with the message that you need to talk.

- When you state your issues, focus on behavior. Frame your concern in a positive way and keep your feedback short. Allow your message to sink in and give them space to digest it and respond. Encourage the rep to come up with a solution to the problem and tweak it if you need to.

- If poor performance continues unabated, or other behaviors crop up that demonstrate disrespect for the sales manager and other members of the sales team—including outright rudeness or dismissive behavior—you have grounds for putting the rep on a Performance Improvement Plan.

- The general rule of thumb is "Salvage first, replace second." For example, if you've set reasonable sales targets and some of your people aren't meeting them, try first to correct the problem through coaching or training. If that doesn't work, then you have to consider replacing them. This is always a difficult decision, and it's a tough conversation. Do everything you can to make it work but, in the end, you have to do what is right for both the person and the company, and assist them in getting a new career.

NOTES

CHAPTER ONE

1. Trip Kucera and Peter Ostrow (Aberdeen Group), "Sales and Marketing Alignment: The New Power Couple," December 2011, http://sellingstrategies. com.au/resources/documents/Aberdeen-Report-Sales-Marketing-Alignment- Oct-2011.pdf

2. DemandGen report, "Breaking out of the Funnel: A look inside the mind of the new generation of b2b buyer," March 2010, http://www.demandgenreport. com/industry-resources/white-papers/430-breaking-out-of-the-funnel-a-look- inside-the-mind-of-the-new-generation-of-btob-buyer.html#.ULKmHaWztH8

3. Nigel Edelshain, Sales 2.0 whitepaper on "Social Selling; 9 Tips on Selling to Today's NEW Customer, 2011, http://www.sales2.com/2011/11/the-social- graph-is-your-friends/

4. Hubspot Blog Post, "What's Wrong with Marketing Automation Today?," http://www.hubspot.com/marketing-automation-information/2012

5. David Elkington (Insidesales.com), "B2B Lead Roundtable: Research from Harvard MIT Pinpoints Hard Lead Conversion Lessons with Easy Solutions," June 2011 Slideshare, http://www.slideshare.net/B2BLeadRoundtable/research- from-harvard-mit-pinpoints-hard-lead-conversion-lessons-with-easy-solutions

CHAPTER TWO

1. Joe Mandese, "MTV Studies Millennials in the Workplace: Uses to Transform It's Own, Even Yours, March 2012, http://www.mediapost.com/publications/ article/169980/mtv-studies-millennials-in-the-workplace-uses-it.html#axzz 2DHaFMIhe

2. *Ibid.*

3. Matthew Philips, "Boomers and Millennials: Who Got It Worst in the Workplace?," May 2012, http://www.businessweek.com/articles/2012-05-22/boomers-and-millennials-whos-got-it-worse-in-the-workplace

4. Mandese, "MTV Studies Millennials."

5. Vorsight and Bridge Group, *Mythbusting Millennials: Separating Fact from Fiction for Managing Gen Y Sales Reps*, 2012, http://www.vorsight.com/mythbusting-millennials

6. Camille Preston, "The Rewired Resolution: Eight Ways to Work Smarter, Live Better and Be More Productive" 2012, https://news.citrixonline.com/wp-content/uploads/2012/06/Rewired_Resolution.pdf

7. Mandese, "MTV Studies Millennials."

8. *Ibid.*

9. Cisco Connected World Technology Report, 2011, http://www.cisco.com/en/US/netsol/ns1120/index.html

10. Dan Schawbel, "Millennial Branding Gen-Y & Facebook Study," 2012, http://millennialbranding.com/2012/01/millennial-branding-gen-y-facebook-study/

11. Matthew Philips, "Boomers and Millennials."

12. Sibson Consulting, "How to Incent Generation Y + Why It's Important," 2012, http://wordisseur.com/wp-content/uploads/2011/12/Wordisseur-How_to_Incent_Gen_Y.pdf

13. Mandese, "MTV Studies Millennials."

14. Matt Wise, "Seven Rules for Getting Started in Gamification," http//www.eprize.com/engage/news/news/2011/12/13/

15. PeopleMatter, "Getting the Best out of Generation Y," 2012 White Paper, http://success.peoplematter.com/download-wp-geny.html

CHAPTER THREE

1. Gerhard Gschwandtner, "What Is Sales 2.0 and Why Should You Care?," 2010, http://sellingpower.typepad.com/gg/2010/02/what-is-sales-20-and-why-should-you-care-part-ii.html

2. Barry Trailer and Jim Dickie, "2012 Inside Sales Performance Optimization Report," 2012, http://www.csoinsights.com/Publications/Shop/inside-sales-performance-optimization

3. David Elkington, Insidesales.com, "B2B Lead Roundtable: Research from Harvard MIT Pinpoints Hard Lead Conversion Lessons with Easy Solutions," June 2011 Slideshare, http://www.slideshare.net/B2BLeadRoundtable/research-from-harvard-mit-pinpoints-hard-lead-conversion-lessons-with-easy-solutions

4. Michael Stelzner, "2012 Social Media Marketing Industry Report: How Marketers are Using Social Media to Grow their Businesses," http://www.socialmediaexaminer.com/SocialMediaMarketingIndustryReport2012.pdf

5. Peter Ostrow (Aberdeen Group), "Streamlining the Top of the Funnel: How Inside Sales Teams Source, Qualify and Close Business" 2011, http://ability-crm.com/wp-content/uploads/2011/07/Streamlining-the-Top-of-the-Funnel.pdf

6. Gartner Research, "Magic Quadrant for Sales Force Automation," July 2012, http://www.sonomapartners.com/Documents/Gartner_2012_SFA_MQ.pdf

7. Bridge Group, "2012 Lead Generation and Compensation Report," 2012, http://www.bridgegroupinc.com/lead_generation_metrics.html

8. IDC Analyst Connection, "Coordinating Marketing and Sales Across the Entire Revenue Cycle," 2008, http://docs.cdn.marketo.com/idc-analyst-connection.pdf

9. Vorsight and the Bridge Group, *Sales Speaks: Perceptions and Ponderings on Marketing Leads*, 2012 ebook, http://www.bridgegroupinc.com/sales_speaks.html

10. IDC Research, "Increasing Mobile Marketing Adoption will Re-emphasize Marketing by Turning Consumer Electronics into Audience Targeting Tools," 2012, http://www.mediabuzz.com.sg/asian-emarketing/february-2012/1488-increasing-mobile-marketing-adoption-will-re-emphasize-marketings-ps-by-turning-consumer-electronics-into-audience-targeting-tools

11. Yahoo Presentation for SF DMA, July 2011, "What you need to know about the Mobile Landscape."

12. Stephen Drake, Raymond Boggs, and Justin Jaffe, IDC excerpt "Worldwide Mobile Worker Population 2009–2013 Forecast," http://www.gotomypc.com/remote_access/images/pdf/How_to_Equip_Your_Company_for_the_New_Mobile_Workforce.pdf

13. Forrester Research, "BT 2020: IT's Future in the Empowered Era," 2011, http://www.forrester.com/BT+2020+ITs+Future+In+The+Empowered+Era/ fulltext/-/E-RES58156

14. Forrester Research, "BT 2020."

15. Jessica Bosari, "The Developing Role of Social Media in the Modern Business World," *Forbes*, 2012, http://www.forbes.com/sites/moneywise women/2012/ 08/08 the-developing-role-of-social-media-in-the-modern-business-world/

16. Forrester Research, "BT 2020."

17. RealityWorks Group (previously Phoneworks), 2011 Inside Sales Metrics Report, http://realityworksgroup.com/learning-center/survey-reports/2011- inside-sales-metrics-report/

18. Gerhard Gschwandtner, "How Many People will be Left by 2020?," 2011, Blog post for Selling Power, http://www.sellingpower.com/content/article/?a= 9452%3frnd=324819

CHAPTER FOUR

1. Vorsight, "The True Cost of Poor Prospecting," 2012, http://www.vorsight. com/cost-poor-prospecting

2. Vorsight and the Bridge Group, *Sales Speaks: Perceptions and Ponderings on Marketing Leads*, 2012 ebook, http://www.bridgegroupinc.com/sales_ speaks.html

3. David Elkington, Insidesales.com, "B2B Lead Roundtable: Research from Harvard MIT Pinpoints Hard Lead Conversion Lessons with Easy Solutions," June 2011 Slideshare, http://www.slideshare.net/B2BLeadRoundtable/research- from-harvard-mit-pinpoints-hard-lead-conversion-lessons-with-easy-solutions

4. DemandCon show in San Francisco.

5. Vorsight and The Bridge Group, *Sales Speaks*.

6. David Elkington, Insidesales.com, "B2B Lead Roundtable."

7. These original findings have since been updated and published in *Inc. Magazine* and *Harvard Business Review* in 2011 and on Forbes.com in 2012.

8. Josiane Feigon, *Smart Selling on the Phone and Online* (New York: AMACOM, 2010).

9. Culpepper and Associates.

CHAPTER FIVE

1. David Elkington, Insidesales.com, "B2B Lead Roundtable: Research from Harvard MIT Pinpoints Hard Lead Conversion Lessons with Easy Solutions," June 2011 Slideshare, http://www.slideshare.net/B2BLeadRoundtable/research-from-harvard-mit-pinpoints-hard-lead-conversion-lessons-with-easy-solutions

2. Sales Gravy Study, "2012 Sales Hiring Trends Report: The Emerging War for Sales Talent," http://salesgravy.web8.hubspot.com/2011-sales-hiring-trends-six-strategies-for-winning-the-war-for-sales-talent/

3. Glenn Fallavollita with Drip Marketing, "The Real Cost of a Salesperson Leaving Your Business," http://myemail.constantcontact.com/DRIP-Marketing-Tip—352—The-Real-Cost-Of-A-Salesperson-Leaving-Your-Business—Part-2-.html?soid=1102452077987&aid=5THfJdid6Jg

4. Barry Trailer and Jim Dickie, "2012 Inside Sales Performance Optimization Report," 2012, http://www.csoinsights.com/Publications/Shop/inside-sales-performance-optimization

5. *Ibid.*

6. Larissa Faw, "How Millennials Are Redefining their Careers as Hustlers," July 2012, http://www.forbes.com/sites/larissafaw/2012/07/19/how-millennials-are-redefining-their-careers-as-hustlers/

7. Bridge Group, 2012 Lead Generation and Compensation Report, http://www.bridgegroupinc.com/lead_generation_metrics.html

8. Scott Edinger, "Why Remote Workers are More (yes More) Engaged," *Harvard Business Review*, http://blogs.hbr.org/cs/2012/08/are_you_taking_your_people_for.html

9. David Elkington, Insidesales.com, "B2B Lead Roundtable."

10. Trailer and Dickie, "2012 Inside Sales Performance Optimization Report."

CHAPTER SIX

1. McKinsey Quarterly, "Getting More from Your Training Programs," http://www.mckinseyquarterly.com/Getting_more_from_your_training_programs_2688

2. Dave Stein, "The Top 7 Sales Training Pitfalls & 7 Solutions for Sustained Success," 2011, http://www.esresearch.com/e/home/document.php?dA=LandingPage_1&PSS=RegFormMini1&SC=DSB01

3. Culpepper and Associates.

4. Barry Trailer and Jim Dickie, "2012 Inside Sales Performance Optimization Report," 2012, http://www.csoinsights.com/Publications/Shop/inside-sales-performance-optimization

5. Lee Salz, *Sales Person Onboarding Best Practices*, ebook 2011, https://www.therevenueaccelerator.com/whitepaper/Sales_Person_Onboarding_Best_Practices_eBook_-_FINAL_-_100411.pdf

6. Trailer and Dickie, "2012 Inside Sales Performance Optimization Report."

7. Bridge Group, "2012 Lead Generation and Compensation Report," 2012, http://www.bridgegroupinc.com/lead_generation_metrics.html

CHAPTER SEVEN

1. Miller Heiman Sales Best Practices Study, Executive Summary, 2012, http://store.millerheiman.com/kc/abstract.aspx?itemid=00000000000007B2

2. Personal communication. Used by permission of Craig Abod.

3. Matt Dixon Adamson, "The Dirty Secret of Effective Sales Coaching," *Harvard Business Review*, January 31, 2011, http://blogs.hbr.org/cs/2011/01/the_dirty_secret_of_effective.html

CHAPTER NINE

1. Barry Trailer and Jim Dickie, "Inside Sales Performance Optimization Report," 2012, http://www.csoinsights.com/Publications/Shop/inside-sales-performance-optimization

2. Bridge Group, "Inside Sales Metrics and Compensation Report," 2010, http://www.bridgegroupinc.com/inside_sales_metrics.html

3. *Ibid.*

4. Penelope Trunk, "Why Gen Y Outperforms Everyone at Work," November 17, 2010, http://blog.penelopetrunk.com/2010/11/17/bnet-gen-y-is-better-at-your-job-than-you-are/

CHAPTER ELEVEN

1. Barry Trailer and Jim Dickie, "Inside Sales Performance Optimization Report," 2012, http://www.csoinsights.com/Publications/Shop/inside-sales-performance-optimization

CHAPTER TWELVE

1. Sales Contestology, "Seven Step Guide to Sales Contests," 2011, http://www.sales-contest.com/wp-content/downloads/sales_contest_web1.pdf

2. Personal communication. Used by permission from PeopleMatter.

INDEX